Eternity and Eternal Life
Speculative Theology and Science in Discourse

Tibor Horvath, S.J.

Wilfrid Laurier University Press

Wilfrid Laurier University Press acknowledges the financial support of the Government of Canada through the Canada Book Fund for our publishing activities. We acknowledge the support of the Canada Council for the Arts for our publishing program.

Library and Archives Canada Cataloguing in Publication

Horvath, Tibor, 1927 July 28–
    Eternity and eternal life

Includes bibliographical references and index.
ISBN 978-0-88920-224-5 (cloth)
ISBN 978-1-55458-497-0 (paper)
ISBN 978-0-88920-768-4 (PDF)

1. Eternity. 2. Future life – Christianity. 3. Time – Religious aspects – Christianity. I. Title.

BT912.H67 1993   236'.21   C93-093989-1

© 1993 Wilfrid Laurier University Press
Waterloo, Ontario N2L 3C5, Canada
www.wlupress.wlu.ca

Cover design by Leslie Macredie

Eternity and Eternal Life: Speculative Theology and Science in Discourse has been produced from a manuscript supplied in electronic form by the author.

Every reasonable effort has been made to acquire permission for copyright material used in this text, and to acknowledge all such indebtedness accurately. Any errors and omissions called to the publisher's attention will be corrected in future printings.

No part of this publication may be reproduced, stored in a retrieval system or transmitted, in any form or by any means, without the prior consent of the publisher or a licence from The Canadian Copyright Licensing Agency (Access Copyright). For an Access Copyright licence, visit www.accesscopyright.ca or call toll free to 1-800-893-5777.

Eternity and Eternal Life
Speculative Theology and Science in Discourse
Tibor Horvath, S.J.

The Newtonian concept of time has been changed by Einsteinian insight. Yet the Einsteinian worldview might make it difficult to appreciate traditional concepts of eschatology, like heaven and hell, death and immortality, life after death and resurrection, last day and final judgments, because these expressions presuppose a pre-Einsteinian view of the universe.

Since theology cannot remain unaffected by the new research in concepts of time, *Eternity and Eternal Life* tries to express the eschatological faith of the Roman Catholic church by using the time language of our age. To achieve this it overviews the research in the nature of time done in geology, cosmology, physics, biology, psychology, sociology, history and philosophy and proposes a notion of time for "timely" Christology and for "timely" eschatology, which, by using the singularity event as literary form, scrutinizes how Christ's time can lead the times of all existing realities through death to "eternity."

This is a pioneering work, one that needs to be tested in the community of interested readers. It is a communal search for an understanding of life, death and eternal life, not only in the light of abstract ideas and cultural linguistic doctrines in the world of religions, but also in the light of science and especially of a person as the horizon of understanding for both time and eternity. Christ as the eschatological union of time and eternity becomes the work's unifying focus and its paradigm, which solves recognized problems and opens our minds to new ones.

Tibor Horvath was born in Hungary, studied in Austria, Italy, Leuven (M.A., L. Phil.), Germany, Granada, Spain (S.T.L.), Rome (S.T.D.), Chicago and entered the Society of Jesus in Budapest in 1946. He was ordained to the priesthood in Granada in 1956. He has been Professor of Systematic Theology at Regis College in Toronto since 1962 and at the Toronto School of Theology since 1968. He is the author of several books and articles, founder and editor of the journal Ultimate Reality and Meaning, Interdisciplinary Studies in the Philosophy of Understanding *and recipient of DBH Deutsche Forschungsgemeinschaft.*

CONTENTS

FOREWORD		vii
1	**INTRODUCTION**	1
	1.1 Core-tenet of Christianity	1
	1.2 History of Christian Eschatology	5
	1.2.1 History–Resurrection–Revelation Link	5
	1.2.2 Eschatology as Expectation	8
	1.2.3 Eschatology as Advent of Salvation	12
	1.2.4 Eschatology as the Theology of Eternal Life	13
	1.2.5 The Teaching of the Church	14
	1.3 Structure and Method	23
2	**CONCEPTS OF TIME**	27
	2.1 Theology of Time After Theology of Being	27
	2.2 Current Theological Notions of Time	29
	2.2.1 Spatialized Time: Before and After	29
	2.2.2 Temporalized Time: Past, Present and Future Tenses	32
	2.2.3 De-temporalized Time	37
	2.2.4 Christological Time	41
	2.3 A New Notion of Time	42
	2.3.1 Current Scientific Notions of Time	42
	2.3.2 Current Notions of Time in Humanistic Studies	52
	2.3.3 Time is a Balance in a Multiplicity of Sub-times Characterized by an Irreversibility Measured Through Uniformly Reversible Changes Pointing to a Self-sublating Singularity Event. Thus in Hermeneutic Language Event Time Can Be Interpreted as Way-making for Eternity	60
3	**THE FIRST PRINCIPLE IN CHRISTIAN ESCHATOLOGY: JESUS CHRIST, THE ESCHATOLOGICAL UNION OF TIME AND ETERNITY**	65
	3.1 The Eschatological Union of Time and Eternity	65
	3.2 Eschatological Union of Time and Eternity: Christology as Soteriology	68
	3.3 Eschatological Union of Time and Eternity: Christology in Sacramental Theology	71

3.4 Eschatological Union of Time and Eternity in the Context
of the Hypostatic Union Christology 73
3.5 Eschatological Union of Time and Eternity:
Christology in the Context of the Trinitarian Mystery 79

4 CHRISTIAN ESCHATOLOGY: SYSTEMATIC PRESENTATION 81

4.1 Time and Eternity 81
    4.1.1 By Virtue of Christ's Eschatological Union of Time
and Eternity, Eternity is the Meaning of Time and
Time is the Expression of Eternity 81
    4.1.2 Jesus Christ is the Conqueror of Death and of
Eternal Life 88
    4.1.3 Eternity is Inalienable Irreversibility Inalienably
Measured by Inalienable Irreversibility 116
4.2 Individual and Eternity 117
    4.2.1 Since Death Is the End of Time as well as the Entering
Into Christ's Time, It Follows that at the Threshold
of Time and Eternity Christ is the Only Judge
and the Only Judge for Everyone 117
    4.2.2 Eternal Life as Heaven is Entering the Trinitarian
God's Eternity: The Time of Christ is My Time 124
    4.2.3 Eternal Life as Hell is an Effort to Hold Up One's Own
Time as Time for Eternity and Time For Others 132
    4.2.4 Resurrection-Time in Time: An Intermediate State 137
4.3 Society, World and Eternity 140
    4.3.1 Christ is the Lord of the Times of History and
Redeemer of the Cosmic Universe 140
    4.3.2 Self-Discovery of the History of Human Society
in the Time of Jesus Christ 142
    4.3.3 Cosmic Times Enter Eternity: Fulfillment
of the Resurrection of Christ 148
    4.3.4 Cosmic Eternity is the Expression of the Uniqueness of
Each of Us by Being Loved by God in the Church of
Christ as No One Ever Before or After 150

5 CONCLUSION 155

REFERENCES 157

SUBJECT INDEX 169

NAME INDEX 172

FOREWORD

In 1978 the late Wilhelm Arnold, former Rector of the University of Würzburg, Germany, and editor of *Lexikon für Psychologie*, invited me as a theologian to write an entry on *Tod*, "Death." I found the complexity of the subject matter fascinating and, having written the article, continued my research.

First, I made up a list of all pertinent concepts and elements which are somehow related to thanatology and the meaning of which might influence the outcome of a systematic presentation of eschatology. During my reading of related literature I discovered more and more the central importance of the notion of time in my research. To my amazement, during that period I found a great number of books and studies published on death as well as on the notion of time. The notion of time has been studied in the most disparate academic disciplines, like theology and geology, philosophy and biology, sociology and physics, and so on. The authors whose names are listed in my references introduced me to a new world. My initial acknowledgment is to them. My work in a certain sense is their work, too, since, by their writings, my horizon has been widened. I became a richer person, thanks to my research, which obliged me to read books that I did not have on my reading list before Dr. Arnold's invitation.

In 1981 I started to teach a course on eschatology. During the course each student was asked to work on one of the 63 topics of the eschatology vocabulary and present the prevailing views reflected in classical and current literature. Meanwhile, I tried to discern and explain the role that the notion of time had in each topic discussed. Progressively, I felt that the difference between Catholic and non-Catholic eschatologies originated in the different concepts of time that each had. My students found such an approach both illuminating and challenging. Their difficulties became further encouragement to me in my work. Thus my second acknowledgment goes to my students, who bore with me as I talked about these ideas in the classroom.

Publication of a few articles on the notion of time followed. "The Theology of Time After Theology of Being," "A New Notion of

Time," "Jesus Christ, the Eschatological Union of Time and Eternity" and "Society, World and Eternity" were originally published in *Science et Esprit* (38:81-96, 40:35-55, 179-92, 43:319-37) and have been included in the present book with the kind permission of Les Éditions Bellarmin. My third acknowledgment is due to Rev. Prof. Gilles Langevin, S.J., the editor of *Science et Esprit*, for accepting and skilfully editing my essays. As an editor of a scholarly periodical, I have long admired Fr. Langevin's talent, dedication and tireless support for academic theological research in Canada.

By 1987 I had completed the first draft of my manuscript, entitled "Eschatology: Eternity and Eternal Life," and began to look around for a publisher. One publisher after another returned my manuscript with the same verdict: its strength is its weakness, at least in terms of a possible audience. Yet during these years the manuscript was constantly being improved. The readers of the various publishers, without exception, through their observations and critiques, helped me to clarify certain points, correct mistakes and errors and detect new connections. In 1989 I turned to the Canadian Federation for the Humanities, Aid to Scholarly Publication Program, Ottawa, to ask about the eligibility of my work for financial support. The manuscript was sent to two more readers, who again made several recommendations and requested clarification of certain parts. The present text should reflect my honest response. My fourth acknowledgment goes, therefore, to all the readers of the various publishers. I appreciate very much their close attention, their actual suggestions and their fair critiques, and I want to thank them all. I am particularly grateful to the Publication Committee of the Canadian Federation for the Humanities and the Social Sciences and Humanities Research Council for having found, after a thorough examination, my manuscript worthy of a CFH subvention. This book has been published with the help of a grant from the Canadian Federation for the Humanities, using funds provided by the Social Sciences and Humanities Research Council of Canada. I am no less indebted to Wilfrid Laurier University Press for the skilful copyediting and for publishing my book.

My next acknowledgment must go to Rev. Angus J. Macdougall, S.J., a classicist, who read the manuscript and made the requested revision of the whole work. He shared with me his gifts as a writer, theologian and understanding friend. I want to thank here also Rev. Henry Hall, who, through the many years of preparation, has helped me to find the right expressions and had time to read the various drafts of the manuscript.

The present list of acknowledgments would not be complete without a word of thanks to the Jesuits of the Upper Canada Province and to Regis College, where I have been teaching systematic theology since 1962 and which provided me with an excellent milieu for theological reflection and scholarly research. My experience at Regis College, a Roman Catholic theological faculty of the English Canadian Jesuits and confederated college of the University of Toronto, as teacher, author, founder and editor of the scholarly journal *Ultimate Reality and Meaning, Interdisciplinary Studies in the Philosophy of Understanding* (University of Toronto Press, 1978-) is without doubt a source for my theology (Leonard, 1988) just as have been my years of study in Hungary, Austria, Germany, Italy, Belgium and Spain.

Finally I would like to make one more acknowledgment: the acknowledgment of all those who are going to read the present book. The reading may not prove easy. This is a pioneering work that needs to be tested in the community of interested readers. It is a communal search for an understanding of life, death and eternal life, not only in the light of abstract ideas and cultural linguistic doctrines in the world of religions (Lindbeck, 1984) but also in the light of science and especially of a *person* as the horizon of understanding for both time and eternity. Christ as the eschatological union of time and eternity becomes the work's unifying focus and its paradigm which solves recognized problems and opens our mind to new ones.

1 INTRODUCTION

1.1. Core-tenet of Christianity

There are many reasons why people are attracted to Christianity, yet the most specific gift that Christ offers to his followers is eternal life. Anyone who wants to live forever should be baptized and become a Christian. This is the tenor of the baptismal rite. "What do you ask of God's Church?" the priest asks the candidate. "Faith." "What does faith offer you?" "Eternal life" replies the candidate. Even though in post-Vatican II liturgies, for pastoral reasons and following the theological worldview of the candidate's family during the reception rite, the words "eternal life" may have been replaced by expressions like "grace of Christ," "entrance into the Church," the profession of faith preceding the baptism and the symbols used, i.e., the anointing, the clothing with white garments and the handing over of the lighted candle immediately following the baptismal rite clearly state that eternal life is the Church's authentic hope.

The God of the Old Testament promised his people fertile land, a country "where milk and honey flow" (Ex 3, 17), and peace and safety from their enemies (Ex 23, 22; Lv 26, 1-46; Dt 28, 1-69; 33, 1-29). The God of Jesus Christ offers above all eternal life. Anyone who follows Christ will never taste death but will live forever, we read in John's Gospel (Jn 8, 51-54). It is God's will that those who believe in Jesus shall have eternal life, since Jesus will raise them up at the last day (Jn 6, 40). John's Gospel is really emphatic (Jn 3, 16,36; 6, 27,54,58; 10, 28; 11, 25-26). But so also are the synoptics (Mt 18, 9; 19, 16,17,29; 25, 46; Mk 9, 42-44; 10, 17,30; Lk 18, 18; 22, 30). And Paul is not much different (cf. 1 Cor 15, etc.).

The earliest Creeds of the Church even in their shortest form never fail to mention "We believe in life everlasting" (Roman Creeds) or "the life of the world to come," "to come quickly" (Oriental Creeds) (DS 1-36; 40-55, 150). Christians have always believed that there is an eternal life, and Christianity would be useless, false and guilty of perjury (cf. 1 Cor 15, 12-19) if there is no heaven, no eternal life.

Yes, eternal life! We use these words, but do we know what we mean by them? Whenever we talk about eternal life we use the language of time to refer to an event of which we have little understanding. Yet we must believe in eternal life, because if we do not believe in eternal life, we are no longer Christians.

Or are we? Could we, for example, without "faith-shaking trauma" remove "eternal life" from our Creed and keep all the other basic tenets of our faith, like the Trinity, the Incarnation, Jesus Christ, the Church, Sanctifying Grace, the Sacraments, etc., as true? Suppose that I believe in everything except eternal life. Am I a Christian? For me, personally and psychologically, which one of the basic tenets of Christianity is more essential: the sacraments or eternal life? the Church or eternal life? Would Jesus Christ make any sense to me if there is no eternal life? Would I be attracted to him if he led me to believe in eternal life when, as a matter of fact, there is no such thing as eternal life? How about my belief in God? Would I care about God if there were no eternal life for me and if death would mean the absolute end of me? And, frankly, do I not sometimes feel that perhaps when I die there will no longer be any me? Do I not consider the possibility that after my death I will never "wake up" and that my faith in eternal life is just a mistake, a pitiable wishful thinking and my love of Jesus an illusion and self-deception? Does this kind of thinking affect my relationship to God? What if there is an after-life, but no Jesus Christ? Would I be disappointed and consider myself cheated by my Church if, for example, after my death, I "woke up" and found myself in a rather different form of life, but with Jesus Christ nowhere to be seen? Do I think that these or similar ideas precede or follow the loss of faith in the living God?

Suppose for a moment that there is no eternal life yet I claim that I know what it means to say "I believe in Jesus Christ" and "I love him really." It is possible that I personally and psychologically may feel that Jesus Christ and my love for him is more important than my faith in eternal life. So much so that, even if I will not "wake up" after death, the love for Jesus Christ which I experience now is so real that I do not care what happens to me after death. The experience of being loved by Jesus Christ and being able to love him is so captivating and joyful that it is worth it, even if for this limited earthly life only. Sometimes I am so "wrapped up" in this mysterious experience that I have the conviction that it is worthwhile to follow him all the days of my life even though there is no eternal life. In other words, so great is this love for Jesus Christ that it means more to me than eternal life.

This kind of testing exercise might reveal what is primary for me psychologically: God and eternal life without Jesus Christ, or God and Jesus Christ without eternal life, or just God without Jesus Christ and eternal life?

To the Christians of the twentieth and twenty-first centuries, the only experiential access to the reality of faith is the experience of the love for Jesus Christ which, after 2,000 years, is still strong enough to capture our hearts and make us wonder how we can so love a person who died 2,000 years ago. The reality of my love for Jesus Christ lets me experience the reality of Jesus Christ and I argue that he is alive since I love him. I just cannot understand how I can so love someone who does not exist. Thus the love of Jesus Christ can subjectively be the most fundamental reality of Christianity. One would be inclined to say that what matters is not that I will live forever, but that I know and I love Jesus Christ here and now. Such an experience is more intriguing after 2,000 years than it was in the time of the early Christians, who were exposed directly or indirectly to the influence of the historical Jesus. For this reason I can perhaps psychologically and subjectively separate my faith in God and Jesus Christ from my belief in eternal life. But logically and dogmatically that is a different matter.

But let us take another example. Suppose for a moment that there is no eternal life, yet I feel that my faith in Jesus Christ provides me with insight, inspiration and courage to promote justice and peace by establishing an earthly paradise on earth. Which one is more important for me: eternal life or a very happy life with no suffering for every human being yet only so long as they live with no life in eternity? Can I separate my faith in Christianity from my belief in eternal life? Individually and subjectively perhaps I could, but logically and dogmatically, I cannot.

Logically and/or dogmatically, i.e., by moving from the *surface* level of the Christian experience to the *deep structure* of faith, charity and hope, where relations are grasped as founded on the *given basic* level, sc., on the life of the revealing trinitarian God, it is not possible to separate faith in God and in Jesus Christ from our belief in eternal life. Thus even though in my subjective personal experience I can make a shift in emphasis or even eliminate one of the three foundational values of Christianity, sc., God, Jesus Christ and eternal life, in the communal and ecclesial life of faith all three are understood as logically inseparable. One includes the other, because God's self-giving means precisely eternal life. Eternal life is the "object" of God's self-giving, because God is eternity. In other words, the language of God's self-giving is the language of eternal life. Therefore it follows that we can understand the meaning of God's self only in the language of eternal life as a gift of God. Only eternal life reveals what the self of the God of Jesus Christ is, and this makes the self-giving of the Christian God different than any other self-giving we know from other human and non-Christian religious experiences. The self-giving of God in Jesus Christ is not just a gift of life after life, but a gift of eternal life.

This should be more evident as we proceed. But we want to make it clear now that the idea or experience of after-life is not the same as the gift of eternal life. After-life and eternal life are two different concepts and two different realities as well. Not after-life but eternal life is the "gift" of God's self-giving in Jesus Christ, and eternal life should not be understood as endless life. Endless time is not identical with the sharing in God's life made possible by the grace of Jesus Christ. The difference between endless life and eternal life is still the same as the difference between created and uncreated reality, between human beings and God.

For a Christian theologian it is imperative to grasp the necessary connection between God's self-giving and eternal life. If God wants to give himself and not something else, he has to give eternal life. If God's self-giving is the core-tenet of Christianity, so also is eternal life, and we should never underestimate the importance of this statement. If we say that Jesus Christ made possible God's self-giving or God gave himself to us in Jesus Christ, we have to say also that Jesus Christ made possible for us eternal life. It is the inner logic of Christian faith that without Christ there is no eternal life for anyone in the world. There could be after-life, but no eternal life. Eternal life is the exclusive gift of Christ to the world, and this is the gift Christians make available to all human beings by their being in Christ.

But how can one legitimize the language of eternal life? How can one know that there is an eternal life, and what is it like? These questions should be the main concern of any research dealing with Christian eschatology.

1.2. History of Christian Eschatology
1.2.1. History–Resurrection–Revelation Link

Each of the three ideas, history, revelation and resurrection, can be traced back to the Old Testament. But their close link as well as their concrete meaning is new in Christian experience. We find this close connection already in the communities of the gospel traditions. The synoptic writers link history—the destruction of Jerusalem, the end of the world—resurrection and revelation with the appearance of the Son of Man closely together as a quasi-single event. And so does the writer of John's gospel.

The early Christians experiencing Incarnation (Jn 1, 14) through the life and resurrection of Jesus Christ became aware that the time of the world became the time of Jesus Christ. His birth, *prōton*, and his resurrection, *eschaton*, became the authentic beginning and end of the world. Christ was not only the first-born of all creation (Col 1, 15) but also the recapitulation (*anacephalaeosis*) of the whole of creation (Eph 1, 10). As a result, both statements are true: revelation is history and history is revelation. The first means that revelation is in time and the second asserts that what is revealed is known in and through history.

Moreover, since the Incarnation is seen in the light of the history of Jesus Christ's resurrection, revelation and history are once and for all inseparably linked with the resurrection. That revelation is history and history is revelation means further that from now on history and revelation together are resurrection and that resurrection is history and revelation as well.

That history and revelation together are resurrection was grasped by the early Christians in the paschal experience, and that resurrection is history and revelation was formulated in the faith of Jesus' final coming. Thus it is understandable that when the early Christians experienced one they were impatiently waiting for the other two. Since resurrection, history and revelation were linked together, it was logical that the cross could become the symbol of the future coming of the Lord and not, as was later the case, the symbol of past suffering. E. Peterson rightly argued that the early Christians used the symbol of the cross on the east wall of their buildings as they were praying towards the east where the sun was rising and from whence they expected the risen Christ to come (cf. Rev 1, 7; Peterson, 1959, pp. 1-14). Thus eternal life was conceived simply as meeting with the risen Jesus Christ, who was coming very soon. The use of the *maranatha*, which was both a prayer "Come Lord Jesus" (Rev 22, 20), and a curse or an oath "this is as sure as our Lord Jesus has come," confirms this (1 Cor 16, 21; Didache, 10, 6; Kuhn, 1969, p. 471).

Now it seems that the early Christians paid less attention to the meaning of the statement "resurrection is history." They emphasized rather that "history and revelation is resurrection." The more so since history meant for them initially the history of Israel, which seemed to come to an end with the destruction of Jerusalem. After having experienced "the end of history" they expected the imminent return of Christ, which meant both the end of the present world and the resurrection of the body (2 Thes 2, 1-12; 2 Pet 3, 10; Mt 23, 43). The return of Christ was heaven for them. They did not think of heaven as a place above. They knew the term "paradise" (cf. Lk 23, 43; 2 Cor 12, 2-4; Rev 2, 7), yet heaven for them was here on earth, where Jesus was expected to return. It is true that heaven was a place where God the Father lived (cf. Mt 6, 9; 1, 11; Mk 11, 25) and where Jesus came from, according to John (6, 33,44,51) and returned, according to Luke (24, 51) and the Acts of the Apostles (1, 9-11). Yet it is remarkable that the followers of Jesus were not concerned with going to heaven to meet the Father there, but rather were eager to meet Jesus here on earth and be with him wherever he was. When Thomas wanted to know the place Jesus was talking about, the answer was "I am the way, the truth and the life. . . . From this moment you know him (the Father) and have seen him." And what Thomas saw was no one else but Jesus, the Lord (Jn 14, 5-7). Philip's further insistence makes it more unambiguous that the Father is in Jesus (Jn 14, 9-11) and that Jesus and the Father are one (Jn 10, 30). Jesus is heaven for his followers. To be in heaven is to be with Jesus. Death is not a curse any longer but the way to be with Christ (Phil 1, 22-26). As a result of Jesus' victory over death, "the way away from God" (Ps 6, 5; 30, 9; 88, 11; Is 38, 11,18) becomes the way to him in Jesus.

The theology of the kingdom of God confirms this. The expectation of the kingdom of God which will have no end was the expectation of being with Christ. Wherever Jesus was, there was the kingdom of God. The identification of the kingdom of God with the "I" of Jesus Christ is already found in the Q sources (Horvath, 1975, pp. 146-47). This might be the reason that, according to the gospels, Jesus did not reveal too much about the heaven from whence he came. A psychologist would think that this was because he did not know anything about it. But a theologian would notice that once Jesus made himself the exclusive centre of all religious concerns, the main concern of the early Christians was who Jesus was rather than what heaven looked like. To know heaven was to know Jesus Christ. Thus it is understandable that the gospel writers did not elaborate on heaven as a place, or even on our spiritual existence in heaven as later Paul was prompted to do in evangelizing the Corinthians (1 Cor 15, 35-53). For the community of the synoptic gospels Jesus had a body, and with that body he was expected to return to them on earth and not some other place. Therefore heaven meant for them this world. And since Jesus was to live and reign forever, their being with Christ, their heaven, was forever too.

That the kingdom of God and heaven were identified with Jesus is an astonishing theology, and we should not pass without scrutinizing it. There is something extraordinary in this exclusive concern with Jesus, who became heaven, eternal life and everything that God meant for the faithful. Why and how the early Christians could think the way they did needs an explanation.

The theological concern focused on heaven as a place above, where all who are saved would go after death, is not archaic. It is a later development. As the return of Christ was further and further delayed, paradise was conceived of more as a place where one is with God, the Father, rather than being with Christ. And since the Father had no body, to be with the Father was more fittingly understood as a sort of spiritual, non-bodily existence, and the resurrection of the body and eternal life became the "last" things. By stressing the transcendence of God (the theology of St. Justin will be a good example) the idea of a new heaven became of greater concern, and a more explicit description of heaven was sought. This kind of theological interest opened the door for a new literary form, apocalyptic literature, with its impressive, imaginative description of heaven, something which the Jesus of the synoptics never tried to offer. Perhaps this is why it took so long before the Church could gain full certitude about the canonicity of the book of Revelation. The apocalyptic literature limited the presence of Jesus Christ on earth to 1,000 years (chiliasm, millenarism), a long time, but not as long as forever (Rev 20, 2). One of the apocalyptic groups, the Montanists, went further and changed Jesus' presence in heaven to the presence of the Spirit in heaven and considered Jesus' followers not as God's sons and daughters (cf. Pauline literature) anymore, but as people endowed with God's spirit who are immortal and, therefore, do not require resurrection.

For the Gnostics and Montanists revelation was neither history nor resurrection. Yet these theologies should not be considered just a Greek type of reasoning. There was a real Judaic Old Testament theological axiom operating in them: anything which is not God, but flesh, must come to an end; otherwise God's uniqueness is at stake. This being so, we should realize that for the early Christians there was not a logical precedent for accepting that Jesus is heaven, the presence of God, the Father, and that there is resurrection and eternal life. Yet for them, as the early Creeds witness, eternal life, resurrection of the dead and the coming of Jesus as the judge of the living and of the dead were all just one event (2 Tim 4, 1; 1 Pet 4, 5; Acts 10, 42, etc.). This suggests that the resurrection was not just a resuscitation for another life in time but rather an entering into eternal life. The act of judgment is the act of rising from the dead and it is done, according to the synoptics, without wrath (cf. Mk 9, 43-44; Mt 25, 46; Paul is the one who used the term "wrath" of God; for an explanation see Horvath, 1979, pp. 47-58, 97-98).

Creating theological synthesis that combined faith that there is one God who is eternity himself (and every created thing is just flesh), and that Jesus who was born and crucified takes the place of God, linking history, revelation and resurrection together, was not an easy task for the New Testament gospel writers. It became even more difficult if instead of simply proposing some new doctrine, they tried to describe the historical existence of the faithful of their communities as they experienced it at that time. And here we find the clues as to why the synoptic gospels differ in describing Christian eschatology.

1.2.2. Eschatology as Expectation

The Greek word *eschaton* has mostly been used since the nineteenth century to signify Christian expectation, following A. Schweitzer, who described Jesus as the one who expected an imminent end of the world. When the end did not come, his followers, the Christians, tried to reinterpret Jesus' message by continually postponing the end (Schweitzer, 1910). But among scholars there was no agreement about what Jesus and the early Christians expected: the end of Jerusalem, the end of the world and/or the coming of the Son of Man.

C.H. Dodd introduced the concept of "realized eschatology," arguing that Jesus did not wait for eschatology, but announced it as already present in his person, in his work, and, more concretely, in his death and resurrection (Dodd, 1935). According to R. Bultmann, the expectation of the immediate end is common to the synoptic writers, and he thought that John was the first who made eschatology independent of the immediate end (Bultmann, 1957). But it seems that Bultmann did not attend to the fact that there is no straight line from Mark through Matthew and Luke to John. The later Matthew, for example, is much stronger than the earlier Mark in expecting immediate eschatology. Thus A. Conzelmann believed that for Luke Jesus is neither the end of time nor the road to the Parousia as O. Cullmann suggested (Cullmann, 1960, pp. 37-118) but the road to the church of the pagans, which Luke called the time of the nations (Lk 21, 24; Conzelmann, 1973).

What the churches of the synoptic gospels really expected is not easy to detect. One way of explaining the differences is to analyze the idea of eschatology and see whether or not it involves expectations of events at some future time for the synoptic churches. According to Bultmann, eschatology meant not time but a way of existence, a decision for or against Christ. Such a decision as an eschatological event transcends the subject-object circle and can therefore be considered as the end of time (Bultmann, 1957). For Barth eschatology meant resurrection and eternity, the eternal "now" (Barth, 1965, pp. 234-35; 1957, pp. 161, 609-11).

J. Ratzinger explains the differences in the synoptic eschatology by the tension between word-schema and the reality itself. Since one cannot describe eschatology as something which has already taken place, there is a distance between the reality and the schema available to express it. The reality is the future, but the schema is taken from the past, with its causal consequences which are not applicable to the future. Yet in the synoptic scriptural language the future is expressed as if it were already past and the literary form of succession is applied to the not-yet experienced reality-in-process. And this future-reality-in-process, sc., the predicted reality, is not an independent commentary on the text but a process of realization which by its realization expresses further dimensions of the words used previously. So John can explain the meaning of the words more penetratingly than the synoptic writers. The schema of text-reality-text brings the reality in-progress into the text, and the future reality becomes *now-reality*. The words later in time are a more adequate expression of the *future-now* reality than the words earlier in time. The only univocal direction in the process is the risen Christ presenting the kingdom of God as future reality. Thus the interpretation-realization process can go ahead safely as long as the Church is the centre of the tension between word-schema and reality (Ratzinger, 1971, pp. 42-50, 60-64).

Such a metaphysical explanation might be correct, but a more simple historical solution is preferable. The differences in the synoptic eschatological texts can be explained by the history–resurrection–revelation link which the three traditions tried to conserve, with each placing a slight emphasis on one part of the triad that reflected the particular interest of each community.

For all three synoptic writers the destruction of the temple in Jerusalem had a decisive role in history. Resurrection obviously meant the end of the world we know, and revelation was understood as the coming of the Son of Man. Indeed, we find all three linked in Mk (13, 1-37), in Mt (24, 1-51) and in Lk (21, 5-38). All speak of the destruction of the temple in Jerusalem, of the end of the world and of the Son of Man's Parousia in such a close connection that it is not easy to separate one from the other two. This close connection is the *crux exegetarum*, and the matrix of so many inadequate interpretations of the synoptic eschatology.

All three synoptics keep the three elements, yet it seems that Mark is more interested in the *revelation* of the Son of Man than in the eschatological end of the world and its historical inauguration by the destruction of the temple in Jerusalem. He does not tell his readers, as Matthew does, that they will not have gone through all the towns of Israel before the coming of the Son of Man, since he does not yet have the sign, of the destruction of the temple, as Matthew will (Mt 10, 23). The sign of the destruction of the temple prompts Matthew to expect the suddenness of the other two, i.e., the Parousia of the Son of Man and the end of the world. For the same reason for Mark those "standing there" (9, 1) will not see before they die the Son of Man coming in his kingdom as we read in Mt 16, 28. Rather they will see just the kingdom of God. According to Mark 13, 30 "this" generation knows about the sign, such as when the twigs of the fig tree grow supple, but in 14, 62 we do not find Matthew's "from now" (Mt 26, 64). All this indicates that Mark did not quite expect a sudden end as Matthew did. And this is quite feasible if we assume that once the author of Matthew's gospel knew about the destruction of the temple in Jerusalem, he could expect the revelation of the Son of Man in the lifetime of his generation. Not the expectation of the immediate end of the world assumedly suggested by Christ, but the particular interpretation of the close connection between history, resurrection and revelation is the explanation of the differences in the synoptic eschatological description. Not Jesus, but the destruction of the temple, prompted the awareness of the immediate eschatology among the members of the post-paschal communities.

Mark was interested in revelation, while Matthew was more interested in *history*. It is Matthew who cares about Jesus' genealogy (Mt 1, 1-17) and about Jesus' relation to the history of Israel. This is why, once he saw the destruction of the temple, he could conclude that the other two, the revelation of the Son of Man and the resurrection with the end of the world, could not be far away.

As Mark emphasized the revelation and Matthew the history, so Luke emphasized *resurrection*. He used apocalyptical terms to describe our preparation (cf. Lk 12, 49) but not to describe what we had to be prepared for, sc., the resurrection. Like Matthew, Luke also knew about the destruction of the temple surrounded by armies (Lk 21, 20) but this was just the inauguration of the time of the nations (Lk 21, 24) which too would end, but not as soon as Matthew thought. For Luke, the death and resurrection of the Lord in Jerusalem is an Exodus (Lk 9, 31) and assumption (Lk 9, 51) described according to the pattern of Elijah's departure from this world (cf. 2 Kings 2, 911; for more details see Lk 24, 44-53). Therefore it is no wonder that Mt 10, 23 is missing in Luke and that in 9, 27 Luke follows Mark rather than Matthew. For Luke the revelation of the Son (cf. Mt 26, 64 and Mk 14, 62) is Jesus' resurrection and ascension.

That Luke gave special attention to resurrection is confirmed by his calling the sons of God the sons of resurrection: "They are the sons of God because they are the sons of the resurrection" (Lk 20, 36). We should notice also that the eschatological expectation of 1 Thes 4, 13-5, 3 is in the line of the Lukan synthesis, whereas 2 Thes 1, 7-2, 5 and 2 Pet 3, 8-16 reflect rather the Matthean tradition.

The source of the triad of history, resurrection and revelation, a common schema for the three synoptic writers, must be pre-synoptic, and might give some hint of the nature of the originating paschal experience which, as the cosmic radiation of the birth of the universe, pervades the early faith in all its manifestations. It suggests an early Christology seeing Jesus Christ as the eschatological union of time and eternity, as we will see later.

Because of the close link between history, resurrection and revelation, the synoptics did not have to use the term *eschaton* in the sense we do now. Though all three knew the term (Mt 5, 26; 12, 45; 19, 30;

20, 8,12,14,16; 27, 64; Mk 9, 35; 10, 31; 12, 6,22; Lk 11, 26; 12, 59; 13, 50; 14, 9,10), they never used it to refer to the last day as John (6, 39,40,44,54; 11, 24; 12, 48), with other New Testament writers (2 Tim 3, 1; Heb 1, 2; Jas 5, 3 and 2 Pet 3, 3), did, or to the end time (cf. Jude, 18; 1 Pet 1, 5,20), or to the last hour, as we find in 1 Jn 2, 18. What the synoptic writers expected was not an *eschaton*, a "last thing" for them, as the resurrection, for example, was for John (6, 39,40,44,54; 11.24) nor the time of stress already experienced (see 2 Tim 3, 4) nor the judgment with the Parousia of the Lord (like John 12, 48; Jas 5, 3 with 7; 2 Pet 3, 3; Jude 18; 1 Pet 1, 5) nor the coming of the Antichrist as for 1 Jn 2, 18. The "last thing" for the synoptics was Jesus Christ himself. Though for the non-synoptic communities expectation was an expectation of something "last," yet they also tried to keep history, revelation and resurrection as close as possible to Jesus Christ, the only true *eschaton* (Rev 1, 7; 2, 8; 19, 22,13), the last Adam (1 Cor 15, 45) whose lifetime was the last time (1 Pet 1, 20) as well as the last day (Heb 1, 2) when he has risen and poured out the Holy Spirit (Acts 2, 17).

1.2.3. *Eschatology as Advent of Salvation*

As time passed, it became more and more difficult to keep history, resurrection and revelation together. With the destruction of the temple in Jerusalem, the history of Israel seemed to come to an end, but that of the nations and of the world did not. Revelation and history were further and further distanced by the steadily increasing time-interval between the two. One way of re-affirming the link was to replace the history of Israel with the history of Jesus' life, suffering and death, which became now the advent-event in the sense of *adventus*. As the historical beginning of the Jewish people became important for the writers of the books of Law, the Pentateuch, so the historical dating of Jesus' birth became important for the early Christians.

Once history and revelation were joined together in a new synthesis, the end of the world (resurrection and eternal life) was brought into the new synthesis, not as a future event but as present salvation from sin, evil and death in a spiritual sense. The theology of everlasting life as expectation gave way to the theology of salvation and justification through Jesus' merits. The Pauline and Johannine theologies supported this new emphasis. The question of the future (eternity) and of the present (time) was replaced by the problem of the relation between the past event of Jesus' work and the present sanctification and deliverance from damnation. The obvious outcome of this development was that the universal judgment when Jesus was expected to judge the living and the dead became just an announcement of the particular judgment which takes place at the moment of each one's death. What was left for the world to come was public announcement of a past verdict at the moment of joining the body to the soul already enjoying eternal life in the beatific vision.

Thus the theology of eternal life was shifted to the far end of the theological spectrum. Not the future but the present was the centre of the theological concern. The crucial question became how the past event of Jesus' work could be effectively present in the sanctification and the salvation of the soul. The treatise *de novissimis* became, indeed, a treatise of the "last things," giving ample room for the treatise on grace and justification. All this was very much in tune with the non-temporal static concept of reality of the first millennium. But once the concept of reality was replaced by a more dynamic one, eschatology again became a central issue for theology.

1.2.4. *Eschatology as the Theology of Eternal Life*

The change was due in great part to the evolutionary worldview. Already in the twelfth century Joachim of Fiore (1130-1202) thought of history as the three progressively developing periods of the Father (Old Testament), of the Son (the present Church) and of the Spirit, the time when the power of the spirit will be at work everywhere. It was based on the mystery of salvation, with special interest in pointing out the distinction between the three divine persons. However, the concept of evolution became widely accepted only through the works of Charles Darwin, Karl Marx and Alfred North Whitehead.

With secularization the search for salvation became the search for good fortune in this world, and the future of the world was seen as dependent on the resources of the natural sciences rather than on the apocalyptic work of the Son of Man. At the same time world wars prompted existential philosophies which made people more and more aware of death as a real event which might prevent us from achieving the desired good fortune. New studies on death became popular. Moreover, the nuclear threat made it clear that we all are responsible for the kind of future we wish for ourselves and for our descendants. Thus the future again became of general interest to everyone.

From this short overview it should be clear that futurology (Marxism is the most popular form of it) and existentialism returned the theology of eternal life from the margin of the theological disciplines to the centre, where it was in the early period of Christianity. The new challenge for Christianity is to say something meaningful to the people of today about the future we expect for the world and for ourselves once we are dead. Consequently, the task for theology is to enter into a mutually fruitful dialogue with the modern sciences, testing the validity of an Einsteinian universe, when humankind acquired the power of bringing its history to an eschatological end by nuclear explosion.

However, in attempting to do this theology must follow its 2,000 years of tradition in keeping the close link between history, revelation and resurrection. Within this tradition theology will have to search for a new concept of time and eternity. Since our age is history, too, neither revelation nor resurrection can float without having close links to our age. Again, because of the close link between history, revelation and resurrection, we have to ask what contribution the insight of the early Christians, discovered in their paschal experience, can make to the world of today. We have to ask ourselves, can our eschatology make some statements of a cognitive nature? If our response is negative, we ignore one of the triad of the early Christian eschatology, sc., revelation. If our response is affirmative, and we assume that eschatology is a sort of knowledge, a claim is made that the eschatological statements are not just emotive, conative, promising, warning, threatening or moral attitude-changing, but informative in the sense of limit-breaking knowledge. The negative or affirmative answer depends on another more fundamental question, sc., if Jesus Christ is the pattern of eternity and the relation of eternity to time, on the basis of knowing him can we know something about future life? In pursuing our question, therefore, we have to scrutinize the concepts of time and eternity in various academic disciplines as well as the mystery of Jesus Christ as the eschatological union of eternity and time.

But before we explain our method at greater length we present the teaching of the Church, expressed in its various councils, reacting to particular problems prompted by historical conditions.

1.2.5. *The Teaching of the Church*

The Nicene-Constantinopolitan creed in 381 professed that Jesus will come to judge the living and the dead and that we expect (πγοσδοκώμεν) the resurrection of the dead and the life of the world to come very soon (μέλλοντος) "to be on the point of doing" (DS 150;

Tanner, 1990, p. 24). The Roman creed from the third century mentions the resurrection of the body (not of the dead) and eternal life (DS 27). The former is more communitarian and cosmic, whereas the latter is more individual and personal.

The Provincial Synod of Constantinople in 543 accepted the edict of Justinian, the so-called *imperator theologus*, against Origenism, proclaiming that there is no pre-existence of the soul prior to bodily existence, that bodily existence is not the manifestation of sin, that the world is not eternal and that there will be no final apocatastasis, i.e., a universal reconciliation of all, demons and wicked souls included (DS 403, 410, 411). Cassiodorus (PL 70, 1111D) claimed that Pope Vigilius, who was in Constantinople at the time (545-555), approved these decrees.

Like Gnosticism, Origenism was a doctrine of Oriental origin challenging the universality of God's creation, the unity of human existence, and the goodness of the material world and of the body. The Church could not accept any of its tenets and rejected the concept of the transmigration of the soul similar to the one we know from Hinduism, and from Orphic and Theosophical worldviews. Therefore, according to the Church, no one lives many bodily lives in other worlds. Unlike Oriental philosophies, the Church, following the Judaic tradition, did not wish to refer the solution of a problem of this world to another, prior world. If there is an original sin, it must be a phenomenon of this world in which we now live. Eternal life begins in time and not prior to it, and heaven or hell as our destiny is decided in this present life of our body and not previously. This reasoning accords with faith in the redemption brought about by the incarnate God as the basic axiom for any knowledge of God and world. Thus the rejection of Origenism is just an application of the synoptic eschatological triad, sc., that there is no revelation and eternal life without history. For the same reason the Church could not accept another tenet of Origenism, which held that Jesus is going to be crucified for the demons in a future world, as he was for human beings in this world.

The Origenist apocatastasis, a doctrine which was defended by great theologians like St. Gregory of Nazianzus, St. Gregory of Nyssa, Didymus the Blind, Diodore Ponticus, Theodore of Mopsuestia and more recently by Karl Barth (1962, p. 478) was rejected by the Church not just in 543 (DS 411) but in 1215 (DS 801; Tanner, 1990, p. 230) as well. The rationale for this lack of "mercy" on the part of the Church is not often understood. Yet there must be a context of revealed "realities" in which apocatastasis does not fit. What this context of "realities" is will be sought later in the analysis of time and eternity complex.

In 1201 in a letter to Yubertus, Bishop of Arles, Innocent III wrote that the punishment of original sin is the deprivation of the sight of God, whereas punishment of actual sin is the torment of hell (DS 780). It was a response to those who objected to the baptism of little children on the ground that baptism cannot have any effect on them, since they had committed no sins. Now the theological argument of Innocent III is interesting. In order to comply with Jn 3, 5 and make baptism necessary for everyone, little children included, Innocent III made a clear distinction between hell, with punishment, and a place without punishment but with no sight of God. However, he did not call this latter place hell. By doing this he succeeded in justifying the baptism of little children, but apparently he made it impossible for all non-baptized people to enter heaven. One problem had been solved but another, i.e., that of the salvation of non-Christian people, had been brought to the fore. We should mention, however, that the same Innocent III had in 1206 made an exception for a Jew who desired baptism but could not be baptized before he died. According to the Pope he went to heaven not by virtue of the sacrament of faith, but by virtue of the faith of the sacrament (*propter sacramenti fidem, etsi non propter fidei sacramentum*, DS 788). The faith of the sacrament can be interpreted as the faith of the dying Jew as well as the faith of the Church. In the latter case the meaning of the Pope's statement would be no more or no less than that no one can be saved without the Church, or what amounts to the same thing, that no one can be saved without Christ, who uses the Church as his sacrament. The baptism of little children is the actualization of one of the basic life-functions of the Church, the faith of which is indispensable to everyone to attain eternal life.

During the twelfth and thirteenth centuries the Cathari, also called the heretics of the apostolic faith, objected to the practice of prayers for the dead because they could not accept the resurrection of the body. They thought that God cannot glorify the body by raising it, since the body is the outcome of sin. They also excluded married people from heaven, allowing only virgins and those who abstained from sexual relations (cf. Rev 14, 4) to enter into God's beatifying presence.

The fourth Lateran Council in 1215 rejected the teaching of the Cathari by affirming that married people will enjoy eternal happiness (DS 802; Tanner, 1990, p. 231) and that everyone, good or bad, will rise with their own bodies which they now have, so that they may receive eternal punishment with the devil or eternal glory with Christ (DS 801; Tanner, 1990, p. 230). The *propria corpora quae nunc gestant* "their own bodies in which they exist" is not to be understood as the numerically identical body in which one died, as if God would have to collect the bones buried somewhere. The condemnation was directed against the thesis of the Cathari, who believed that God will give us another new body, which is not of this universe, but of another world, that is, of a pure spiritual existence. The Council insisted on the identity of the earthly body each individual has in this life, because the reward or punishment will be measured to the deeds performed in this world to which the present body belongs. History and resurrection, time and eternity were held together. The mystery of our time entering into eternity was upheld by the Council. In 1274, some versions of the Second Council of Lyons insisted again that everyone will appear before Christ with "their" bodies to give an account of their own deeds (DS 858).

Since the question of time and eternity was not considered, there is some inconsistency in this teaching. On the one hand, the importance of the body for any human person living in this world was rightly defended but, on the other hand, the importance of the body for purgatory was ignored. Why is it that we cannot merit except while living in our bodies in this world, yet we can make satisfaction by expiatory suffering in purgatory without our bodies and obtain remission of venial sins *parva et minuta* while being cleansed after death (Innocent IV, Letter to the Bishop of Tusculum, DS 838)?

Notwithstanding, the purification after death in purgatory should not be interpreted as a sort of Upanisadic philosophy of transmigration (Raghavan, 1974, pp. 73-78; Dange, 1984, p. 268; 1978, pp. 76-79), transferring the redemption from the consequences of sins committed in this world to another world. Keeping the mystery of the Incarnation of Christ as the most powerful problem-solving paradigm, the Church always tries to solve problems of this world in this world, and holds that salvation or damnation depends on the deeds performed in the body in this world, an axiom which the final-option theory does not take sufficiently into account (Rahner, 1961; Boros, 1965). The mystery of purgatory, as we will see, is related to the reality of the present world.

Innocent IV (DS 838) mentioned two texts as the scriptural foundation of the doctrine on purgatory. One is 1 Cor 3, 13-15 where Paul says that certain teachers will be saved on that day but only through fire (Gnilka, 1955). Paul places expiatory punishment at the final judgment. Now expiation at the end of the world when history and resurrection are united is understandable, but the case of expiation after death without the body is a different matter because revelation, history and resurrection cannot be separated from each other.

The other scriptural text used by Innocent IV is Mt 12, 32. The text says that there are sins which cannot be forgiven either in this world or in the next. Consequently, the pope argues, there are some sins which can be forgiven in the next world, sc., in purgatory. With similar logic one could argue from Mt 12, 32 with Mt 16, 16 that there are some sins which can be forgiven in heaven which are not forgiven in this world, i.e., without the power of the keys given to Peter. Such an argument could be used to solve the problem of the salvation of nonbelievers, whose sins would consequently be forgiven in the next world, without baptism and without any mediation of the Church. But such a view would run into difficulty, since no one can be saved outside of the Church of Christ and therefore there is no forgiveness in heaven without forgiveness on earth.

Both the Greek and the Roman Church agreed that prayers for the dead are efficient, and therefore the intercession of the living faithful for the dead is useful and the soul after death can be further purified. The difference was rather about the name of purgatory, conceived as a place between heaven and hell. If there is no body, there can be no place. Here is another example of dogmatic disputes being prompted by the various concepts one has of time, space and eternity. It seems that unless some further research is done on the notion of time, space and eternity, theological and dogmatic differences between the Greek and the Roman Church will find no satisfactory solutions. This is further confirmed by another conciliar statement which caused lengthy disputes in the thirteenth and fourteenth centuries.

In 1245 Innocent IV declared that the souls of those who are cleansed fly *protinus* "at once" to their eternal home (DS 839). The Second Council of Lyons in 1274 used the term *mox* "suddenly" or "immediately" in the case of both those who are saved and those who are condemned (DS 857-58). Yet everyone should appear again on the last day before Christ with their bodies to give an account of "their own deeds" (DS 859). There is an assumption that everyone from heaven and everyone from hell will be judged again, now that each has his/her body. This is a logically consistent declaration, since judgment must be given to people in the body for the deeds committed in their bodies. Otherwise we have to sympathize again with the Hindu and Orphic way of solving problems, sc., in another world without the bodies in which the sins are committed. Yet we should call to mind that the judgment on the last day is expected to take place in this world and not in the other since, according to early Christian tradition, to judge the living and the dead the Lord was returning to this world. History, indeed, cannot be separated from revelation and resurrection. But is there any point in bringing to judgment again all those who have already been enjoying the vision of God in heaven?

The profession of faith given for the Greek-Russian Church by the Council of Florence in 1445 adds to the doctrine of the Council of Lyons II that the souls who are cleansed will not only be received in heaven but will clearly see the one and triune God as God is in himself. However, some will do this more perfectly than others, according to their different merits. And those who died with mortal sin or with original sin will go immediately to hell but will be punished by different punishments (DS 1305-06; Tanner, 1990, pp. 527-28). The Council of Florence used the term "hell" and thus excluded the idea of "limbo" for those who died only with original sin, a possibility left open by Innocent III, who did not use the term "hell" (DS 780) except for the punishment of actual sins.

The vision of God as part of eternal happiness was already mentioned in the Council of Vienna (1312) by affirming that it cannot be without *lumen gloriae* "the light of glory." Therefore the Brothers and Sisters of the Free Spirit, the male Beghards and the female Beguines, were wrong in claiming that any spiritual intellectual being is able to see God and enjoy him without the grace of the light of glory (DS 895; Tanner, 1990, p. 383).

After the Second Council of Lyons (1274), it became the teaching of the Church that the vision of God is possible immediately after death, before the resurrection of the body. However Pope John XXII wanted to underline the importance of the final judgment with the resurrection of the body and preached that the vision of God will take place only after the final judgment and not before. It seems that Rev 6, 9 supports this conclusion by saying that the souls of all the people who have been killed on account of the word of God await judgment beneath the altar. Under pressure from the King of France and the theologians and cardinals, the Pope was willing to revoke this doctrine and prepare a statement, but his sudden death prevented him from making it public. His successor, Benedict XII, published it in 1336 in the Apostolic Constitution entitled *Benedictus Deus*. According to the *Benedictus Deus*, which is recognized as *ex cathedra*, infallible teaching of the Magisterium of the Church, all those who are purged immediately after death, and all those who are to be purged after death will, before the final judgment and the resurrection of the body (once they are purged), "see the divine essence intuitively and face to face so that as the object is concerned no creature acts as a medium of vision, but the divine essence is shown to them plainly, clearly and openly" (DS 1000; see Tanner, 1990, pp. 527-28).

Here we find a new problem-solving paradigm. If history and resurrection are separated, one problem-solving paradigm remains for eschatology, sc., the idea of the existence of the separate soul, independent of the body, having a sort of angelic existence. Such an understanding of human existence presupposes that there are two parts in every human being: one is mortal and the other is immortal. The latter safeguards personal individuality after death. The existence of the soul separated from the body is an intermediary state. So was purgatory, which was never called heaven, although the deprivation of the sight of God caused by original sin (which Innocent talked about), was later called hell by the Council of Florence. The Council of Trent in 1563 in its decree on purgatory reaffirmed the doctrine of the previous councils: there is a purgatory and souls are aided by the suffrages of the faithful (DS 1820; Tanner, 1990, p. 774).

The Second Vatican Council, by its *Dogmatic Constitution on the Church* (1964 Tanner, 1990, pp. 849-98), recaptured the idea of eschatology as expectation of the promised restoration which has already begun in Christ and is carried forward in the mission of the Holy Spirit through whom it continues in the Church. The eschatological nature of the Church is seen in its pilgrim state as it performs the task committed to it with "the hope of good things to come" (*Dogmatic Constitution on the Church*, no. 48; Tanner, 1990, p. 888). The eschatological statements concerning heaven and hell are not affirmative and judicial, but rather optative, saying that "when we have finished the one and only one course of our earthly life *we may* enter into the marriage feast... that *we may not* be commanded to go into eternal fire like the wicked and slothful servant (cf. Mt 22, 26) into exterior darkness where there will be the weeping and gnashing of teeth (Mt 22, 13; 25, 20) (*Dogmatic Constitution on the Church*, no. 48; Tanner, 1990, p. 888). Mary is both the image and the first flower of the Church to be perfected in the world to come, since in her the Church has already reached that perfection, and thus she is a sign of sure hope and of solace for God's people on pilgrimage (*Dogmatic Constitution on the Church*, nos. 65, 68; Tanner, 1990, pp. 896-98).

Following the Second Vatican Council, the theology of eschatology tried different solutions to problems touched upon in our survey of the history of the theology of eternal life. In 1979 the Sacred Congregation for the Doctrine of Faith made public a document entitled *Letter on Certain Questions Concerning Eschatology* (*AAS* 71 [1979]): 939-43). The document lists three points as centres of recent theological controversies: (l) the existence of the soul separated from the body; (2) the meaning of life after death; and (3) the question of what happens between the death of a Christian and the general resurrection.

About the first it is stated that the individual human self, a spiritual element, subsists after death, and there is no valid reason to reject the use of the term "soul" for this human self. In regard to the second point, i.e., the meaning of life after death, the letter restates the belief of the Church in the happiness of the just and eternal punishment for the sinner yet with the possibility of a purification different from the punishment of the damned for the ones who are saved. This is what the Church means when it talks about hell and purgatory.

Finally, concerning the question of what happens between the death of a Christian and the general resurrection, we are told that there is a fundamental continuity between our present life and the future life as well as a radical break between the two. The document argues for the difference between the resurrection of the dead at the glorious manifestation of our Lord and the situation of people after death and that the two must be distinct and different. But it would not exclude an explanation which would try to link the bodily resurrection with individual death and entry into eternal life following the pattern of Jesus' own death and resurrection, if distinction is made between the bodily glorification of the Virgin Mary by her assumption and the bodily glorification of all other saved faithful before the glorious manifestation of our Lord on the last day.

The language of purgatory as "possibility" was used to respect the difference between the Oriental and Occidental churches. The same term "possibility" was not used in regard to hell, yet some theologians think that the official teaching never affirmed more than the concrete possibility for each person, without stating that there is anyone in hell. Eternal punishment as a mere possibility is considered as identical with "traditional doctrine, provided that the possibility is not reduced to a mere abstract consideration necessarily believed by God's victorious grace, but is considered as a concrete eventuality in the life of all men, in whose power it is to close themselves to God's gift of salvation" (Dupuis, 1979, p. 534).

The subtle distinction between two possibilities (abstract consideration and concrete eventuality) could perhaps be applied to humans, but the question of the devil and of the demons is another matter, unless their existence is denied. To make hell empty one has to deny the existence of the condemned angels, which implies a special interpretation of the Fourth Lateran Council (DS 800; Tanner, 1990, p. 230). It is true that the main thrust of the doctrine is to refute the doctrine of the Cathari and the Albigenses, who believed that the devil is eternal. Therefore we can argue that no one would disagree with the Council by saying that demons, whether they exist or not, are not eternal but created by God, and if they are bad they become bad of themselves and were not created so.

This is a valid hermeneutics for the teaching of a council in general. But our present case is different. The conciliar text in question is a *creed* and the sentences of a creed affirm existence, sc., God revealed that "it is" or "they are," because God does not reveal possibilities. Thus the various sentences of a creed are to be interpreted not in the context of a paragraph but as an individual affirmation or sentence which says "we believe that God revealed that demons became bad of themselves and were not created so," etc. The accent is primarily on what God said and not on what the next sentence says. Thus it seems that the creed more explicitly states the existence of bad angels than that of the good angels. Thus the actuality of hell remains a real issue.

Finally, the letter of the Sacred Congregation for the Doctrine of the Faith touches the intriguing question of time and eternity, the relation between the two, of the possibility of sharing in God's eternity and the problem of the difference between shared eternity and historical existence in time. But no directions are given. Yet these problems are the central issues of recent discussion, and further contribution to it is a welcome challenge for any creative research in eschatology.

1.3. Structure and Method

The traditional outline of the *de novissimis* had two main parts: the "last things" of persons and the "last things" of the world. The first part dealt with death, particular judgment, heaven, hell and purgatory, whereas the second with the resurrection of the body, the second coming of Christ, universal judgment and the end of the cosmic universe.

These are the main topics. But there are many other themes and concepts which make up the vocabulary of a thorough eschatology. All the pertinent concepts are interrelated and determine mutually each other's meaning. Unless we consider the hermeneutic function of these terms, there is a risk of using them in a sense foreign to the language of eschatology, and the treatise on eschatology might look like a book mixing English, French, German, Russian or other words in the same paragraph. A well-determined vocabulary and the analysis of the meaning involved is important. Not taking into account the different elements forming the field of the research means that particular observations will probably not be accurate. Suppose, for example, that one fails to consider angels in the treatise on eschatology. There is then the danger of structuring an eschatology which does not link history, revelation and resurrection, and therefore will not be in line with the eschatology of the early Christians. Without considering angelology we may be tempted to understand after-life as a sort of angelic existence, and death will be just like "changing horses" at a station of our existential pilgrimage. In such a case my personal "I" would not die, but only my body. Yet death is not a dream. It is real, and my whole being, not just my body, has to die. Death is the end of me and not just that of my "imprisonment" in my body.

A more or less adequate treatise on eschatology has to consider a number of topics which make up the field of any research in Christian eschatology. There are about 63 traditional topics which make up the basic language of eschatology and which we tried to build into our systematic presentation. As a *leitfaden* we list them here in alphabetical order.

Aeon	Apocalypse
After-life	Apocatastasis
Anacephalaeosis	Ascension
Angels	Beatific vision
Antichrist	Beatitude

Body
Cosmic eschatology
Death
Descent into hell
Devils, evil ones
Dialectical tension between universal cosmic eschatology and individual, existential eschatology
End
Eschatology
Eternal life
Eternity
Expectation of what is to come
Faith, charity and hope
Future
Futurology
Glorification
Grace, sanctifying
Heaven
Hell
Hermeneutics of eschatological statements
Historicity
History, theology of
Holy Spirit
Imminence of the end
Immortality
Intermediate state
It is not I, but Christ who lives in me
Jesus Christ, the eschatological union of time and eternity
Judgment universal and particular
Kingdom of God
Last things
Limbo
Mary, the first "flowering" of the Church
Millenarianism
Non-Christian eschatology
Now
Paradise
Parousia
Person
Purgatory
Resurrection of the flesh
Sacraments
Satan
Scientific picture of the world
Second coming of Christ
Self
Sheol
Soul
Spirit
Temporality
Time
Trinitarian God
Utopianism
World

These traditional concepts serve as a language which is given to us beforehand, and we have to use them as a medium of understanding. In the light of Hans-Georg Gadamer's theory of hermeneutical experience, these terms may have an effectiveness, a quality of newness in our time, which they never had before (Gadamer, 1975, pp. 235ff.). The sensitivity to this newness "involves neither 'neutrality' in the matter of the object nor the extinction of one's self, but the conscious assimilation of one's own fore-meanings and prejudice" (Gadamer, 1975, p. 238). Our fore-meanings and prejudices come from an Einsteinian worldview which is just as much part of the effective history of the eschatological texts as any previous time after the Christ event, and we hope that the new concept of time after Einstein will bring forth the newness of the early Christian eschatology.

The concepts of time and eternity are fundamental for Christian eschatology and for Christian faith in general. The Newtonian concept of time has been modified by Einsteinian insight. The Einsteinian worldview might make it difficult to appreciate traditional concepts of eschatology, like hell and heaven, death and immortality, life after death and resurrection, last day and final judgment, etc., expressions which rather presuppose a pre-Einsteinian view of the universe. Yet the end of the Newtonian worldview cannot mean the end of the theology of Christian eschatology. Theology cannot remain unaffected by the new research in the concept of time which is going on in the various disciplines, like geology, cosmology, physics, biology, psychology, etc. We should try to express the eschatological faith of the Church by using the language of our time and communicate Christ's message to the world of tomorrow. It is possible that Christian faith has a good deal to offer those who are concerned with the mystery of time.

Since this is our hope we will try to give an overview of the research in the nature of time which is going on in geology, cosmology, physics, biology, psychology, sociology, history and philosophy in order to be able to propose a new definition of time. This overview will make up Chapter 2 of our book. In Chapter 3 we contrast our notion of time with the mystery of Christ, suggesting a new Christology that considers Jesus Christ as the eschatological union of time and eternity. Christology should always be the principal part of eschatology. The revelation of Christ is the pattern by which we are entitled to make valid statements concerning our future and the future of our universe. Only in the light of Christ can an eschatology fulfill its twofold task: (1) to say something about what kind of life eternal life is, and (2) to show its possibility.

In the search for a modern language of eternity explaining our cosmos-sharing eternity, the singularity event, or black holes, will be used as literary form. According to modern cosmology, singularity events are formed when the mass of a dying star collapses into a kernel of matter so dense that, whereas its size is minimal, its gravitational attraction is enormous and so overpowering that nothing, not even light, can escape it. Deep inside of black holes, in the singularity event, the laws of physics break down. A few physicists think that a singularity event leads to a passage through which energy and matter pulled into a black hole might exit into another, different universe. This opening is called the white hole. Thus it is possible that another universe, a different cosmos, exists within our universe (Taylor, 1975; Dyson, 1988, pp. 20-23). Although it is possible that one day the way the present universe began will be described by the laws of science (Hawking, 1988), the "laws of physics" of the other universe will, however, remain always a mystery for the outsider to the singularity event.

Such a language can serve as a literary form expressing how Christ's time as a singularity event can lead the times of all existing realities through death to his time. We know now that all that enter into a singularity event appear to be dead to those in time, since that was the last light which escaped from the attractive force of the singularity event and reached us back in our time and space. But in reality that which is dead in our sight, and in our time and space, entered and lives in a world which is not perceptible from the world of time and space except by those who entered into the horizon-event of Jesus Christ, the eschatological union of time and eternity. This is a paradigm we introduce in Christian eschatology.

The systematic presentation of our eschatology forms Chapter 4 of the present book, under three headings: (1) Time and Eternity; (2) Individual and Eternity; (3) Society, World and Eternity.

2 CONCEPTS OF TIME

2.1. Theology of Time After Theology of Being

The theology of being made it possible for methodical thinking about faith to enter into a meaningful dialogue with the human sciences and thus become a science in the proper sense. The notion of being served as a bridge between faith and reason, between this world and the world beyond, between humans and God. Being was considered to be a real transcendental notion, since no reality could ignore its necessary conditions except non-being, the nothing, unworthy of any scientific investigation.

It is more than 700 years now since Thomas Aquinas saw this and gave a solid foundation to theology as a real science. The notion of being was a brilliant problem-solving paradigm since, in addition to solving many problems of that time, it was open-ended enough to leave all kinds of questions open for further discussions. What the notion of being is or should be was disputed by scholastics for centuries afterwards. But as time passed, the strength of the notion of being became its shortcoming. Since it is transcendental, too abstract and non-empirical, the emerging new sciences found it irrelevant, and turned first to the concrete, empirical notion of measurable space as a new paradigm and, then, after Einstein, to the notion of time. As a result, theology lost its link with the world of science, the world of "realities."

To resolve the "anomaly," new theologies, like positive theology, dialectical theology, process theology, theology of history, theology of liberation, etc., have been proposed to replace the abstract, lifeless, non-biblical "outmoded" theology of being by some concrete, lively, biblical, updated system, possibly as universal as being previously had been. Theologians tried to register for other disciplines like philosophy, literature, history, psychology or sociology, etc., in order to gain status for their discipline in the academic world. Yet all fell short, and none of them could establish such a universal paradigm as the notion of being. The new theologies became just provincial theologies affiliated with a passing local insight and concern.

Following the example of the *philosophia perennis*, which took the basic complete unity of human language, the judgment, as affirmation of being, and built its transcendental method on it, some theologians have recently turned to language as a universal problem-solving paradigm. Thanks to the Whorfian and Chomskyan revolution, language was discovered in its deep structure as a universal and useful paradigm for both the humanities and scientific research. Experiments in the natural sciences were interpreted as new language formation and the language of understanding was distinguished from the language of discovery. The first was the dialogue of the scientist with his colleagues, the latter, the dialogue of the scientist with nature, when nature replied to the discoverer's question not in the form of understanding, but in the form of force by setting free certain amounts of energy in order to cause alterations in the environment which could be measured, and thus "perceived." The language of discovery was seen not so much as a communication of self as self to self (language of understanding), but as that of energy performing a definitive task. The so-called natural laws were no longer considered the immortal ideas of an abstract Platonic world, but statistics relative to a specific language conditioned by certain paradigms (Horvath, 1980, pp. 157-68). As a consequence of this change, the new linguistic studies were not influenced so much by space-imagery as the historical and structural linguistics had been but by the notion of time. This close relationship between language and time experience is well expressed by V. Nalimov, professor of the Laboratory of Mathematical Theory of Experiment, Moscow State University, in his book *Realms of the Unconscious: The Enchanted Frontier*; he wrote: "our conjecture is that the category of Time arose from the necessity to overcome the barrier between the deep inner sensation of the continuous nature of the world and the discrete re-presentation of its verbal expression" (1982, p. 52). Thus it seems that both the natural sciences and the humanities are converging in their concern for the notion of time, and "spatialized" time is gradually being replaced by "timed" space.

This new awareness of the notion of time should not be confused with the Heideggerian existential fundamentality of time (Heidegger, 1962, pp. 274-488; Hodgson, 1971; Lehmann, 1970). The interest in time is noticeable not only in a Husserlian analysis of human consciousness but in all sciences. Studies dealing with the nature of time are numerous in geological, cosmological, physical and biological studies. Time has now become as fundamental and universal as being was in the medieval period, and theologies are turning to this new universal and fundamental paradigm in order to enter into a dialogue with other sciences and to release a new understanding of time and eternity, central concepts operating in revelation and redemption.

2.2. Current Theological Notions of Time

The current theological views of time can be classified by three models: spatialized, temporalized and atemporalized, or ontological, concepts of time.

2.2.1. Spatialized Time: Before and After

One of the most current theological notions of time is the one based on the biblical lexical meaning which is identical with the popular intuition of time, sc., the linear span limited by its beginning of birth (creation) and by its end or death (eschatology). Eternity is then conceived as an endless time (cf. Gen 21, 33; Ps 90, 2; 102, 12; Is 40, 86, etc.) not limited either by birth or by death. The image underlying this definition is spatial, and thus eternity does not differ from time. Eternity is endless, infinite time. McTaggart called statements of this kind F statements. They are static, tenseless ways of talking about time in the form of "earlier than" (McTaggart, 1967).

The New Testament applies this notion to Jesus who is said to be before and after ages (Jn 8, 58; 17, 24; 1 Cor 2, 7; Eph 1, 4; 3, 9: Col 1, 26; 1 Pet 1, 20). We should note here with J. Barr that neither Hebrew nor Greek had an exclusively proper term for time (Barr, 1962, pp. 20-21). The initial meaning of the term was not what we understand today by the word "time." And this is quite understandable. Time is not something one can point to; therefore, it is not a first denotation for the human mind to reflect upon. Barr is right when he concludes that from the lexical stock of the Bible it does not follow (though many writers uncritically say so) that Greek had an abstract notion of time and Hebrew a concrete one. Both J. Marsh (1952) and J.A. Robinson (1957) defended the distinction between *chronos* and *kairos* in the sense that *chronos* is the measured time independent of events which take place in it and which exists on its own, whereas *kairos* is an event or opportunity appointed by God and filled with its own specific content. But one can say with J. Barr that *chronos* and *kairos* practically had much the same meaning (Barr, 1962, pp. 31, 44).

John R. Wilch found that *eth* was used in the Old Testament "in order to indicate the relationship or juncture of circumstances, primarily in an objective sense and only secondarily in a temporal sense, and to direct attention to a specifically definite occasion or situation" (Wilch, 1969, p. 164). *Eth* refers to the occasion itself, and temporal relationships are expressed by terms like *az*, "then," a successive relation without any definite temporal relationship (e.g., Jgs 5, 11), *mo ed*, "an appointed" feast (Hos 2, 11) and *yom*, "day" (Num 9, 22). The most interesting and perhaps the most original expression is *ques*, which means the eschatological end (e.g., Gen 6, 13: "I have determined to make an end of all flesh"; cf. Dan 8, 17; 11, 35, etc.).

From both the lexical-grammatical and the semantic use of the biblical terms related to our concept of time we can conclude that time in the biblical sense is rather a quality of an event, which makes the event special, outstanding among others; and, therefore, it has a sort of reference-role for other common, ordinary, unimportant events. This is the obvious meaning of the term "day," the span which has its beginning with sunrise and its end with sunset, since day was an outstanding event opposed to the dark night, when nothing except menace and fear were dominant. Later on, the unity of the day was measured by sunsets. The Mesopotamian division of the day into 12 hours was not familiar to the people of the Old Testament, and the biblical Hebrew has no word for "hours." This sense of time is further confirmed by the use of *ques*, emphasizing that the event in question is outstanding in relation not just to some, but to all possible events, since it is the end for all. From this comes its unique importance. Such a meaning of *ques* is the foundation of that theological view which holds that Hebrew time is linear and not cyclical. All this, however, does not mean that the Hebrew mind had discovered a new philosophical notion of time, and that there is a deeper understanding of time and eternity involved. The biblical notion of time is no different from any other contemporary notion of time and eternity: it is spatialized time. The so-called biblical linear and non-cyclical concept of time originates not from a deep insight of what time is but from the belief that Yahweh is the only God and he is God alone. Therefore, time is just a creature in the hand of God. It is "flesh" which has an end. It cannot go on and on, because then it would be like God, having no end and no beginning.

We should note here that the Newtonian absolute, substantial notion of time as a limitless great receptacle is also inspired by the same imaginative process of spatializing time. It is understandable that the strongly monotheistic Hebrew faith instinctively sensed idolatry in such a view of time. Since only Yahweh is eternal and everlasting and there is no God besides him, there must be an eschatological end for time. Thus the Hebrew faith in one God changed, not the concept of time, but its duration.

This innovation is the raison d'être of the prophetic mission and of its limited duration. Once faith in limited, finite time, i.e., faith in an eschatological end, had been firmly established, the purpose of prophetism was fulfilled, and prophets were no longer needed. And what the Hebrew prophets did for the Jewish tribes, Muḥammad did for the Arab tribes. His faith in one God transformed the impersonal eternal force of *dahr* "fate" into a creature of God. W. Montgomery Watt sees in this event one of the reasons for Muḥammad's great success (Watt, 1982, pp. 26-28).

For Israel and Islam time is assessed in reference to God's eternity, which was seen as endless time. Indeed, the two Hebrew words which are translated into English as "eternity" are both negative: *olam*, "something hiding, limits of which are not perceptible and/or non-existent" is a negative, and *nesaḥ*, "something shining forth, superior to all limits and which therefore cannot be seen," is a positive negation of limits. Thus from the biblical studies of time and eternity we cannot affirm that there is a concept of eternity qualitatively different from the concept of time (cf. Ecc 3, 11: [God]—"has put eternity into man's mind, yet so that he cannot find out what God has done from the beginning to the end"). When J. Marsh (1952, p. 139) claimed that from biblical studies one can conclude that there is a notion of eternity qualitatively different from that of the totality of time, one can agree with him, affirming not a difference between time and eternity, but a difference between God (eternity) and man having an eschatological end (time). Consequently, in the Old and New Testament, we find no concept of real immortality, but just the concept of the eternal God. Any immortality would challenge the uniqueness of Yahweh as God and the belief that time is his creature, which, as such, must have an end. This is what "flesh" (creatureliness) means. It is true that certain events or people have a singularity or uniqueness which arises from their encounter with God. The encounter with God gives to them a special quality in regard to the others but this special quality cannot mean immortality, since that would be blasphemous. Belief in life after death should not be confused with immortality, and anthropological studies provide us with many examples. According to the Bible, everything is mortal except God (1 Tim 6, 15). Thomas Aquinas succinctly expressed this biblical truth "God is eternity.... Eternity is nothing else but God himself" (*S. theol.* 1, 10,2 and 3; *S. Contra gent.* 1, 15,3; 3, 61,3; *Comp. theol.*, 4, 5; 2,8; 7, 80).

2.2.2. Temporalized Time: Past, Present and Future Tenses

Temporalized time has three varieties: reduction to the past, reduction to the present or reduction to the future. McTaggart called these A statements. They are dynamic, tensed ways of talking about action (McTaggart, 1967).

2.2.2.1. Past-Oriented Time

Faith in the event of Jesus Christ has revolutionized the concept of spatialized time. As a unique event it was not subject to repetition, yet it was not lost in the past forever, like other events known from human experience. According to faith its real uniqueness was that even though it was a past event it never remained just past event. It is and it will be always present and it is and it will always be already future. In contrast to ordinary history "where the past is sublated by the remembering present, the historical 'now' is reached and vanquished by the event of the transhistorical past which becomes the redeeming standard for the present as well as for the coming future" (Horvath, 1971, pp. 45-46).

But how is such a constant re-presentation, *Vergegenwärtigung* "making-present" of a past event for future generations possible? To explain the possibility of such a constant re-presentation, various replies have been given. Each one was conditioned by the author's concept of time, which in turn determined the kind of theology he/she was doing. In general, the key point of the research was Lk 22, 19 (cf. 1 Cor 23, 26) "Do this in remembrance of me" with *zkr* and *bkr* "remembering and blessing" in the Old Testament and Ex 13, 8-10: "You shall tell your sons ... you shall keep ... this ordinance." But the interpretations are many. For illustration we will mention about 20 "solutions" proposed by different authors.

To explain how the past can meet new generations, G. von Rad (1965, p. 104) used the expression *Historizierung*, "historicizing" of the myth through cultic dramatization. It was a form of remembrance but dramatized in words and actions in order to capture and impress the audience more deeply. Through these acts the past events of Israel did not come to rest but continued to meet and become contemporary with each generation, as B.S. Childs has explained (1962, p. 83).

However, one can question von Rad's assumption that dramatization is a real re-presentation or actualization of the past. As commemorative remembrance the dramatization is not a past dimension, but rather a renewal of the past in the present. Thus C. Westermann insisted that we should not talk about re-presentation of the past but rather about a present answer to a past act of God (Westermann, 1964, pp. 306-55). Since the objective distance between the present and the past is maintained, the contemporaneity of the past with the present is just existential.

The concept of time that was available to theologians prevented them from being able to say anything more. M. Noth admitted that the solution to the question of re-presentation is not to be sought in a special concept of time in the Old Testament (Noth, 1952). According to H.H. Schmid (1967, pp. 1-15), the change is not in time but in generations following one after the other. The past generations of the parents are successively replaced by the present generations of the children. The subjects of remembering, i.e., fathers and sons, are changing, and there is no need to look for any new concept of time.

H.W. Robinson (1936, pp. 49-62) hoped to explain the impact of the past on the present by introducing the concept of corporate personality. Not the generations separately, but the unity of generations extending both back into the past and forward into the future is the guarantee that the past never becomes merely past. Much more simple is the solution proposed by H.B. Huffmon (1906, pp. 31-37). The renewal is nothing else but the keeping of God's commandments here and now. It is obedience to past generations that any human society would allow and demand.

G. Ebeling stands for a more metaphysical re-presentation which transcends the biblical notion (1950, pp. 11-17). He finds justification for this in the fact that, unlike the Old Testament, the New Testament does not recognize various renewals of a covenant but the transmission of a once-and-for-all binding covenant which is not to be renewed. It is done once-and-for-all and one is related by it to the history of God, which obliterates the biblical distance between past and present. The once-and-for-all *extra me* is applied to a new historical situation and becomes *pro me*, "for me" (Schmidt, 1970, pp. 100-109).

Without an adequate concept of time, Ebeling's stress on the once-and-for-all event of Christ cannot avoid a tensed way of talking of the past event and of its effects for the future. An appeal to the "history of God" is not enough to establish the difference between the redemptive work of Christ and the redemptive work of Yahweh in the Old Testament, unless one can show that the redemptive work of Christ made a real difference in the history of God. Otherwise it is just another re-presentation of an absent presence (Strasser, 1964) of God known in the Old Testament and in the historical consciousness of various peoples.

Because the time-concept was much the same, none of the proposed replies could really overcome the barrier of the temporal-chronological separation. Some hoped to find a solution in the distinction between chronological recording and historical consciousness. Such a distinction, indeed, can be justified by the example of the Old Chinese civilization, which had excellent chronological recording without any historical consciousness. Though the distinction is valid, it cannot make the re-presentation of the Christ event different from any other culture event where historical consciousness is reached.

All the solutions proposed so far rely on Plotinus's concept of time. In his *Enneads* 3, Plotinus criticized Aristotle for defining time in terms of motion and motion in terms of time. As a result, Plotinus believed that time must be identified with the creative activity of the soul. Time is nothing else but the life of the mind passing from one stage of experience to another. Time is therefore not a substance but the creative memory of the mind.

Both the substantial and the subjective definitions visualize time in space. The difference is that one considers it in a slow, and the other in a quick, motion. If one conceives Plotinus's memory operating as a modern computer, one could turn Plotinus's objection to Aristotle's notion against Plotinus himself. A new concept of time distinct from chronological recording as well as from historical consciousness is needed. But let us see a few more authors.

Unlike Luther, the Council of Trent did not find it sufficient to believe that the redemptive work of Christ is a past event and that only its effects transcend the limits of the past. In order to see the redemptive work of Christ as an act not only of the past, but of the "here and now," the council of Trent tried to sublate the difference between the past and present by affirming that the same Jesus Christ who died on Calvary is the one who offers, e.g., the Mass here and now (DS 1743; Tanner, 1990, p. 733). The Mass is, therefore, not just the work of the remembering faithful, but the work of Jesus Christ, who, by virtue of his resurrection, is believed never again to be a "past." But without a more adequate concept of time the doctrine of Trent can easily be interpreted as an act of God (cf. *virtus divina* in Wegenaer, 1958) or of the Holy Spirit (Mühlen, 1964 and Congar, 1983) in Jesus Christ who does his own work over and over again. But would this not obscure again the once-and-for-all aspect of Christ's redemptive work?

To eliminate such a misunderstanding, O. Casel (1962) developed the theory of *Mysteriengegenwart* "the mystery-present." According to Casel, the re-enactment of the mystery of Christ does not multiply Christ's redemptive work in time and space, but makes the once-and-for-all cross and resurrection event present here and now, not under its own past space and time instances, but under that of the here and now of the bread and wine as "species." In other words, it is a quasi-borrowing of space and time from the eucharistic bread and wine. The past event is really present by entering the space and time of something else.

Casel's proposal is the first which assumes a new concept of time. Otherwise his theory remains just another myth. But Casel never elaborated a new concept of time which would help to overcome the Catholic and Protestant differences concerning the real presence as well as the doctrine of sanctification, and perhaps that of papal infallibility included. With the old concept of time the Catholic doctrine seems to multiply the redemptive work of Christ, whereas the Protestant doctrine seems to fail to underline sufficiently the here and now effective value of the Cross-event and reduces it to a mere will of God extrinsic to the Jesus of the past.

As H.W. Robinson did through the concept of corporate personality, so K. Rahner broadened the sacramental presence of Christ through the idea of the Church as sacrament extending itself from the past into the future (1966). The Mass is not only a sign of Calvary, but also the present work of the Church receiving Christ's redemptive work and offering it to the Father, and as such is not repetition. It is not a leasing of time and space but a certain co-extension of the time and space of Christ with that of the Church. As a sort of lasting balance of two different times Mass can be understood as both propitiatory and eucharistic "at once."

The assumption that the Mass can be the offering of the Church as well as that of Christ presupposes that the time of the faithful can become the time of Christ during the Mass. In explaining the "how" of this co-acting "at once," the authors mostly tried to underline the *here* (real presence) rather than the *now* of the redemptive act of Christ. But after Vatican II there is a slight difference in emphasis. The vocabulary seems to be moving from "space" words like "repetition" and "renewal" to "time" words like *perpetuare* "perpetuate" (*Constitution on the Sacred Liturgy*, chap. 2, nn. 47, 48). Although even post-Vatican II authors did not pay much attention to this (see, e.g., Eisenbach, 1982) the new terminology points to a promising future for theology.

2.2.2.2. Present-Oriented Time

For K. Barth, eternity, not time, is central, yet his concept of eternity reflects a present-oriented concept of time. He wrote:

> Time is distinguished from eternity by the fact that in it beginning, middle and end are distinct and even opposed as past, present and future. Eternity is just the duration which is lacking to time as can be seen clearly at the middle point of time, in the temporal present and in its relationship to the past and the future. Eternity has and is the duration which is lacking to time.... (God's) *stare* is also a *fluere*... the *fluere* of empirical time.... If an unmoving, persistent present is distinguished from our fluid and fleeting present which can be understood only as a mathematical point, this distinction rightly describes the problem of our concept of time... the problem of our *"now"* (Barth, 1957, pp. 608-11).

Briefly, time is a "now" with separation, contradiction, distance, due to its extension to the past and to the future, which are distinct and even opposed. The various times manifest God's freedom to create various times.

For H.U. von Balthasar and O. Cullmann, the Christ event, which took place in horizontal time, is a "vertical now" present to every point of history (Balthasar, 1971, pp. 22-58; Cullmann, 1960). R. Bultmann, too (1960) sees the "now" as the key word for the New Testament in which human life is lifted above the stream of time, perhaps in something like the community for Müller (1949).

P. Tillich (1963, p. 406) posits time primarily as "the mode of becoming finite freedom." For Rahner it is a realization of the potentiality of one's own being, "attaining the unique, irrevocable completion of its institution" (Rahner, Vorgrimler, 1965, p. 46). Freedom is simultaneity symbolized by the "now."

2.2.2.3. *Future-Oriented Time*

Process theology and existential theology in their description of time both focus on the future tense. Time is a flux, a process, an existence which is suspended between a definitive beginning and a definitive end mutually determining each other. Process theology as well as existential theology are future oriented, with the difference that whereas process theology sees the future positively, existential theology is more impressed by its tragic end, death.

The theologians of hope, too, like W. Pannenberg (1968) and J. Moltmann (1967), place more emphasis on that aspect of time which the future tense expresses. Time is a realm of possibilities that lies ahead, full of promises rather than of achievements. The British theologians H.D. Lewis (1981), H.H. Price (1972) and J. Hick (1976) defend the validity of the chronological future. Time continues, and its durational quality is argued on an empirical basis as a sort of endless succession of one "after" the other.

The theologians overviewed so far thrust the reality of time to the realm of the historical discipline, and their concept of time is hardly a challenge to the hegemony of the Kantian understanding of time.

2.2.3. *De-temporalized Time*

Early classical theology influenced by the Platonic worldview could not find too much value in time. Time was considered as a sort of necessary evil to be endured and for which one would receive eternal life as a reward. Since the visible thing, the outer nature, is transient, wasting away, one should not care about it but instead look to things which are not seen but which are eternal and whose weight of glory, i.e., reality, is beyond all comparison. This kind of Platonic view which J. Stinson calls reward theory (Stinson, pp. 49-62) is reflected in 2 Cor 4, 16-18.

N. Lash, in his discussion with B. Hebblethwaite, "sought to avoid speaking of 'timeless participation in the glory of God,' preferring, instead, to speak of participation in God's timeless glory" (Lash, 1979a; 1979b, p. 63). Thus Lash's concept of time seems to be more in line with the classical tradition than Hebblethwaite realized (Hebblethwaite, 1979).

It should be noted that the classical view just mentioned is not totally alien to the findings of anthropological studies, which know not so much about immortality, in the sense of eternity, but rather about an "after" life, in the sense of survival after death as long as one's memory is kept alive among the people who knew one. The *Sasa* and *Samani* tenses among the Akamba and Gikuyu of Kenya as well as the *Kituki* and *Tene* tenses of the Kikamba languages are proofs of this (Mbiti, 1969, pp. 19-28; 1971, pp. 26-28). Personal "immortality" in preliterate cultures lasts as long as one is remembered by one's own name. Once no one remembers the dead, the dead survive only in "spirit form," in a state of collective immortality, a concept not too different from Platonic immortality or from the Buddhist concept of heaven, without a "belief in a permanent self or soul" (Malalasekera, 1974, p. 172; see also Barnhart, 1992).

The assumption shared by many in the past that the Greeks believed in immortality and that the Hebrew doctrine of "personal immortality" owes its origin to the Greek belief has recently been seriously questioned. First of all the doctrine of immortality should not be considered a Greek doctrine, but merely a Platonic concept, since not too many Greeks shared it. Plato's contemporary, Thucydides, for example, knew only of the immortality of those who died for their country. It was an incentive given to young men to despise death. Moreover, immortality in Plato cannot be interpreted simply as "personal" immortality. It was, instead, the survival of eternal ideas which did not have too much in common with the shadow-reality of a human person existing in time. Plato's dialogue about Socrates' death in the *Phaedo* does not convey more than a philosophical immortality, which is not a quality of nature, but of action. Only Christian writers under the influence of their faith were disposed to see more in it, an interpretation not unusual in patristic theology (Horvath, 1975, p. 32). One should remember also that in Plato *psyché* "the soul" and *thymos* "the consciousness" do not necessarily mean the same thing. W. Jaeger, in his book, *The Theology of the Early Greek Philosophers* (1947, pp. 73-89), sees the Orphic soul theory as a direct precursor of Plato's view of the divine nature of the soul, and he does not exclude the possibility of the influence of the Oriental shamanistic idea of the transmigration of souls. In any case the Platonic doctrine of the divine nature of the soul should be distinguished from any doctrine about the eternity of the human person. The incorruptibility of an idea should not be confused with the eternity of a human person. Such a confusion might lead one to misinterpret the meaning of the scholastic thesis, which holds that *anima humana immortalis est*, "the human soul is immortal" (Sagues, 1958, pp. 685-94), which was taught also by the fifth Lateran Council.

The fifth Lateran Council (1513) contradicted the Neo-Aristotelians in its statement that the soul is immortal (DS 1440; Tanner, 1990, p. 605) but without any philosophical explanation of the term "immortality." As a matter of fact, no scholastic theologian ever thought that the human soul is essentially and metaphysically immortal, but only as *non absolute* and *gratuite* "not absolutely" but "gratuitously," which means that the human soul by itself is mortal, since only God is essentially and metaphysically immortal. The many distinctions offered by the authors, like *de facto, de iure, necessario inamissibilis, conditionate inamissibilis*, etc., with the consequent endless disputes among B. Beraza, C. Boyer, A. Deneffe, G. Huarte, L. Lercher, D. Palmieri, F. Vernet, etc. (Sagües, 1958, pp. 685-94) served only one purpose, i.e., to indicate the essential difference between the "human" and "animal" forms from the point of view of the scholastic philosophy. The disputes were prompted by the fact that 54 years after the fifth Lateran Council, Baius was condemned for having said that the immortality of the first man was his natural condition and not a gift of grace (DS 1978). From this condemnation it follows that for the Church only God has immortality in the real sense (cf. 1 Tim 6, 16) and if human beings share in it, it is a special gift of God which is not contrary to the nature of the human soul, since the human soul is not just a substantial form in the Aristotelian sense, but subsistent in the Platonic sense as well. Now we have seen that the meaning of the subsistent form for Plato is not "revolutionarily" different from the Buddhist view of eternity. Indeed, for both, temporal and personal have no particular value. Since time and the personality closely related to it are essentially illusory, Nirvana must be the end of time as well as of the human being as person (Brandon, 1965, pp. 1-5; Badham, 1987).

Thus we venture to conclude that the systems just mentioned, Platonism included, could never seriously consider the possibility of applying the concept of eternity to a human individual or, in other words, the compatibility of eternity and human existence.

In 1899 R.H. Charles, in his *Eschatology, The Doctrine of a Future Life in Israel, Judaism and Christianity*, summarizing 2 Maccabees, stated that "as regards the resurrection, its nature was as follows. It was to be to an eternal life. . . . [T]he resurrection was not only to an eternal life, and that an eternal life in the body, but also to a life to be eternally enjoyed in the community of the righteous" (Charles, 1970, pp. 276-77). But recent biblical studies find it unlikely that the doctrine of "eternal life" as found in 2 Maccabees can be interpreted in any way different from that "eternal life" which was known to the Akamba, Gikuyu or the Kikamba of Kenya, i.e., a survival after death with a "spiritual" body in a collective immortality as long as one's memory is kept alive among the people of God (Collins, 1974).

Martin Hengel shares the view that "the indications of the historical origin of resurrection are on the one hand in the direction of Iranian religion, where they are already attested by Theopompus (fourth century BC), while on the other hand conceptions of resurrection communicated by the dying and rising of vegetation deities had certainly been known in ancient Israel for some time" (Hengel, 1974, 1, p. 196).

In the period of intertestamental times we find more numerous texts for spiritualized after-life (e.g., *Book of Jubilees*, 23, 30ff: "their bones shall rest in the earth, and their spirits shall have much joy"), yet references to "resurrection" are very few in the Old Testament. Leaving aside Is 26, 19, which is difficult to date (Martin-Achard, 1960) and is interpreted metaphorically by some (Hasel, 1980), Dan 12, 2 is the first clear reference to the the resurrection of the dead (Hengel, 1974, p. 196). Nickelsburg gives a plausible form-critic and history of tradition analysis of the text. In contrast to the Trito-Isaiah's promise (Is 65-66), during Antiochus's reign many Hasidic Jews were slaughtered, whereas some of the Hellenizers had died and were not burned in Gehenna. By creating a new theodicy, the author of Daniel 12, 1-13, justifies Trito-Isaiah's prophecy by a "come back to life" (Nickelsburg, 1972), when some come back to life "unto life everlasting," and some to "everlasting disgrace" as everlasting proof of God's words' validity. In the Bible this is the first occurrence of the term "life everlasting."

From the context it is clear that the author of Dan 10, 1-12, 13 was not particularly interested in the "resurrection of bodies" but in justifying the truthfulness of God. This is why, unlike in the Christian literature, the references to the resurrection of the body remain scarce in the Judaic sources (Fischer, 1978). Therefore, we can assume that what the author of the Second Maccabees who lived after Christ had in mind was that the Jewish nation would never die as long as the world exists and, therefore, there would be Jews in the world "all the time" (cf. Ez 37, 1-14; Hos 6, 1-3; Is 53, 10-11). The author of Dan 12 certainly did not elaborate on how an individual who died for Israel would exist after death. His concern, too, was the fidelity of God rather than a share in God's eternal life (North, 1972). Evidently, resurrection from the dead is not identical with eternal life, which is God's own life and there is no indication in the Old Testament that God was willing to share his life (eternity) with anyone and jeopardize his uniqueness. The real breakthrough came only with the New Testament's faith in "God became man."

When Jesus' followers began to believe that this human person here and now, i.e., Jesus of Nazareth, is sharing God's eternity, they had a special basis for that. The faith that God became human and will remain human forever as the only one redeemer for everyone has prompted the belief that being human—being in "flesh" (in time)—is compatible with being a human forever, without ceasing to be at all. The compatibility of eternity and a human being was conditioned by the belief in the eternity of the Incarnation, where eternity and time were united in an "eschatological union." The belief in the everlasting Christ-event was the ground of the belief in the eternity of a human being. Later on, in order to make the faith in eternal life more credible, the Christian mind searched and found support in the popular belief in survival after death, which was interpreted as eternal life in Christ. As a result, immortality was mistakenly seen by some as the natural condition of humanity and the importance of the Christ-event lost its validity for our immortality, as Baius's case exemplifies.

2.2.4. Christological Time

To hold eternity and time together without jeopardizing the role of either one, K. Barth and N. Berdyaev both looked to the mystery of the Incarnation (Slaatteg, 1980, p. 27). In their quest to develop a new concept of time they relied strongly on biblical theology instead of following J. Barr's suggestion that, if the Christian doctrine of time has to be developed, "such a work must belong not to biblical but to philosophical theology" (Barr, 1962, p. 149). We intend to work out a new notion of time based on the speculative theology of Christ, which at one time was a great inspiration to philosophical thinking.

For an authentic philosophical mind the two concepts, God, and man, must be incompatible. Aristotle rightly knew of univocal and equivocal concepts but never thought too much of analogy as a bridge joining the created world and the uncreated God together (Jüngel, 1964, pp. 6, 28-29; 1967, pp. 94-97). By maintaining that for Thomas Aquinas, Christ, the God-man, was the ultimate hermeneutical principle in the light of which he understood whatever he understood (Horvath, 1966, pp. 7-9, 279-83), one can assume that when Aquinas made the first extensive use of the concept of analogy for a possible human knowledge of God he could rely on the creative formulation of the Council of Chalcedon, combining God and man in one subject, "unconfusedly, unchangeably, undividedly and inseparably" (DS 302; Tanner, 1990, p. 86). The statement that Christ is God and at the same time that he is not God, since he is really man, and that Christ is man but at the same time he is not man, since he is really God, required the concept of analogy as an indispensable addition to univocal and equivocal concepts. The recent use of symbolic knowledge implying the threefold dimensions of the visible, intersubjective and divine world is a further development of the early analogical concepts (Schupp, 1974) which affirm a real disagreement in a real agreement.

As the unity of God and man in the Incarnation through the concept of analogy made a contribution to a better understanding of being, so we hope that the same union can make some contribution to a better understanding of time and eternity. We are going to analyze what time is for Christ and what impact his time has made on the time of the world. Since we are interested in speculative theology, we will turn to the concept of time in modern physics because, as Rahner suggested, "we have to learn from modern physics how to think, in terms that are abstract and non-imaginative" (Rahner, 1971, p. 162). For an introduction to the notion of time in modern physics, we will begin with the science of geology, and from there we will progressively construct our notion of time.

2.3. A New Notion of Time

Traditionally there are two basic views of time: (1) absolute time, which is like a great container independent of all that exists and in which everything flows (cf. Newton or Locke); and (2) relative time, which is derived from events: events are time. Recent studies have amplified this twofold division.

2.3.1. *Current Scientific Notions of Time*

Time has become of special concern for almost every discipline we know today. Here is a glimpse of the ongoing reflections.

2.3.1.1. *Time in Geology*

By using data from superposition (principle of superposition) and succession (principle of faunal succession), geologists can determine eras, periods and epochs of relative times not by the motion of the sun but by establishing geological events and their succession. To determine the beginning and the end of these events, geologists have to establish their sequences by means of geological clocks. The basis for the so-called geological clocks are the regularities observed in geological research. But regularities, e.g., intervals of mountain-building activities, intervals of glacial extensions, seas changing positions, etc., are irregular. Seas, for example, do not ebb and flow with regularity. Such irregularities may result in an inaccuracy of a few hundred million years for a geological age.

Early geological inaccuracy was diminished by the discovery of the radioactive disintegration process, which is not affected by other geological events, like changes in heat, pressure and chemical conditions. The rate of its decay is described in terms of half-life and is determined in each radioactive element as the time required for half of the original amount to change into another element.

In this objectively observable phenomenon we can discover three elements which are the basis of what geologists call geological time: first of all there is a certain alienation (e.g., uranium changes into lead), then reversibility (alienation is repeated again and again, constantly; thus it functions like a clock) and finally irreversibility (all the repeated changes are in one direction, since it flows from uranium to lead in 4.51 billion years, from rubidium to strontium in 47 billion years, from potassium to argon in 1.31 billion years, etc., but not the other way around) (Matthews, 1971, pp. 103-107).

The alienation means the transformation of one element into the other, which creates a certain affinity, i.e., a family relation among elements. It is remarkable that this alienation is a constant structure of geological realities. Except for uranium and thorium, all other radioactive elements are produced from other elements by some nuclear reaction. Within the regularity there is an irreversible orientation towards the other as other, which is often labelled a "run-down." This regular run-down was confirmed by the radioactive run-down in the dead organism discovered by William F. Libby in 1949 (Matthews, 1971, pp. 105-106). As long as the organism lives a balance is maintained between the ordinary variety of carbon and the radioactive carbon. But once the organism dies, it ceases taking in more carbon 14, and since the decay of radioactive carbon proceeds at a regular rate, the age of the organism can be determined.

Thus we observe instances of alienation with an irreversible run-down in which a returning reversibility serves as a measurement without affecting the irreversibility manifest in reversibilities. There is an element which seemingly functions as a balance between the various alienations, each with its irreversible alienations (Gould, 1987), yet each within its own reversible repetitions. And this is not just a mental measurement but rather the basic nature of the earth and of its constitutive elements.

We can say, therefore, that geological time is not only real, but it is the most basic and universal constituent nature of that reality which we call the earth. Time is, as it were, the ultimate reality of the earth, and as we will see later on, that of the universe, too.

It should be noted also that earth-time is not one single time, but a sort of balance of many constitutive event-times, all submitted to one time which governs the earth-time as well as its sub-times (Stever, 1983), sc., the cosmic time (Whitrow, 1975, pp. 64-82; Matthews, 1971, pp. 140-41). The concept of time in geology, therefore, must be validated by the concept of time in cosmology.

2.3.1.2. Time in Cosmology

In cosmology the strength of the 21cm line of the neutral hydrogen atom is measured on a 300-foot aperture telescope and is interpreted as an indicator of the mass of 140,000 million suns of the Spiral galaxy NGC 1961 (de Vaucouleurs and Olson, 1982). The wide broadening of the spectral lines is the result of the high velocity of a spiral galaxy (ca. 400km per second), which suggests that the galaxies are moving further away from the earth at a speed at of several million miles an hour. Knowing the speed at which the galaxies are moving apart from each other, the cosmologists venture to calculate the lifetime of the universe and translate it into solar motion-time as nearly 20 billion years.

Such a translation of the lifetime of the universe into earth-time is misleading, since earth-time is conditioned by the time of the universe, and not vice versa. Earth-time, as the measurement of the universe, projects time as space, where a large place is measured by the multiplication of smaller spaces. Such a multiplication is not possible for cosmic time, since the components of cosmic time are not exact replicas of earth-time. To illustrate this let us take the spiral galaxy of Andromeda, the nearest large galaxy which, the experts claim, contains two billion stars and satellites. And the spiral galaxy in Andromeda is just one of the many galaxies, each composed of billions of stars. Thus the cosmic time of the universe cannot be the sum of the times of the participating stars, but rather the balance of all the galaxy times which again are the balance of the many star-times and so on. What this balance amounts to we cannot measure by our time, which is conditioned in its turn again by a much greater cosmic unit. Measurement by years makes sense to us, but it is unrealistic and would mean nothing to one living outside our solar system. Yet the time of the universe is real even though our measurement is inadequate. Time is simply not what we measure by our time-scale, whatever type that might be.

The notion of time which emerges in our analysis is equally valid whether we conceive the universe as oscillating, i.e., as cosmic cyclic expansion and contraction or as a once-and-for-all expansion. A cyclic universe is not identical with cyclic time unless time is understood as pure measurement and not as we propose it, sc., a balance of a multiplicity of sub-times of different kinds. If we consider the language of cosmic time as a "dialogue" with the cosmos in which the cosmos replies, as it were, to our question by releasing more and more energy, the language of cyclic time must include the presently experienced time which is not cyclic. The technical success of the laws of thermodynamics and of Einsteinian physics supports this request. Cosmic time as we experience it relates all the different experienced time-levels to a unity which corresponds to a process which, according to the law of thermodynamics, flows from a maximum level of energy to a maximum level of entropy. Within this astronomical flow there is a uniform vibration and a basic unique rhythm functioning as an "atomic clock," which, through reversible rhythmic vibration, realizes as well as expresses the irreversibility of cosmic time. An exclusively cyclic language of time would be a language ignoring this experiential datum, and would suppose a view of time which identifies the measurement of time with the nature of time. Such a simplistic view of time is operative in theologies which consider apocalyptic destruction as the dividing line between the present life and the life of resurrection. But to speculate correctly on the relation between the time we know and the time we do not know, the Incarnation should act as the problem-solving paradigm for a speculative theologian. The Incarnation as problem-solving paradigm suggests that time is once and for all, because the Incarnation itself is irreversible and once and forever.

G.J. Whitrow, who claims that there is no certainty that the universe never passed through a contracting phase and that the laws governing the known forces and interactions in physics are compatible with the reversal of time's arrow, admits that in the basic building blocks of the universe, in the case of the weak interactions involving neutrinos, time reversal is doubtful (Whitrow, 1975, pp. 128-32). If we conceive of time as a balance of sub-times, there can be no reason why the macrocosmic arrows of time would be different from the microcosmic arrows of time. All the more so, since, if with David Layzer (1975) we relate the three macrocosmic arrows of time, i.e., the thermodynamic arrow, defined by entropy and the historical arrow, characterized by increasing information-generating process, with the cosmological arrow, described by the recession of galaxies, we have to say that the universe is unfolding so that the future is not predictable, and though it is growing out of the past, it contains much more than the past. If this is the case, physical time seems to control any kind of time, psychological time included, even though the two cannot be considered as identical. Consequently, irreversibility should be considered as the most specific nature of time (Penrose, 1990, pp. 391-417, 454-65). We experience time as the transitional irreversible reality of everything we are aware of and express in our language. Now language manifests the characteristics of irreversibility. Thus even the concept of cyclic time cannot be expressed except through irreversible language.

A definition of time which says that time is continuity in existence is insufficient. I. Barrow, in his *Geometrical Lectures*, noted that things rising and perishing together have different times (Barrow, 1735). Two events which continue in existence together with a common beginning and with a common end can still have different times, because each implies a different multiplicity of sub-times with a different balance irreversible in the reversible basic rhythms. Even in the oscillating universe such an irreversibility through reversible basic rhythms is the guarantee that none of the reversible basic rhythms will ever match what is called proto-time, when the whole universe, with its billions of galaxy systems, was just a very small intensively energized spot which exploded and the gravitational force became separated from the other three basic forces, that is, from electromagnetism and from strong and weak atomic forces. The more so, since in that proto-time there is nothing changeless. As the experiment of bombing accelerated particles into the centre of the atom indicates, even the smallest known elements of material things, like protons, quarks and leptons will split and decay into energy. But at the same time there is a unique natural period of an atom the duration of which was defined as the duration of 9192.631,770 periods of the cesium-113 radiation and is known as the cesium atom clock (Whitrow, 1975, p. 75).

If we use the expansion of the universe to explore the concept of time, the concept of time will evidently depend on the gravitational force as well as on the amount of the mass in the universe, since it was found by Einstein that time, space, energy, acceleration and mass are interrelated. Therefore, the future of the expansion of the universe depends on the average density of the universe. If there is enough mass in the universe the expansion will stop and will reverse. The amount necessary to stop the expansion is called critical density. The presently known visible matter supplies about one-hundredth of the critical density, and if there is no more matter in the universe some say that the universe can continue to expand indefinitely, slowing down only slightly. This is called the "open universe" (Melott, 1981, p. 71). There are others who claim that the universe is not open. Stephen Hawking believes, e.g., that the discovery of the black holes provided one more argument against the open universe. According to him it is possible that the black holes may contain a significant quantity of mass which could reverse the expansion and move it toward a big crunch (Hawking, 1976; Park, 1981, pp. 94-95; Penrose, 1990, pp. 427-47).

But the black holes may be considered as an argument for an open universe as well. Some believe that a black hole on this side may have a white whole on the other side and be a connecting link between our universe and a neighbouring one, between our times and other times existing within our times (Gribbin, 1979).

At the point of black holes where the gravitational drawing force surpasses the velocity of light is the singularity event, where, because of the great density, the mass with its time and space is crushed until it reaches a point similar to the proto-time with its irreversibility. Thus at singularity the uniformly reversible changes are sublated, and irreversibility is radicalized. It seems, therefore, that the description of time as irreversibility can be valid even in the passages of singularities and eventually in the other universes as well.

In considering cosmic time our time shrinks to a small spot, yet it receives a special importance on account of Einstein's relativity theory, supposed by most of the ideas referred to thus far. So we should say a few words about Einstein's theory and time in modern physics.

2.3.1.3. Time in Modern Physics

We have seen that time is a fundamental property of the relationships existing among stars, galaxies and universes. Yet according to Einstein's theory the observer cannot be disregarded.

Einstein united time, space, mass and gravitation. According to his general relativity, gravitation influences the speed of light and bends space and time. Strong gravitational fields can bend time and delay the travelling time of light. Time, therefore, cannot be considered as an independent absolute receptacle (Newton), or as a mental category (Kant). Einsteinian time is neither substantial nor relational. It is relativistic, since it is related to gravitation. Now the gravitation force is the feeblest of the four basic forces, but still is the most effective over unlimited distances. It influences all forms of matter and it pulls and never pushes. Any system of gravitating bodies has a definitive space-time so that the gravitational effects of the systems are properties of the space-time.

In other words, according to the gravitation of each system, there will be a special space-time for each. And since the gravitations are intermingled, so too will the times be, making times always an intermingling of times, or, if we prefer, a balance of times, a term which conveys more dynamics than, for example, equilibrium does. One of the empirical tests of general relativity is the gravitational red-shift effect. Einstein noticed that a gravitational field has a slowing-down effect on clocks of nature. Studying the spectrum light emitted by a massive body, one can see that the color becomes more red when the gravitational field of the body slows down the frequency of the light. J.A. Wheeler especially argued that we should give up thinking of nature as a machine that goes on independent of the observer. He devised a thought-experiment to suggest how the observer helps determine the reality that he/she perceives. The universe is a participatory universe (Wheeler, 1980).

But again Einstein was the first to notice that all measurements of duration involve judgments of simultaneity which depend on the relative position of the observed distant event and on the relative position of the observer and the mode of connecting the two. The observer relates the external event to some previous instance in his/her own experiences (e.g., the special position of hands on a watch) and the speed of the signal connecting the event and the perception of the signal and the instance of the experience. Now the instance of one's own experience is evidently not the same for all. Einstein found that a moving clock would appear to run slowly compared with the identical clock at rest with respect to the observer. The closer to the speed of light the speed of a moving clock gets, the more slowly it will appear to run compared with the clock of the observer. Thus he concluded that the inertial mass of the body will increase as its velocity approaches the speed of light, and the time will dilate as a result (Whitrow, 1975, pp. 96-98).

The phenomenon of time dilatation is applicable to living organisms as well. Provided that the motion takes place with approximately the speed of light, an organism, after a long flight, would return little changed to its original position, whereas one remaining in the original position would age a great deal.

The idea of dilation has interesting applications for time. It is possible that something could appear to one observer as later while appearing to another as locally simultaneous. If A and B experience F together and then B moves faster than A in the direction of E, then A, the first observer, can perceive B as perceiving EF locally simultaneous. Furthermore if one observer whose velocity exceeds that of the other, sees E and F simultaneously but his/her speed is less than that of light, F can be seen by the first observer as prior to E. Thus the order of certain events can be reversed by the changes of the observer, because the duration of time between two events depends on the position of the observer.

If time is conditioned by the observer and the universe, different data can be assigned to the same event, depending on the choice of the observer. Thus Einstein's theory would challenge the possibility of an objective sequence of temporal states of the universe, since each observer has his/her own sequence of these states, and so there is no one absolutely unique privileged observer. There is, however, a privileged class of observers in the sense that those in uniform relative motion or at rest can be considered as inertial. In this case the Newtonian law can be considered as valid (Einstein, 1961) and the temporal order of events is seen as absolute, i.e., independent of the observers. Theologians in the past knew only pre-relativistic theories of time and considered the temporal chronological order as absolute. But the Einsteinian time dilatation and the relativity of the temporal order could serve as a paradigm to solve the problem of the "how" of perpetuating the once-and-for-all Christ-event. Unlike in pre-relativistic time theories, for relativistic time theories time depends on the observer as well, who is a multiplicity of sub-times trying to establish a balance and create his/her own time. This will become more evident by considering the nature of biological time.

2.3.1.4. *Mathematics and Research into the Nature of Time*

Considering real time in physics, Stephen Hawking believes that the universe has an end. It will end up in the universal singularity event which forms a boundary to space-time, and the laws of physics will be broken down. Thus "real time" has a definitive boundary.

But Hawking's mind cannot stop there. His mind, like any human mind, wants to transcend any experienced boundary. To answer questions emerging further in his mind he looks for a problem-solving paradigm. He turns to mathematics, the only exact science reflecting the unlimitedness of the human mind, and inspired by the model of the "imaginary number," he introduces the notion of "imaginary time" (1990, p. 134). "Imaginary time" is not a real time. Thus it has no beginning and no end. Yet like the imaginary numbers that may be applied to real numbers and open the way to a solution of new problems, so may imaginary time be applied to real time and open a way to solve some problems of real time. Imaginary time is, therefore, a hermeneutical device. It is like the language event which, as we will see later in the section on Philosophy, Time and Language (2.3.2.3), may legitimate talk about "eternity."

The notion of imaginary time as a hermeneutic device makes the string theory of an infinite two-dimensional world plausible for Hawking. Such a world would not have boundaries and could be considered as a self-contained eternal world with neither beginning nor end (1990, pp. 157-69), where there is no need for a creator (1990, p. 141).

Such a conclusion is conceivable if time can be reduced to space as to its ultimate reality and meaning. The space component of time is obviously the proper field of mathematics and thus can be expressed by the basic operation of mathematics, the equation. Space is mathematical, and mathematics is spacelike, since both are based on the assumption that left and right, or up and down, are reversible. In such a self-contained equational system obviously there is no need for a creator, for the simple reason that the creator is not a mathematical figure.

But if we believe that the distinctive characteristic of real time is its irreversibility, then we have to say that its most basic constitutive element is not mathematical and, therefore, time cannot be expressed

CONCEPTS OF TIME 51

adequately by equation. The future will never be past and the past will never be future, unless we want to reduce time to space as to its ultimate reality. Consequently, we think that imaginary time should not be modelled on imaginary numbers. The more so, since in a two-dimensional world there is no room left for real time. Therefore, we have to look for another problem-solving paradigm for our mind to transcend the boundaries of the experienced space-time.

As a kind of "imaginary time" a theologian may propose the time of Jesus Christ, who, after one has considered relevant data, can be conceived as the eschatological union of time and eternity. It seems that the eschatological union of time and eternity "model" would safeguard the most basic distinctive feature of time, irreversibility. Futhermore, by presenting Christ not only as a hypostatical union of human and divine natures but as an eschatological union of time and eternity, we are able to open a "universe with no boundary" where time will be the foundation of space as well as the expression of eternity.

But first let us continue collecting further data by sketching briefly the notion of time in biology, psychology, sociology, history, philosophy and language. As a conclusion we will then try to summarize the common features of all the data in a statement about the nature of time which hopefully is not only accurate, consistent and concise but, above all, by its ability to generate more theories, to a certain degree, validates itself.

2.3.1.5. Biological Time

Living bodies contain different biological clocks, whose functions are to enable the organism to bring about the required response at appropriate occasions. The evidence for this internal timing mechanism comes from the observation of animal navigation and photoperiodism and of daily and other periodic rhythms in the behaviour and activity of living organisms. These biological clocks do not depend on purely metabolic processes, since then they would depend on temperature. Plants shows no evidence of any central regulator of periodicity conditioned by heat. The nine months of human gestation does not follow solar time. Charles Ehret argues that each cell has its own clock (1983; 1967) and the synchronization of the cellular clocks is regulated by some rhythmic control centre, the master clock.

The human brain itself is subject to rhythmical activity, due to electric currents with special frequency range (Arnold, 1985). Brain oscillators produce a well-timed complex system. Some local oscillators show a capacity for pulling others into synchronization. The importance of biological time in personal life becomes more and more important. Our cognitive-time senses (cf. psychology of time), which are controlled by social and psychological factors, are superimposed on the rhythm of the innumerable biological clocks that are within us, below the level of the consciousness. Research on progeria will teach us more about how our time is built into our genes which regulate our growing and aging process.

The time-experience, which can be described as the systematic organization of the various time-levels or sub-times into one's time, and warranting a common beginning and a common end with an irreversible course, is not independent of the laws of thermodynamics. How this systematization or unification takes place is the mystery of a person's lifetime. Our time-concept formation evidently comes to an end at the moment of death, when we lose the balance among the constituting sub-times, and our time will be alienated by other times that, as sub-times, were dominated by "our" time in the course of our life.

2.3.2. Current Notions of Time in Humanistic Studies

2.3.2.1. Psychology of Time

The goal of the psychology of time is to discover the laws underlying the means by which one forms his/her time-experience. Time-experience is the result of establishing a relationship between oneself and the events which affect one as accomplished (past), or as engaged in action (present) or to which one orients oneself (future), thus building the sense of personal identity. Human ideas of time are emerging, as Piaget has demonstrated, and can be analyzed and understood in the perspective of their development and their relation to purposeful action (Fraisse, 1964).

One of the greatest problems of the psychology of time is the way memory operates and retains information. Memory is the psychological basis of our consciousness of self, since, by producing a sequence of past events in chronological order, it presupposes different time-levels in which one's irreversibility is experienced and realized. Each of us experiences time differently, because each time is an insertion in the "combat" of times provided by the biological, sociological, cultural and philosophical irreversibilities experienced through reversibilities. The geological, biological or psychological, etc. times constitute our personal time conditioned by the permanent organic rhythms of the universe of which we are part.

Some psychologists, like W. James (1890) and H. Münsterberg (1916) spoke of "internal clocks," analogous to biological clocks, as a measure of individual duration. Piaget (1971) distinguished four major stages in the emergence of human awareness of time: sensorimotor (from birth to 2 years), preparatory (2-7 years), concrete operational (7-11), formal operational (12-through adulthood). This schema, however, reflects Western education and its school system and is therefore socially conditioned. But all genetic psychologists will agree that awareness of time develops slowly, "with graduational establishment of coordinated motor activities from repeated goal-oriented encounters with the world" (Gorman and Wessman, 1977, pp. 2-3) and conditions the Ego-identity.

Ego-identity is an interpretation of self-perceived and self-accepted consistency over time. There is a progressive continuity between what the person was, has become and promises to be (Gorman and Wessman, 1977, p. 3; Hartocollis, 1983, p. 221). It is a unification of past, present and future which forms the structure of personal time. It is unlikely that any two people will develop exactly the same cognitive structure of time, but a general pattern can be set up, like that of Charlotte Bühler (1968):

1. before self-determination (0-15)
2. tentative self-determination of life goals (15-25)
3. more specified and definitive determination of life goals and their implementation (24-45/50)
4. assessment of the foregoing life and its relative degree of fulfillment (45/50-60/65)
5. final phase of rest and retirement (65-90/death).

2.3.2.2. *Time in Sociology and History*

The multiplicity of time is the central problem in sociology (Gurwitch, 1964; Sorokin, 1964). Gurwitch defined social time as "the convergency and divergency of movements of the total social phenomena giving birth to time as well as elapsing in time" (Gurwitch, 1964, p. 30). The different social activities like the religious, technical, economic, cognitive, moral, judicial, political, etc., are manifestations of one total social phenomenon, the "collective acting" (Gurwitch, 1964, p. 28). History and sociology are in dispute as to which one of the two is able to arrive simultaneously at the multiplicity and the unity of time. Historians such as Fernard Braudel (1958, pp. 96-97) favour historical time over social time, whereas sociologists like Gurwitch adopt social time over historical time. The argument of the historians is that they are able to comprehend both the narrower issues of time as well as the longest duration. But sociologists will argue that, unlike historians, who reconstruct the continuity of time, they work on typology, emphasizing the discontinuity of types and the hierarchies of the multiple manifestations of time.

We are inclined to see social and historical time as different, yet we deal with both under one heading, because the two together illustrate the paradoxical nature of time. Scrutinizing various types, like types of societies, clans, movements and the times of all of these, sociology observes the reversible measurement, whereas history marks instead the irreversibility of the phenomenon. Yet this general statement does not mean that social time is just a manifestation of historical time. Sociology is dealing with language, which, as we will see, is the home of time, a society-creating factor. Thus the concern for time in sociology is critical. Sociology will find this more so than it has in the past.

The historian's concern with time can be seen as a truism, but we should note that history is just one aspect of the reality of time. History is human time considered in abstraction from geological, cosmic, physical, biological and even psychological times, though it is never independent of them. Human time is that of culture (development of intellectual and moral talents) and of civilization (application of human talents for mastering the surrounding world) from the viewpoint of temporality. Time in history is a time which had a beginning and an end, and one is as important as the other. Time which has no end is not a time for history. The "actuality" of non-being and the irreversibility of it make history the most obvious discipline of time. But human time is both a balance of the multiplicities of sub-times, and a sub-time in another balance of many "other" multiplicities of sub-times. In addition to non-human times, history implies the times of all individual human beings who form the total human time. Each person has his/her time, his/her own history. Yet the personal time includes also the time of other peoples. No one's time can be achieved without others' time. The totality of people's time is history, and history is the fulfillment of one's time.

Now the balance of the multiplicity of sub-times itself is in time. Disequilibrium can be brought about by changes in the ecological habitat of those who share in the same historical "period," by the confrontation of two different cultures or by evolutionary changes within the same society.

Concerning the process of culture changes, there are two points of view. One finds the reason for change in the individual member of the society, the innovator. The other sees the basis of the change in the social milieu. The first uses the model of the stable equilibrium versus constant changes (Durkheim, 1954; Radcliffe-Brown 1961), and the second employs the model of changes against stable equilibrium. The first model is based on the classical organism analogy, whereas the second considers the laws of thermodynamics. Changes against the stable equilibrium model are operating in one-to-one dialogue in parliamentary systems and in international relations in contests between two different culture-types, which end up in the surrender/defeat of one of the two. Yet on an individual or communal level it is always the same progressive dynamic of the human spirit which refuses to be repetitious without creative affirmation of itself. On account of its indefinitely progressive and at the same time universalizing tendency, the human spirit lifts up and breaks down what has been built. It brings life as well as death to itself and to its surrounding society and world.

In this time-forming process we can distinguish four instances detected in the history of individuals, societies, systems, beliefs, etc. (Horvath, 1976, pp. 449-51). The first instance is discovery, discovery of something which is new, different from anything seen, heard or existing before. It is a new value, which gives new identity to the inventor or discoverer. Such a discovery takes the form of vocation as a result of a religious experience as in the case of prophets, founders of religions, etc., or the form of scientific, technological or economic innovation, as a result of inventive insight, or that of simple human individualization resulting from personal encounters, falling in love etc. Now every discovery is self-discovery. Values and self-values are germane.

The next step is the proclamation, the communication of the discovery. If one finds the discovery valuable, one has to tell someone else about it. This can be done by proclaiming the experienced new event as something worthwhile, valuable for others, for the rest of the human race (cf. apostolic need for preaching, propagating ideas, campaigning, publishing or talking about "being in love"). The third instance is organization, institutionalization of the communication.

Organizations, institutions, corporations and companies are formed to make the communication of the discovery more effective.

Finally, when the organizations and institutions are weakened and lose their initial vigour and effectiveness in constant confrontation with newly emerging discoveries and their respective communication and organizations, the fourth step is taken, sc., the philosophical trans-historicization or dogmatization of the institutions in order to make them permanent, immortal, in a word, secure against time. The aim of philosophizing about a system or institution is to argue that the proposed discovery and communication with its institutions is so indispensable to the world that, without them, the world cannot survive. The philosophizing or dogmatizing process is especially accelerated by the appearance of new prophets, seen as heretics, of new rival inventors or of individuals who, by their proclamation and structuralization, become a menace to the previously established culture-types, inventions, products, markets, family lives, etc.

Throughout these stages the human spirit constantly brings about challenges and responses which in their turn will be challenged and replied to by other culture-types, inventions, products and markets. Throughout these four stages the new ones label the previous ones as old and try to transform or absorb them, in order to establish themselves as the only immortal ones.

The four instances—(1) discovery of self, (2) communication of discovery, (3) institutionalization of the communication and (4) philosophizing the institutionalization—make up the structure of social time, which gives birth to the different philosophical notions of time grasped and expressed in language.

2.3.2.3. Philosophy: Time and Language

No analysis of a notion of time can be complete without considering the close relationship between time and language. Language introduces us not only into the personal differentiation between me and you, him/her and them but also into the world of present, past and future and reveals the speaker's awareness of time. The tense-structure of a language reflects the time-awareness of its speaker. The English language probably has more tenses than any other language spoken in our world (Nalimov, 1982, p. 52), and it seems that English-speaking people are the most time-conscious on earth.

The close relationship between time and language can be scrutinized by the historical diachronic study of the reconstruction of the past of a language or by the descriptive synchronic studies of its structure. Since the latter makes no explicit reference to the past of a language it is more apt to illustrate how time-experience is a linguistic event.

The descriptive synchronic study of a language is divided into three branches: the study of a sound system (phonology), the study of rules governing the arrangement of meaningful elements (grammar) and the study of meaning (semantics). The phonology is described in terms of articulatory processes (e.g., contacts of lips, bilabial-vibration of the vocal chord, voiced form of closure-stop) or in that of acoustic impression (pitch, high and low, falling frequency of vibration). The role and function of time in phonology is the one which we find in musical experience. In music it is called rhythm. In language it creates a certain balance of different sounds, each with its own time, facilitating the semantic event. Grammar, with its morphology (inflection, conjugation, declension) and syntax (arrangements of the parts of speech) can provide the generation of an infinite number of sentences based on a finite set of utterances and of rules. As a result, the speakers constantly make up and understand sentences which were never encountered in previous experience. Such a definition of grammar is already semantic.

A non-semantic approach to grammatical categories can be obtained in terms of morphological behaviour. The two basic units are the phoneme and the morpheme.

Morphemes are the smallest elements conveying meaning. Phonemes are the smallest sound units without meaning. With a limited number of phonemic units humans are again capable of forming endlessly different meaningful units and signal meanings. They can ask questions, make hypotheses, discuss past and future and so on. According to Joseph H. Greenberg, this makes humans "time-binding animals," since anthropoid beings can signal only about here and now (Greenberg, 1971, p. 266). The grammar which generates the deep structures of languages and converts them to surface structures by means of transformation is the transformational grammar (Chomsky, 1957). In his *Aspects of the Theory of Syntax*, later called standard theory, Chomsky described how surface emerges from the transformation:

> A grammar contains a syntactic component, a semantic component, and a phonological component. The latter two are purely interpretative; they play no part in the recursive generation of sentence struc-

tures. The syntactic component consists of a base and a transformational component. The base, in turn, consists of a categorical subcomponent (the phrase-structure rules) and a lexicon. The base generates the deep structures. A deep structure enters the semantic component and receives a semantic interpretation; it is mapped by the transformational rules into a surface structure, which is then given a phonetic interpretation by the rules of the phonological component. Thus the grammar assigns semantic interpretations to signals, this association being mediated by the recursive rules of the syntactic component (Chomsky, 1965, p. 141).

Time-experience can and does influence the generation of sentence structure. The language is therefore the event, where time can be observed and its nature further described. The surface structure has a diversity which, in its relation to the deep structure, is characteristic of human language, but both are derived from a more abstract underlying structure. Now the pluralism of the surface structure of time has been indicated in the previous section dealing with time in geology, cosmology, physics, biology, psychology and sociology. The different surfaces of time systems are derived from an underlying structure of the language which receives semantic interpretation from the different disciplines, and the multiplicity of the surface structures, in turn, shows a richer interpretation of the deep structures, the transformation of which are precisely the great variety of time notions we found in different disciplines.

Such a great variety indicates that the transformation function of the deep structure cannot be reduced to one time interpretation, because time appears always as a balance in a multiplicity of subtimes, which points beyond the times of the surface to a ground where times find their "homes" and the language of eternity is introduced mostly by philosophers, poets and religion founders. Heidegger once called language the home of being (Heidegger, 1971, p. 135) but more fittingly language should be called the home of time. It is both the home of time and the way-making for eternity. The language of the Johannine Jesus is the most classical use of linguistic reality as way-making for eternity by transforming irreversibility into inalienability (Jn 13, 1-18, 1). Language as the home of time and the way-making for eternity is an effort to bring about as well as to express oneself as being loved uniquely as an individual for all eternity. Language in its basic level is aiming to achieve the event which is commonly known as "being accepted, loved." Every speaker using language intends to be unique and inalienable and accepted as such indeed. One could simply say that language is love and love is language because both are a sort of way-making for eternity.

Language and time interconnections can be further analyzed. Language bridges not only temporal distances, but also various times operating in different disciplines, as we have already noted. Language makes communication between sciences possible, and lets scientists of different disciplines talk about the various times operating in their research fields. Furthermore language reveals the time of the language itself. Both the multiplicity of sub-times and the irreversibility of the balancing of the multiplicity of sub-times are expressed in language. One would venture to say that time without language is non-existent. To say that time is related to the observer is correct, because the observer is a speaker. An animal is neither an observer nor a speaker. The non-human has time, yet its time is not a language event. The time of a non-human being does not have language, and this is why it is not a way-making for eternity either. Language is the home of time, because language constitutes time as a hermeneutic event, i.e., bringing light to its own obscurity. In language time becomes time for itself, time of times. Once one is speaking a language, one is not only speaking but is spoken by the language. By speaking a language the speaker enters into a world which is pre-given, so that the speaker gives up some of his/her individual uniqueness and the time of languages appropriates his/her time. The speaker of time, otherwise called observer of time, is taken up into the plurality of times.

Language makes it possible to express time as a multiplicity of times and to experience it as universal, actively present in everything and everywhere. It is language that makes one experience that time exists and that time exists in time because language is made up by time and time is revealed in language. By saying that language is the home of time, we touch an important element in language which might shed further light on time, sc., the semantic nature of language.

To speak is to say something. And to say something is both communication and invitation to communicate and accept communication. To speak is to come out of the solitude of loneliness and to enter into the world of someone else. It is an offering of something and oneself in that something in order to let that something be accepted and with it the speaker as well. Every language, that of physics, mathematics, or another, implies if not a demand, at least an opening to be listened to, to be respected and accepted. Language as home of time means also that the acceptance of one should be an acceptance of one as unique, "personal," related to his/her time, in a word, inalienable. And this is true about any language which is serious. But the language which is not serious is just a camouflaged negative language which determines the positive language, as non-being does being. To be a determinate entity is to be this and not that. Gadamer rightly noticed that Plato saw that element of non-being in being as that which "really made it possible to speak of existent at all" (Gadamer, 1975, p. 409). So too negative language makes it possible to speak of what is positive and existent.

Language appropriates the characteristics of time and time assumes those of language. As a result, language transforms uniqueness and irreversibility into inalienability: "I am irreversible" expressed in the hermeneutic language event implies both an affirmation of being in time and a negation of being in time by making an opening to be listened to and respected as someone absolutely unique who cannot be challenged by any other time. It is in this sense that language is the way-making for eternity and eternity turns up in time. Yet it is not eternity that enters into time. Rather, time expressed in language is opened up to enter through its own sublation into eternity.

After having seen the different notions present in geology, cosmology, physics, biology, psychology, sociology, history and philosophy, we are now in a position tosummarize the new notion of time operative in the research and observations in these disciplines.

2.3.3. Time is a Balance in a Multiplicity of Sub-times Characterized by an Irreversibility Measured Through Uniformly Reversible Changes Pointing to a Self-sublating Singularity Event. Thus in Hermeneutic Language Event Time Can Be Interpreted as Way-making for Eternity

We have seen that time has a proper meaning in geology, cosmology, physics, biology, psychology, etc. It is not just an abstraction or measurement but the result of the co-activity of various constitutive elements called sub-times mutually determining each other. In other words, we can say that time is always a conflict of times (Fraser, 1978). The different sub-times or time-levels are interrelated in a sort of combat of times aiming at the sublation of one by the other. As a matter of fact, each being, from the smallest cells up to the whole universe, has its own clock-forming interaction with the clocks of the other beings.

Thus so-called external and internal time, personal and real time, etc., are all interrelated and finally grounded in cosmic time, which suggests the velocity of light as an absolute speed variant. But the speed of light is really not absolute. The interrelations of time-levels will undergo a considerable alteration because of gravitation, which might bind the speed of light. Thus gravitation is the time-grounding force which makes the great variety of time-levels possible, as well as the black holes bringing about a singularity event which, according to the internal observer, seems to occur at a finite time, whereas according to the external observer it occurs in an infinite future.

Time is, therefore, always hierarchically interactive, realizing in different degrees what time fundamentally means, i.e., irreversibility. The influence of the gravitational force on the speed of light and the observable features of the black holes point to a singularity event when uniformly reversible changes are sublated and irreversibility is radicalized, since beyond that event the idea of "reverse" is nominal, prompted by mental images of an observer from this side of the time-horizon.

That time fundamentally is irreversibility means that time does not have two reversible sides in the way that space, for example, has. It is once and for all, and when it is made reversible, time is no longer time. This suggests not only that time is going in one direction or that there is run-down with no return, but also that time is a force not letting itself become obliterated by anything else but itself. This makes time a sort of ultimate reality of every reality whatever, wherever or "whenever" that exists, gravitational force included. Or, using the terminology of another philosophical system, we can say that time makes each reality of being independent, individual or subsistent.

Yet time is not just an irreversibility, but an irreversibility measured by uniformly reversible changes. And this is so because the irreversibility itself is realized and expressed in and through such uniformly reversible changes. Consequently the uniformly returning changes are not external to the nature of time. Rather, they are its constituent elements. On every level of time there is a constant uniformly returning change in which a no-return irreversibility breaks through. Thus the nature of time is composite and cannot be studied without studying both the constant uniform changes and the irreversibility actualized precisely in the uniformly returning changes. Irreversibility and its measurement, the reversible changes, both discernible and verifiable by the different Newtonian and Einsteinian observers, should be considered and understood as the reality of time itself.

Time is the axis of opposites, which can be illustrated somewhat by relating time to language and showing that language is always a language of time. Language implies a reference to the irrevocable by revocable symbols. The speaker constantly understands and makes new sentences which he/she never encountered in his/her previous experience. The abstract repeatable symbols make possible the indefinite varieties of sentences, which are not just the combination or summary of the meaning of the various terms, since they involve reference to something irrevocable experienced by the speaker. Thus language is not only dependent on time, but it is revelatory of the speaker's time.

The irreversibility of time through reversible changes and the irrevocability of the language by revocable symbols point to the fullest realization of time and language as to their ultimate of ultimates when irreversibility and irrevocability take the form of inalienability. But this cannot take place on the surface structure of the language of time, where Zeno's paradox and McTaggart's contradictions move, but at the deep structure, where irreversibility appears as inalienability, i.e., denial of end or death as radical alienation, which on the deepest basic level is nothing else but eternity and can only be just one person, and one person only. On this level language posits subject over object, inalienability over irreversibility, eternity over time, subject over subjects.

An analysis of the generative transformation grammar suggests that language is not only the record of finitude (Gadamer, 1975, p. 415) but a special hermeneutical event where time is radically questioned by time itself and the supporting ground of the balance of the multiplicity of sub-times can be interpreted by one word, eternity. The word "eternity" is the hermeneutical significance of time in its basic structure where the balance of the multiplicity of sub-times is rooted.

Now eternity can be approached in a hermeneutical experience of language only if time is conceived essentially as a balance in a multiplicity of sub-times, as we have defined it. Since time is a transdisciplinary event without univocal meaning, the balance of sub-times of the various fields is not a simultaneous or successive co-existence. Its actuality can only be experienced when one language evokes a multiplicity of languages, since every word affects the whole of languages, so that the speaker is related to the whole of language. As a result, the speaker discovers him/herself as being spoken by all the languages mediating times. As one language is related to the whole of languages so is one time to the whole of times. In such a hermeneutical experience of time the meaning of time is interpreted in a dialogue which moves from speaking of times through being spoken by times and ends up by having uttered one word which is more than the sum of all words expressing times. It is unmistakably one word which denies at once both the reversibility and irreversibility as ultimates, exhibiting the balance of times, rooted not in time but in the negation of time. When time is experienced thus, language becomes the home of time as well as the way-making for eternity. At this instant the speaker finally is able to utter the word expressing comprehensively him/herself once and for all by overcoming the barrier he/she experienced in life between his/her times and their verbal experiences and reach the time-horizon which has most intensively inspired poets, prophets, artists, religionists and theologians.

In this sense we can say that eternity is fully realized time. It is not infinite time. It is not timeless, either, because it has time. Yet it does not include time, since time comes to an end in eternity. Eternity, however, is not unrelated to time, since time includes eternity as something already real. Thus the meaning of time is eternity and time is an expression of eternity (cf. divinity of Christ as the meaning of his humanity and the humanity of Christ as the expression of his divinity).

Time exists since eternity exists. True we do not know eternity without time, because time reveals eternity by its own sublation when we are still in time. As irreversibility is measured, expressed and realized through reversibility, so eternity is measured, expressed and actualized in time through the times of various observers. If we take time as irreversibility measured by uniformly reversible changes, eternity makes sense to us from our point of view as reversible uniform changes made irreversible (see permanence as the Aristotelian concept of eternity) or as irreversibility made uniform flux (process philosophy, pantemporalism). In other words, eternity differs from time as inalienability measured by inalienability differs from irreversibility measured by uniform reversibility. Thus time is more paradoxical than eternity.

Since time is both real and multiple we must say that there is no univocal notion of time. But from this is does not follow that the notion of eternity and time are equivocal notions. As we cannot point to anything when we speak of time, much less do we know what we talk about when we use the word "eternity." Yet when on the deep level of language we use the word "time" we use it to express its fulfilled reality as well, and so time as irreversibility points to inalienability, sc., eternity, as to its ultimate reality and meaning. The notion of time and eternity are hermeneutical notions.

With our notion of time we can hold with Davies (1976) Prigogine (1980) and Morris (1984) that time has reality in the fundamental laws of physics. With process philosophers like Whitehead (1969) and Griffin (1986, pp. 21-26), we can subscribe to pantemporalism. But since we stress the multiplicity of time, the balance of which, by means of hermeneutical language experience, points beyond time, we admit the legitimacy of the language of eternity.

3. THE FIRST PRINCIPLE IN CHRISTIAN ESCHATOLOGY: JESUS CHRIST, THE ESCHATOLOGICAL UNION OF TIME AND ETERNITY

3.1. The Eschatological Union of Time and Eternity

The purpose of the kerygma of the early Church was to transcend the time between the "past," when Jesus preached, and the "now," when the proclaimed word was announced, by bringing both into the future, which was not the future of men and women but the future of God, a future made by God. And this was possible because in the kerygma God's eternity appeared as power related to Jesus' presence. Thus the kerygma was not only a preaching about Jesus but the realization of the presence of God in the word of the community of Jesus Christ. The eternal God was associated with the time of Jesus, and the time of Jesus Christ became the "eternity" of the presence of God.

The possibility of the kerygma as the presence of the past historical Jesus together with the presence of God's future meant that through the kerygma of Jesus Christ everyone's time could be related to eternity. The discovery of this possibility opened the door for the evangelization of the Gentiles with no exception whatsoever. Through Jesus' time, God's time, i.e., God's eternity, became available to every time. The universal dimension of the kerygma was a necessary outgrowth of experiencing Jesus, the proclaimer, in the proclaimed word anywhere and at any time. Jesus was not only a fact of the past, but a word-event now and the two could be identified.

The identification of Christ as word-event (the proclaimed Christ) with Jesus as past event (proclaiming the *eschaton* of God) meant that Jesus' time had conquered the present, and therefore, it became the time of God for everyone. The latter was experienced in the conversion of the Gentiles which revealed through the kerygma that Jesus' time conquered times that had before been considered as times outside of God's time. Thus Jesus appeared in the kerygma as the eschatological union of God's time and our time or, in other words, the eschatological union of time and eternity, the core of all Christologies.

Jesus Christ, as the eschatological union of time and eternity, was experienced in the kerygma of his followers yet detected as such in Jesus' own time, too. By proclaiming the kerygma that stated "The Kingdom of God is at hand," Jesus brought the future of God close to his time. He not only brought the *eschaton* of God and his time close, but he identified himself with the *eschaton* of God. God's *eschaton* and *prōton* were taken up as his *eschaton* and *prōton* by proclaiming that God is his father. Thus his time was united with the time of God. This was conveyed in his behaviour as well as in his words, making the relation of other times to his own time identical to God's time, or eternity. He proclaimed that whatever is done to him is done to the Father, and that believing in him is eternal salvation whereas rejecting him is eternal damnation. The identification of his time with God's time was the reason that any action, word or behaviour performed in time was expected to have a real impact on eternity. In other words, on account of him, time reached eternity. The intransigent determination to make himself the centre of salvation on the one hand, and his concern for the Father's time, expressed as the Father's will on the other, could be explained only as a manifestation of the eschatological union of time and eternity taking place in Jesus of Nazareth. Unless he is seen as an eschatological union of time and eternity, a sin committed against him cannot be a sin committed against God with consequences for all eternity.

The same Christology operated also in Jesus' identification of God's love with the neighbour's love. Once God's eternity is made available in his time to all times, one can reach eternity in any time. What one does not do to one of the least of one's brothers and sisters one does not do to him. And what is not done to him, is not done to the Father. In other words, sinning against one's time is sinning against God's time, sc., eternity.

The clarity and obscurity, the simplicity and complexity of the parables are further hints of understanding Jesus as the eschatological union of time and eternity. The recurring theme of all the parables is the arrival of the time of God, which requests an immediate response. Now this personal response cannot be delayed according to the doctrine of the parables, because it is a moment of once and for all. The kingdom of God announced by Jesus takes up the characteristics of the future. There will be no other future, since eternity has entered into the present time "now." Therefore there cannot be a "once more." This is the mistake of those who do not see in the words of

Jesus anything more than the present time of the parables and miss the presence of God's *eschaton* in them (cf. Mt 13, 10-15; Mk 4, 10-12; Lk 8, 9-10 with Is 6, 9-10; Mk 8, 18 with Jer 5, 21 and Ez 12, 2).

In the parables of Jesus one should not separate the way it was told (in time) from that what was said (talk about eternity). The union of time and eternity takes place in both, because the relation between eschatology and the parables is not an analogy of concepts. The kingdom of God is "like" (Mt 13, 31) which really means that it "became" like (Mt 13, 24). It "is" (Mk 4, 26) the language event in which the reality of the kingdom is expressed and made present to the audience. The kingdom as eternity is brought to an "at hand" in the immediacy of the parable. Therefore, the parable is not just a puzzle to be solved, but a summons to give up one's time and take up the time offered by Jesus. It is a call to all those whom God has chosen to follow Jesus. And as such the parable itself was a discovery of the kingdom for Jesus too. Since the kingdom was a grace of God, he discovered eternity by entering into his time as a gift of God.

As a result of this "parable-test," Jesus became the history of the kingdom of God and the history of God's future for himself and for his audience as well. Precisely the identity of the kingdom of God as proclaimed with the history of Jesus the proclaimer made possible that the crucified Jesus and the risen Christ could become the object of the proclamation of the kingdom of God. Thus the history of language event moved from Jesus' proclamation of the kingdom of God to the proclamation of Jesus' death and resurrection as the language of eternity developed through the language of time. The eschatological union of time and eternity is expressed in the language of death and resurrection in a more explicit way. Death and resurrection, the most obvious eschatological language, became the language of eternity in time where the *eschaton* of God became the *eschaton* of time.

Since the identification of the kingdom of God, the proclaimed, with the history of Jesus, the proclaimer, made possible that Jesus could become the object of the proclamation, the proclamation of Jesus was the constructive foundation of the Christ kerygma of the early Christians. In this process of eschatological language we discover the history of the identification of revelation with resurrection and history. By connecting revelation with resurrection and history, Jesus was unambiguously expressed as the eschatological union of time and eternity indicated by several formal expressions of the kerygma bringing time and eternity into union in Jesus Christ (Mk 13, 11;

Mt 24, 35; Lk 21, 33: "Heaven and earth will pass away, but my words will not pass away," Rev 1, 4.8.17; 4, 8; 11, 17; 16, 6; 21, 6; 22, 13—notice that the author applies to Jesus what was said of God by changing the usual "who will be" to "he, the one who was dead, who is to come"—Heb 13, 8).

If language can be described as both the home of time and the way-making for eternity, eternity can be experienced in hermeneutical language event, which opens by *speaking out* in time and ends up by *being spoken to* in time by one word which is unmistakably one and only one word. And this one word invokes the ground of the balance of all the sub-times which is beyond time. It is the negation of time in affirmation. Thus language makes eternity for us experiential.

According to the fourth gospel Jesus is the word who calls us listeners to open up to a dialogue which is a conversation with him in time. Yet in him and in his words eternity can be approached. By virtue of his words he brought his listeners into hermeneutical events which became both the home of time and the way-making for eternity. Moreover, he presented himself as that word. He revealed himself not only as both the home of time and way-making for eternity, but identified himself with eternity. As the word he calls everyone to himself as eternal life (Jn 3, 15-16,36; 4, 14; 6, 40-47; 10, 28-30; 12, 50).

Also according to the fourth gospel, one has to listen to his words, which make eternal life present here already (Jn 5, 24-25). He is the bread and drink for eternal life (Jn 6, 54-58). But there is one condition: one has to lose life now in order to have life which is eternal. The grain must die to yield eternal life (Jn 12, 25). The evangelist, indeed, presents Jesus as the one who is very much aware that eternal life is in his power (Jn 17, 21) because eternal life consists in knowing him and the Father who, again, cannot be known but through him (Jn 1, 3; Jn 1, 2; 1 Jn 2, 24-25; 5, 11-13,20; Jude 21). It is obvious in John's gospel that Jesus, the word who became flesh, presents himself as the eschatological union of time and eternity. He is both the realized and the future eschatology.

3.2. Eschatological Union of Time and Eternity: Christology as Soteriology

Christ as the eschatological union of time and eternity reveals sin as well as redemption from sin. Christ's redemption is to be understood as deliverance from suffering and death and from its tenant, sin, which, as it were, rented death as the final domain of its victory (Rom

6, 23; 5, 21). Suffering, death and sin are closely related in Pauline theology, yet sin is more transcendental than suffering and death. The power of sin is manifest in its capacity to change everything it affects. It changes suffering and death into a suffering and death *of* sin by preventing both from becoming an expression of eternal life, i.e., the actualization of generosity, integrity and authenticity by making them the final and irrevocable act of greed, incontinence and pride (Horvath, 1977, pp. 309-11).

But where the reality of sin is specially manifest is in its effect on time. Sin denies the "timely" nature of time and proposes it as a substitute for eternity. It closes time upon itself by an effort to eternalize it. Sin posits reversibility as the central reality of time. As a result, time is driven by sin into a sort of schizophrenic self-contradiction with an attempt to eliminate sub-times as other times (sin against generosity) by imposing one's time as the measure of all other times (sin against authenticity) and by extending one's own time to other times which are not one's own times (sin against integrity). Thus sin is an attempt against the multiplicity of times, which can take the form of killing, raping, hijacking, taking hostages, blackmailing, promoting social injustice, etc. Because of the close interactions among times, any form of eliminating other times as other strengthens the reality of sin (cf. original sin and the sin of the world).

Now Jesus Christ is the one who has broken down the dividing wall between eternity and time (cf. Eph 2, 14) that he might reconcile time(s) with God and bring hostility to an end in one body (Eph 2, 16). He established the authentic reality of time, which by its own sublation opens itself to eternal life. By virtue of Jesus' eschatological union with eternity his time is a unique time which can never be sublated by a future "present." Rather, Jesus' time is the one which reaches all the future times and becomes a true redeeming standard for every present as well as for every past and every coming, future time. If we can say that the humanity of Christ is the potential of any human being as well as the perfect humanity, since it reached and exhausted the openness of human nature (Rahner, 1964, pp. 110-15), we can also say that the time of Christ is the potential of any human time as well as the real perfect time since it reached and exhausted the irreversibility of any time and thus became the only time fully irreversible in the eternity of God. Thus Jesus' time as a unique time is representing (representation soteriology) and, in solidarity with all other times (solidarity soteriology), substitutes (substitution soteriology) our sinful time and invites us to enter into his time, where the presence of God is the presence of eternal life. In an atonement he reconciled time and eternity. He became time that we might be "made" eternal.

On account of the internal connection of all times Jesus has to be the redeemer of all the times of the whole of humanity and of the entire cosmos. Christ cannot redeem my time alone without taking up other times of which I am a "balance," cosmic time included, since we are all part of it. He is not only the redeemer of all times but he is the only redeemer, since without him there can be no sharing in eternity.

Jesus as the eschatological union of time and eternity also makes understandable one of the most intriguing features of the early Christian faith, sc., that Jesus of Nazareth is recognized as the one without whom there is no salvation for anyone. Indeed, there is no one beside him who can offer eternity, i.e., salvation from sin and its wage, death, because there is no eternity besides God, and his eternity is now in union with Christ's time. And this was revealed precisely in Christ's resurrection.

Moreover, the recognition of Christ as the eschatological union of time and eternity logically implies that Christ will remain and live forever and with him all those who are related to him, sc., who believe in him. Thus faith in eternal life is just a corollary to Christology. The faith that Jesus remains forever has a logical priority over the faith in eternal life of the faithful. The first Christians did not believe in Christ because they wanted to live forever. Rather they realized that they live forever because Jesus will remain forever, since he conquered the times of the created world and made them share in God's eternity. By virtue of Jesus' eschatological union of time and eternity there is no time, whether on earth, heaven or hell which is left untouched by him. This is the meaning of his resurrection here on earth, of his descent into hell, and of his ascension into heaven. Since time is united with eternity in Jesus, all human beings are predestined effectively and antecedently to any human merit to live forever. That Jesus is the only one who saves any human being and that there is no salvation without him means that he is the only one who saves any human person from being absorbed by other times. Jesus of Nazareth is the only one who makes eternal life possible for any created being. Thus the most specific and most exclusive gift Christianity can offer to the world is that of eternal life.

As a result of the Christ event the only alternative to the eternity of God is the "eternity of human being," sc., hell, which according to

Thomas Aquinas, is not eternity, but rather endless time (*S. theol.* 1, q. 10, a. 3 ad 2). Rightly understood, faith in the eternity of hell as well as faith in eternal happiness with God is a further corollary to Christology. Since Christ is the only one who established a relation between time and eternity no one can enter into eternity without him. Faith in Jesus Christ as the only Saviour is the positive, and faith in hell the negative formulation of the same doctrine. Thus the problem of eternal hell finds its solution in the mystery of Christ as the eschatological union of time and eternity. Christ has established a relation between time and eternity and thus the time of the world will never be the same. We all are predestined to live "forever." After Christ there is no choice between living and living forever. The only choice left is to be with Christ or without Christ. Thus hell has Christological meaning, which is expressed in the article of faith professing that there is no salvation without Christ.

This does not mean that one has to recognize Christ as such (cf. Mt 25, 44: "Lord when did we see you hungry"). It means that Christ is the turning point, who is identified with the times of all of us (cf. you neglected to do it to me, what you did not do to one of the least of mine, Mt 25, 40). Eternity can be touched in every time, and therefore we have to take the world and people we live with very seriously. They are not just temporal beings, something or someone passing away which are present today but gone tomorrow. Each time is imminent, since in it we encounter eternity. For some Christologies time, as a secular, not a theological concept, might be irrelevant, a passing futile condition of the "eternal nature" of human existence, which consequently does not demand redemption. Redemption affects only the "eternal," the "immutable" human nature, but not its time. It is only for an eschatological union of time and eternity, Christology as salvation, that time is of central importance (see the importance of "time," "hour," "day," the "time of harvest" for the New Testament, and especially John's distinction between Jesus' time and our time, Jn 7, 6, etc.).

3.3. Eschatological Union of Time and Eternity: Christology in Sacramental Theology

The purpose of the kerygma is actualized and expressed in the sacraments. The theology of the sacraments reflects, therefore, the theology of the kerygma. We have described the kerygma of the early Church as a challenge to the ordinary notion of time. It was the power of the proclamation that the future of God appeared in the present overpowered by the "past" of the historical Jesus. Now the history of sacramental theology is an ongoing effort to translate this mystery of the proclamation into the language of time.

The doctrine of the everlasting (indelible) character, the threefold historical orientation of the sacraments (commemorative sign of the past, demonstrative sign of the present and prognostic sign of the eschatological future, cf. *S. theol.* 3, 60, a. 3) and particularly the efficient causality of a future event on an event in the past (cf. the influence of the sacrament of penance on the disposition of the penitent, *S. theol.* 1.2, 113, 8; 7, ad 4) are the corollaries of an eschatological union of time and eternity Christology. Considering the sacraments christologically as the revelation of Jesus Christ saving us by his beatifying presence (Horvath, 1970, pp. 393-94), Jesus Christ's eschatological union of time and eternity is "sacramentally" present and operative in each sacrament. And since the Christological consideration of the sacraments is hermeneutically prior to the anthropological and ecclesiological considerations, the eschatological union of time and eternity interpretation of the sacraments is a leading problem-solving paradigm for issues pertinent to sacramental theology, both in its existence and development. This is precisely why sacramental theology must have a decisive role in discussing cosmic eschatology (cf. 4. 3. 3).

It is through the sacraments, the visible extensions of Christ's risen body in time, that people, Church, societies and cosmic world are "saved" and are on their way to entering into eternity. There is no grace without the sacraments because the sacraments are the eschatological realizations of Christ's redemption. Each grace is sacramental, since each grace is eschatological. Consequently both are true: there is no salvation without Christ and there is no salvation without the sacraments, i.e., without the Church, the primary sacrament of the risen Christ. Yet this does not mean that everyone has to receive the sacraments. Rather, it means that no grace is given to Christians or non-Christians which is not communicated through the sacraments (for the sacramental marriages of Christians as a means of communicating sacramental grace to the non-sacramental marriages of non-Christians, see Horvath, 1979, pp. 160-61). This is a logical necessity of the Christology considering Jesus Christ as eschatological union of time and eternity, who is taking up all times into the eternity of God. He is the Saviour for all, and there is no time which is not affected by his redemption. The concept of time operating in sacramental theology is an indication that the nature of time is already under the influence of the resurrection, and eternity is incarnated in time.

3.4. Eschatological Union of Time and Eternity in the Context of the Hypostatic Union Christology

We have seen that in biblical understanding God is eternity and creature is time. Now according to the faith of the Church, Christ is the hypostatic union of God and man. If we replace the term God by "eternity" and man by "time," we could say that Christ is the hypostatic union of eternity and time, an insight which opens new ways for understanding Christ.

The obvious meaning of Jesus as the hypostatic union of eternity and time is that one and the same person lives in eternity as well as in time. God, who is one and identical with eternity, assumes and becomes time like any created being. He becomes a balance in a multiplicity of sub-times characterized by an irreversibility measured through uniformly reversible changes. Therefore for faith time and eternity are not mutually incompatible realities as human reason would conclude. Time is not eternity and eternity is not time, yet Christ is both: time and eternity. Consequently neither eternity nor time should be considered without the other, because in Christ time became the revelation of eternity and eternity is revealed as the origin and the end of time. Christ through the mystery of the Incarnation has established a relation between time and eternity in the sense that God's eternity can be revealed in the time of the world. Or, using another paradigm, we can say that the humanity of Christ or the time of Christ is God's point of observation of other times whence all other times are measured. Christ's time reveals eternity as his humanity does his divinity. His time is the expression of God's eternity.

In stating that Christ is the hypostatic union of time and eternity we notice at once the difference between the two Christologies, sc., Christ as the hypostatic union of man and God, and Christ as the eschatological union of time and eternity. Since we have identified eternity with God and time with creatures we just cannot say that there is a reality we call a person who can be separated from both, sc., eternity and time, and as such could exist both in time as well as in eternity. Time cannot be separated from the human person and eternity from God as nature can be separated from personhood. Otherwise God would not be God, but an idea. And human beings would not be real beings but a set of abstractions. As a consequence, both God and man would cease to be what they are. Obviously we can create an abstract notion of time and eternity, but such a notion can only exist abstractly and does not correspond to the reality of time as we have found it in our analysis.

Time is not something in which we live. Time is what we are. If time could be removed from us we would not be what we are and, more importantly, we would not be who we are. We can say the same for God. God is not just someone who lives forever. He is eternity, which is not just an adjective applied to God. We cannot say that time lives in eternity and eternity lives in time, like a person who as an abstract concept can be conceived as a created person living in time and as an uncreated person living in eternity. If this reasoning is correct the Christology of eschatological union of time and eternity opens new depth for the Christology of the hypostatic union.

Hypostatic union means personal incommunicability (see John of Damascus, *De fide orthodoxa*, 1, 8; PG 95, 828), and *eschaton* means "last." Now in the New Testament writings *eschaton* can refer to anything which is last in a line, like penny, labourer, disciple, fraud, day of feast, people, enemy, trumpet, plague, etc. (cf. Mk 9, 35; 10, 31; 12, 6,22; Mt 5, 26; 12, 14,16; 19, 30; 20, 9; 27, 69; Lk 12, 59; 13, 30; 14, 9,10; Acts 1, 8; 13, 47; 1 Cor 4, 9; 15, 8,26,45,52; Jn 7, 37; 8, 9; Rev 2, 19; 15, 1; 21, 9). It can refer also to a new state different from the previous one (Mt 12, 45; Lk 11, 26; 2 Pet 2, 20). It means also, especially in Johannine literature, the last day, the day of resurrection (Jn 6, 39,40,44,54; 11, 24), the day of judgment (Jn 12, 48; Jas 5, 3), the day of pouring out of the Holy Spirit (Acts 2, 17). In the epistle literature it means the day of stress (2 Tim 3, 1), the day of Jesus appearing in the flesh (Heb 1, 2; 1 Pet 1, 20), the end of times, the day of scoffing about Jesus' coming (2 Pet 3, 3; Jude 18), the last hour when the Antichrist appears (1 Jn 2, 18) and the last time of revelation of salvation (1 Pet 1, 5). Finally, in the book of Revelation, Jesus Christ himself is called the *eschatos*, the first and the last (Rev. 1, 17; 2, 8; 22, 13).

Eschaton can mean, therefore, something which is the last in the same continuous succession and something which breaks with the preceding and opens a new beginning. The New Testament use of the term *eschaton* supports both eschatological schools: one which believes that eschatology should be regarded as something from outside the human and sacred history, since the last day brings a complete break (McKenzie, 1957; Wellhausen, 1961; Mowinckel, 1956) as well as the one which sees eschatology as simple conclusion of the history, since *eschaton* is already part of present history (Gressmann, 1905; Lindblom, 1963).

Indeed, if we relate *eschaton* to Jesus, he is both: the last in the line of all times and the one who is also outside of the present order of time. As the eschatological union of time and eternity he is the end of the present world as well as the new beginning of the world's transition to eternity. The fulfillment of Jesus' eternity in time is the meaning of all creation, the end of which is the realization of Jesus' eschatological union of time and eternity. As an *eschaton* he is the *prōton* of all times (creation). Time reached its "end" at the moment of the Incarnation, when eternity entered into time but it did not take up Jesus' time completely until Jesus died. His death, as the end of time, affected his time and its union with eternity.

In the eschatological union of time and eternity Christology, both the Incarnation and the death have an important role. Before death his time was just an irreversible expression of his eternity, but after his death his time became an inalienable expression of God's eternity. In his resurrection from the dead, the eschatology initiated at the moment of the Incarnation has been completed. It was precisely in death that Jesus' time entered into eternity and as the realized *eschaton* set all history and the cosmic world in motion in order to redeem the whole by assuming it into the eternity of God and to let it share in the life of the sons and daughters of God (Rom 8, 1-25). The history of the world before Jesus was the "process" of realization of the eschatological union of time and eternity, but after his resurrection the process entered into Jesus' realized eschatology.

The change which took place in Christ as a result of his death can be further illustrated by using the hypostatic union's removing-replacing paradigm for expressing Christ's mystery in time-language.

It is known that conciliar theology used the removing-replacing paradigm to solve the problem of unity between "natural" and "supernatural," between divine and human. For example, in the case of the mystery of the Eucharist the substance of the bread and wine was removed and replaced by that of the body and blood of Christ. Similarly, in the case of the hypostatic union the reality of the human person was removed from the human nature of Christ and replaced by the reality of the second divine person, the Son (Horvath, 1971, pp. 40-49). If we use this problem-solving method for the mystery of Christ as the eschatological union of time and eternity before his death and after his death, we can ask if there is anything in Christ's time which can be removed and replaced by his eternity following the model of the hypostatic union. A pertinent instance can be found in the theological "I" of Jesus Christ, or expressed in time-language, in the "theological time" of Jesus Christ. To clarify this we propose the following consideration.

Unlike God, any human being is just time named variably as Self, as Ego, as Body and/or Soul or person. The *Self* is understood in psychology as the source and objective of motivation, the organizational centre of behaviour and experiences, the totality of experiential content and behaviour patterns (Pawlik, 1972, pp. 313-19). The *Ego* as the psychic centre goes deeper than the Self, since the Ego is known as the centre of the primitive and unorganized desires, which as structure is not identical with experiences and the experience of the Self (Toman, 1972, p. 316).

Human being as *Body* can enter into the domain of other disciplines like physics, biology, etc. Body can be considered as a unified field of energy which, by balancing a multiplicity of biological times, creates its own time, its own individual biological time. The consideration of body as a field of energy implies the spatialization of time which functions as a secondary element in time. It provides the reversible changes which serve as measurement of the irreversibility of biological time. Time and space are inseparable, since space is the measurement of time, though time is more fundamental than space. What makes body "body" is the unity or rather balance in a multiplicity of biological times.

Biological time is conceived as a synchronization of a number of cellular clocks regulated probably by some rhythmic centre (master clock) not independent of the *cosmic* time which follows a linear direction commended by a "run-down" flowing from a maximum level of energy to a maximum level of entropy according to the laws of thermodynamics.

The *Soul* can be considered as that ability of the Self, Ego or Body which, by balancing the multiplicity of biological times, creates cultural, philosophical and theological times. *Cultural* time is a system of controlling or coping with the contingencies of time, whereas *philosophical* time is a system for forming concepts and a language of time and eternity. Finally, *theological* time in our view is the solution to the problem of time and eternity.

In the light of these considerations a *human person* can be understood as the one, who by balancing biological, cultural, philosophical and theological times, creates his/her own time, demarcating it from times which are not his/hers by distinguishing experiences which are gone (past) from the ones in process of taking place (future) and thus building up "I" as the last stronghold of the self-defence mechanism against the alienating force of time.

If these considerations are acceptable we can say that a human being, or person, is an Ego and a Self as much as he/she creates his/her biological, psychological and cultural times. He/she is or has a soul as much as he/she creates his/her philosophical and theological times. It is on the level of philosophical and theological times that the so-called philosophical and theological "I" as a self-defence mechanism against the alienating force of other times builds up. The philosophical "I" is the human person who realizes the challenges of time. The theological "I" differs from the philosophical "I" in that the theological "I" is seeking a defence against the alienating force of time in the mystery of eternity and not in the paradox of time.

What all these times have in common is that they are balancing a multiplicity of sub-times in order to realize and express a unique irreversibility through uniformly reversible changes. Before death, therefore, time has space as its co-ordinate, providing reversibility as measurement for irreversibility. Death, as the end of time, affects all the different forms of time, the biological, psychological, cultural, philosophical and the theological time as well. Death is a real end, therefore the biological ego, the psychological and cultural self, as well as the philosophical and theological "I" die. The theological "I" dies inasmuch as eternity, in which a defence against time was sought remains out of the reach of time. Eternity cannot enter time to save time, since eternity is the end of time by its "nature." The only bridging is the eschatological union of time and eternity in Jesus Christ.

The risen life after death brings about a difference. By virtue of Christ's redemption the irreversibility of one's time is measured by Christ's time and made inalienable. The theological "I" finds the solution of the problem of time and eternity in Christ's realized eschatology, that is, in eternity: the theological "I" understands itself after death not through the reversible changes but in Christ's eternity as its foundation. And this is resurrection.

If we try to apply this schema to Christ before and after his death, we find an important difference between him and other human persons. The difference can be grasped by asking whether, following the removing-replacing problem-solving paradigm used in the theology of the hypostatic union, any of the above-mentioned times are missing in Jesus Christ so that it has to be replaced by the eternity of the second divine person.

As a real human being Christ had a Self, an Ego, a human body with a human soul and consequently a human time which, by balancing the multiplicity of biological, cultural and philosophical times, was demarcated from any other human times which were not his as such. In this sense one can think of Jesus Christ as a real human person. He had a biological and psychological Ego, a cultural Self and a philosophical "I" (i.e., forming concepts and a language of time and eternity). Yet all these "times" were balanced as well as measured by a theological time which was not his creation; rather, he was the creation of that theological time. The problem of time and eternity appeared to him not from the side of time but from the side of eternity. It was the problem of eternity rather than the problem of time which made up Jesus' theological "I." This is why the evangelists describe him as the one who is not only more concerned with eternity than anyone else, but also as the one who has a particular conviction of being unique, different from any other human persons by being freed from the dialectic of past, present and future. His theological "I" was not like our theological "I": Christ's theological "I" was not only a solution to his problem of time and eternity but the foundation of the reality of his time and of the reality of his eschatological union of time and eternity.

Yet before his resurrection this theological "I" was so immersed in other times that the spatial correlates of the other times, sc., the uniformly reversible changes, appeared as its measurement. As a result, the theological "I" before resurrection could not appear to Jesus as the foundation of the reality of all times. But at the moment of death space was no longer a co-ordinate of his time, and eternity was not measured, except by eternity itself, and Christ's time became not only irreversible and inalienable but also the revelation of God's eternity as well as the foundation and the "end" of all times which are to enter in it as the eternity of God. This eschatological Christology was forcefully expressed in the post-paschal kerygma: the Logos became flesh, eternity became time. The Word, the image of the invisible God (Col 1, 15, 16-20), the integrity of God, the Son of the Father was unambiguously manifested as the one who together with the Father sends and gives the Holy Spirit to all.

3.5. Eschatological Union of Time and Eternity: Christology in the Context of the Trinitarian Mystery

The post-paschal time is presented in the New Testament as the age of the Holy Spirit, who is the authenticator of times by means of the kerygma of Jesus Christ. The revelation of the Holy Spirit made the revelation of the Triune God complete. Since we have identified eternity with God, the mystery of eternity cannot but be the mystery of the Trinitarian life of God. Thus if there is any revelation of eternity, it must be found in the revelation of the Triune God. The life of the Triune God holds all that we can know now about what eternal life, what eternity is. And the revelation of the Triune God was given by no one else than by Christ, the eschatological union of time and eternity. Christ is the answer to Qoheleth's question "who can bring one to see what will be after him/her" (Eccl 3, 22).

An analysis of the mystery of the revelation of the Triune God will shed light on both the mystery of Christ, the eschatological union of time and eternity, and on the mystery of eternity. The trinitarian life of God the Father, the Son and the Holy Spirit can be expressed by non-spatial terms as the inalienable generosity of God (i.e., the Father who gives life), as the inalienable integrity of God (i.e., the Son as the perfect otherness of the Father), and as the inalienable authenticity of God (i.e., the Holy Spirit as guarantee and revelation of the Son as real God by being the expression of the Father). Thus God the Father's eternity means that God's generosity is measured by God's inalienable integrity (the Son) and that both God's integrity and generosity are measured by God's inalienable authenticity (Holy Spirit), which means that none of the three can be sublated by any of the other two. Now if we relate generosity, integrity and authenticity to the triad of faith, charity and hope, our entering into Jesus' "time" means taking up Christ's integrity in faith with the generosity of the Father in charity and the authenticity of the Holy Spirit in hope. In other words, eternity is the fulfillment of the authenticity, generosity and integrity of human existence in the faith, charity and hope of Christian existence by overcoming the challenges of incontinence, greediness and pride, the sins against faith, charity and hope, as well as against the integrity, generosity and authenticity of human existence.

Incontinence is the decay ("run-down") of one's authenticity, i.e., losing one's own time by being absorbed by other times. Greediness is the decline of one's generosity, i.e., the elimination of others' time as other time. And finally pride is the deterioration of integrity, i.e., the negation of the proper interdependence among human beings as "others," of the interdependence of each human time with the other human times.

If authenticity means being conformed to the original, that is, being not a fake or substitute, but guaranteeing oneself as oneself, incontinence means its opposite. It means not containing, not holding oneself together in oneself, but extending oneself to something which is not him/herself. One alienates, dissipates oneself and becomes something else by losing oneself. It is the inability to hold together the different levels of sub-times. Similarly, if generosity is readiness to give in an unrestricted way with the desire of reaffirming the other as other, greediness is its opposite. It is an unrestricted craving for what belongs to another with the desire of eliminating the other as other. It is the desire of simplifying the different levels of sub-times.

Finally, if integrity means being complete, having all the qualities, excellences, etc., that are requisite to its kind without defect or lack, it implies unity and interdependence of the members and their completeness. In a word, it affirms the totality in its totality. And pride as its opposite is a conceit of high opinion of oneself with the contempt and disdain of others, an arrogance rooted in a repressed feeling of incompleteness. It is imposing one's time as a measure for all other times.

If eternity as salvation is entering into Trinitarian life by achieving one's authenticity, generosity and integrity in faith (sharing Christ's integrity), charity (sharing in the Father's generosity) and hope (sharing in the Holy Spirit's authenticity), then eternity as damnation is the rejection of the Trinitarian life by seeking one's authenticity, generosity and integrity in pride, greed and incontinence. It is upholding time against eternity, the possibility of which is due not to any immortality of the soul but uniquely to Christ's eschatological union of time and eternity, which, by virtue of his universal redemption, has opened the eternity of God to all times without any exception.

4 CHRISTIAN ESCHATOLOGY: SYSTEMATIC PRESENTATION

4.1. Time and Eternity

Christ as the eschatological union of time and eternity is the paradigm which solves the problem and determines the relation between time and eternity in Christian eschatology. From it, as from a fundamental axiom, we can deduce a few basic assertions which are the elements of any Christology and Christian eschatology as well. We propose 13 such basic eschatological statements, which are the foundations of the fourth part of our research.

4.1.1. By Virtue of Christ's Eschatological Union of Time and Eternity, Eternity is the Meaning of Time and Time is the Expression of Eternity (I)

Our first eschatological principle sums up the second and third part of our research. It serves as a guiding hermeneutical principle for the following traditional topics of Christian eschatology: apocalypse, end (*telos*), eschatology, hermeneutics of eschatological statements, Future Studies, imminence of end, death, time and eternity. Terms like future and end, last things and eschatology, time and eternity, are understood often as synonyms within Christian eschatology. Yet each has a definitive meaning in the ordinary use of language which both clarifies and conceals its Christological meaning in Christian eschatology. For example, we all have a future at least as long as we live. We all are interested in knowing it and spend considerable effort to influence it or at least get ready for it. The effort to know our future prompted a human discipline called Future Studies, which is not completely foreign to Christian eschatology. However, Christian eschatology must be distinguished from Future Studies.

Christian eschatology is essentially a Christology. This does not mean some sort of spiritual (angelic) existence achieved by a liberation from the body. Nor does it mean immortality as a natural condition of the human soul, nor even the idea of a universal resurrection from the dead as the axiomatic interpreting principle in the light of which we understand the meaning of Christian future, end, imminence of end, eschatology, last things. Rather, it means that, by a hermeneutical twisting, Jesus Christ, the conqueror of death and eternal life, determines and defines future, end, eschatology and the like.

4.1.1.1. Future Studies, Futurology

Future Studies is one of the more recent branches of scientific investigation. Edward Cornish, together with the members and staff of the World Future Society, published a handbook for Future Studies in 1977 with the title *The Study of the Future: An Introduction to the Art and Science of Understanding and Shaping Tomorrow's World* (1978). Other pioneer books worthy of mention are: H. Kahn and B. Bruce-Briggs, *Things—to Come* (1972); A. Linstone and W.H. Clive Simmonds, *Future Research: New Directions* (1977); T. Peters, *Futures-Human and Divine* (1978); D. Loye, *The Knowable Future: A Psychology of Forecasting and Prophecy* (1978); (cf. *Zeitschrift für Zukunftsforschung*).

The purpose of Future Studies is (1) to explore systematically the possible future for national and international communities, (2) to ascertain how much of the possible futures is desirable and why, and (3) to seek means by which the probabilities of their occurrences can be enhanced (Cornish, 1966). Workshops of this kind are named think-tanks.

In this age of great discoveries, mass production and mass communication, we are aware that we do not just move to a predetermined future world. Instead we consider ourselves as active participants in the creation of the future world. The ones who are planning, projecting, forecasting and providing the future are the futurors, and the beneficiaries are the futurees. Using this language Christ could be considered as the futuror and believers as futurees (Ferkiss, 1974, pp. 258-63; Strawson, 1970; Schwartz, 1971, pp. 347-64).

There are three basic principles operating in Future Studies. The first is the assumption of the unity and interconnectedness of reality, which means that it is impossible to comprehend any single entity without considering its place in the whole. Unlike the traditional view, the new holistic thinking sees humans as part of the unity of the universe. The world of the future is going to be created out of the present one. The second basic principle is that time is of central importance, and the third is that ideas are the tools of the future. Since the future does not exist it must be invented. "Ideas as futuribles are the tools of preparing the world to come" (Cornish, 1978, p. 97).

To invent the future two methods are employed: the fragmentary and the holistic methods. The fragmentary method breaks things into their smallest parts and then reassembles them in a logical manner. It is expected that collecting a great amount of data and processing them will give a key to the future. The holistic method begins with an idea of the future and works backwards to establish a feasible relation to the present.

Both methods rely on two principles: the principle of continuity and the principle of analogy. The principle of continuity suggests that the future will be like the present (e.g., our globe, with its oceans, mountains, etc., will be here even a few hundred years from now). The principle of analogy assumes that certain patterns of events are recurring. So, for example, in discoveries, concepts and theories are conditioned by sensory data as well as by projecting the possibilities. Both methods use models, simulations and games. The assumption is that we can learn something about anything by studying something similar yet easier to deal with.

The research is then carried out by operation (research techniques and information gathered from other sciences and applied to a different set of problems) or by system analysis (i.e., selecting among alternatives by comparing alternatives). A system is an abstraction from identifiable replicate patterns of experience. It is made up of a group of interacting entities and resources with a definitive objective. The state of a system is everything we can possibly know about a system at a particular time (e.g., the state of an atom, state of health, state of mind, state of economy, state of the world).

"There are again two fundamental assumptions concerning the state of a system: (1) a state of a system can be specified by a limited number of observables; other observables can be determined if these key observables are known, (2) the state of a system changes with time in a predictable manner, and the dynamical principles by means of which the time evolution may be predicted are knowable" (Gilbert, 1985). As a concrete task for the state of the environment Thomas L. Gilbert listed the greenhouse effect, the acid rain problem, and (for the state of the world) the possibility of a nuclear explosion, and effective measures to prevent it.

4.1.1.2. Apocalypse

Future Studies admit a logical as well as a certain causal connection between future and present but reject fatalism, which is the fundamental assumption of one of its earlier ancestors, the apocalypse. Apocalypse as a disclosure of the future favoured fatalism and divine libertarianism, which claims that what the future will be owes nothing to what our activities at the present are. The truth value of these statements depends on God's will. There is a discontinuity between the future and the present and asymmetry between statements about the past and statements about the future. Time leads to its own end, which is not emerging from time. The nothingness of time will be unveiled at the end, and from that comes the name "apocalypse."

Future Studies, unlike apocalypse, see a logical connection between what will be and what the present is, though admitting that there is uncertainty and that the future will be what it will be not solely because of what at present is. In other words, the future is logically but not causally determined. It will not be what it is going to be because of what happened before it. Now apocalypse defends divine libertarianism for present-time statements and absolute certitude for future statements, which are free extrapolations from the future in the present.

The origin and growth of the apocalyptic literature in Jesus' time were due to the history of Israel's conflict with other nations. Israel, being subjected to foreign powers with no realistic hope of attaining political independence, expected not from its own effort but from God's intervention that God's kingdom would be established in Israel by destroying Israel's enemy (Hanson, 1975). It is from this tradition that some New Testament passages present Christ as coming down with heavenly agents, like the angels and the stars, and descending upon the earth to judge the world in the midst of a cosmic cataclysm.

The Future Studies of our time and the apocalyptic literature of the past are two ways of mastering the future according to their two different contexts: one is of a successful and powerful group and the other is of the oppressed and powerless mass. The former tries to influence its future by its own skill, whereas the latter does so by winning a lottery, by dreaming of a sudden cosmic cataclysm destroying the oppressing power or preparing bloody revolution.

4.1.1.3. End

In influencing the future the range of time is of critical importance. The immediate (up to one year from now), the near term (1-5), the middle range future (5-20 years) and long range (20-50 years) or far future (50 or more years) cannot be shaped by human planning in the same degree. The far future can be much less affected by the power of the action performed now and much less the end of the future. To dominate the future means to dominate the end of the future, otherwise the mastering is not effective. This is why the question of the end has fascinated humans as much as the question of the future. Obviously the two are connected.

End means the terminal point of any material thing that has a length. The end of the material world is the cosmological end beyond which no further extension can be conceived, like the one described by Jastrow (1977, pp. 52-57). It is the end of our cosmic world. But the end of our cosmic world is different from the end of biological beings, which is called *telos*. *Telos* is the limit where the potentialities that one biological being has are actualized. Thus the end of one biological being can be the beginning of another biological being in a biological evolution, for example. Thus Samuel Alexander would talk about empirical evolution (Gotesky, 1978), whereas Bergson's favourite term is "creative evolution" (Bergson, 1914). Whitehead speaks mostly of emerging evolution (Whitehead, 1969), and Dyson of the expansion of human life in the universe (Dyson, 1988, p. 297).

For the end of a personal being we use words like destiny, progress, history, death or eschatology. Destiny is that to which one is ordered. History is the meaning of destiny, and progress can be the meaning of history. If a God-given meaning is added to history, the end of history is an eschatological end, which later was called "last thing(s)."

4.1.1.4. Eschatology

Eschatology is a Western term and refers originally to Judeo-Christian beliefs about the end of history and of the world in its present state. But the term has been extended by historians of religions and includes similar topics in the religions of pre-literate people, ancient Mediterranean and Near Eastern culture and Eastern civilizations as well (Moltmann, 1980., p. 958.; see also MacCulloch, 1920, pp. 373-76; Abel, 1969). Eschatologies are divided by experts into two general classes, sc., mythical and historical eschatologies. Mythical eschatologies emphasize the reproduction of the origin of the world at the end of the present one. End time is a return to the innocence of the beginning. Historical events are interpreted as a representation of eternal return. In a word, mythical eschatology is the myth of the eternal return (Gunkel, 1885; Eliade, 1954).

Historical eschatologies are based on historically datable events considered as fundamental for the progress of the world. They are not repeatable, just remembered. History is not abolished. It inaugurates the end, which is the fulfillment of the past. Redemption is redemption from cycles having no beginning. The redemptive heroes are impersonal representations of the ultimately universal. Buddhism and Hinduism do not have a historical eschatology (Moltmann, Werblowsky, 1991, pp. 401-404). The idea of purification from guilt and the idea of the Reincarnation of souls are mostly found together. Yet it is not easy to establish or exclude, for example, the connections between the non-cyclic eschatology of the Micmac Indians or the belief in the resurrection of the bones in the Andaman Islands and of Semang pygmies in Malacca and the Christian linear eschatology with the resurrection of the body (Lunear, 1979, pp. 15-21; Mbiti, 1971). Recent descriptions of eschatologies are not concerned with causal influences anymore.

Eschatology in the Christian tradition is not identical with apocalypse, since eschatology is an extrapolation from the present into the future, rather than the extrapolation from the future into the present, which is apocalypse (Rahner, 1966, p. 337).

Christian eschatology is not futurology. It is a Christ-event already determined and presently operating in history, and human history and progress can never bring it about. It is offered in the cross-resurrection of Jesus Christ, as gift to everyone (Stanley, Brown, 1968, pp. 777-82; Mckenzie, 1968, pp. 464-67).

4.1.1.5. Imminence of the End

Since Christian eschatology is a God-given event and is free of human planning, no one can know the day, or the hour, when God will bring it about. It is God's secret (Mk 13, 3; Acts 1, 7; Pet 3, 8, 10; 1 Thes 5, 1). Being so, it is always imminent. Whenever it comes, it will come shortly: it is at hand any time (1 Thes 4, 17; Phil 4, 5; Lk 9, 27; Mk 9, 1; Mt 10, 23; 1 Jn 2, 18; 1 Pet 4, 7; Jas 5, 8). The imminence of eschatology is further enhanced by the fact that it has happened already in the Christ event.

4.1.1.6. Hermeneutics of Eschatological Statements

There is a difference between statements about the past and between statements about the future. The statements about the past are disjunctively true or false and singular. The statements about the future are neither true nor false and are not singular. Now the statements about the Christ-event are to be taken as either true or false and refer to an event which is singular. Thus the statements of Christian eschatology have simultaneously the characteristics of past and future statements. They carry the expectation of a future with a definitive recognition of a past event. Thus eschatology implies both faith and hope because Christ has come and Christ is the one who will come again. This was the reason that, by introducing a new term, sc., *elpis*, Paul replaced the Old Testament dyad of faith and charity by the New Testament triad of faith, charity and hope. Hope for Paul meant not so much an idle expectation, but a trust, a cheerful alacrity, a power working for an arduous goal on account of the complete assurance that God would not fail to help him in his enterprise of working with Christ (Horvath, 1977, pp. 286-89).

Thus it seems that the Pauline eschatology does not reject the method used by Future Studies. Yet the goals at which they are aiming are so different that the Pauline eschatology used rather apocalyptic terminology to express the end for which the faithful are working, with an effort similar to the one recommended in Future Studies. Consequently, if one would like to express correctly the Pauline eschatology one needs to make two statements: I expect the coming of the Lord Jesus Christ by waiting and I expect the coming of the Lord Jesus Christ by trusting absolutely in God that his help will never fail to let me bring it about as a God-given end. Since faith, charity and hope characterize Christian existence, Christian eschatology is to be described not only as "the last things" but as the last things not independent of human effort.

Since human existence can be described as a process moving from inauthenticity (hopelessness) to authenticity (hope) in order to be generous (love) in integrity (faith), Christian existence, as an existence of faith, charity and hope, is the real ground for the legitimacy of eschatological statements. Indeed, "there can be no eschatological assertions which cannot be reduced to the assertions concerned with Christian existence" (Rahner, 1966b, p. 337) of faith, charity and hope, the formal principles of eschatology. Christian eschatology is, therefore, not an evolution already fixed. It is not even a history dependent on human freedom but a history of salvation promised by God which is to be achieved in Christian existence. Christian existence is an existence which, first being received in faith asserting the gratuity of the God-given Christ-event, moves ahead to reveal God's love in charity by relying always on the help of God, who will never fail. We know the *eschaton* in faith, charity and hope which communicate to us God-given promises in Christ, on whom we rely to make decisions within the context of salvation history.

Since Christian existence as an existence of faith, charity and hope is the ground for the legitimacy of Christian eschatological statements, these statements are calling for a structural change in our human existence, not only in terms of warning, threatening, promising, but also in terms of factual information about the events and places which break the limits of our knowledge. This factual information is about Christ, in whom time and eternity are united. Christology is the new knowledge stated in and by eschatological affirmation. Statements of Christology are transformed into statements of eschatology and thus make up the state of our system specified by a limited number of observables provided by faith, charity and hope experienced in Christian existence.

Our second basic eschatological principle is such a Christological statement. It is the soteriological formulation of Christ as the eschatological union of time and eternity for the meaning of death in Christian eschatology.

4.1.2. Jesus Christ is the Conqueror of Death and of Eternal Life (II)

Through his death on the cross Jesus Christ has conquered the death of every human being. This victory had been revealed in his resurrection when the time of the historical Jesus had been sublated by eternity, the time of Jesus Christ, the incarnate God. As a result, through death every human being enters into Christ's death. In death one's time definitively comes to an end and each human being enters into Christ's time. Eternity is exclusively Christ's way of existence as God, whereas time is exclusively a creature's way of existence. Without Christ, the incarnate God, there is no eternity for a created being.

In the Christian theological search for what future, what end, what eschatology, what the basic principles of hermeneutics of eschatological assertions and the ground of their legitimacy are, Christ as the conqueror of death and of eternal life is the highlight which distinguishes

Christian eschatology from any other eschatology and at the same time makes it transform all other eschatologies. Jesus Christ in person is the eschatology for everyone not by abolishing but by conquering death and making eternal life possible for every human being. Christ conquered death without denying its reality. People will die with him and after him. Yet the victory of death becomes now its own defeat. Death which was, and is an end, becomes precisely the revelation of eternal life as a gift of God. Because of Christ, eternal life, the exclusive way of existence of God which is beyond the reach of any creaturely existence, now falls as "a prey" to anyone. The future is not going to be what our actions will bring about, and yet we know what that end will be. It is not determined by our past but by the past of Jesus Christ.

We can therefore admit logical determinism. The future is going to be what it is already in one person. But there is no fatalism, no logical necessity and no logical libertarianism. The end is here without the end of the end, because Jesus is not only the end, but also the "end" expected in trust and actively participating in the fulfillment of his promise. And the fulfillment of promise is not a promise of endless life but the promise of God's life, God's eternity in regard to which everyone is powerless except Jesus Christ, the conqueror of death and bestower of eternal life.

The way death and eternal life have been conquered by Christ is clarified by the following basic assertion.

4.1.2.1. *Death is a Real End of Time as well as a Real Entry into Eternity. At the Moment of Death, the Self, the Ego, the Body, the Soul, the Philosophical and the Theological "I," in One Word "I" as a Person Comes to an End by Being Sublated by Christ's Time, sc., Eternity (III)*

Our third basic eschatological assertion implies the following traditional topics of eschatology: death, after-life, immortality, self, Ego, body, soul, the theological "I," Christ's descent into hell. To scrutinize the mystery of death we will deal with the rationale of death versus the non-rationale of living forever, distinguishing between dying and death, between clinical and biological death, legal and psychological death. Then we shall interpret the scriptural notion of death, the teachings of the Church about death, note the understanding of death by a few theologians, and finally analyze death as a real end and a real entry into eternity.

4.1.2.1.1. The Rationale of Death Vs. the Non-rationale of Living Forever

In spite of its sad and terrifying reality, death appears as a rather suitable problem-solving device for facilitating constant progress, bringing peace, providing democracy, balancing monopolism and overpopulation, revealing evil and above all making people unselfish without choice. Humans, as they grow older, become dedicated to one ideal, to one purpose, to a one-sided way of life which they would not easily give up for any new risky un-tested alternative. Death removes old conservative elements and lets ideas die with people. Once the old fighting guard is gone, the young ones, not having experienced past injuries and quarrels, ignore the past and are willing to live in peace until new wars are nourished by new injustices and new quarrels.

Furthermore death makes every human being equal, without exception. No one can buy off death. Victim and killer will sooner or later meet the same fate: "You kill me now, but you will come after me, whether you wish to or not" is any victim's verdict upon his/her murderer. Good and bad, poor and rich, American and Russian, Jew and Moslem, black and white, all end up in death. In addition, death balances the monopolism of private wealth. With death one's accumulated wealth will pass on to others. Death balances overpopulation as well. What would we do if people remained with us from early history? How could we relate to them, since we have difficulty relating ourselves to people living today? Thanks to death, earlier generations disappear from the surface of the earth, leaving room for others.

Death stills anger, lowers or cancels demands and makes concessions. Death marks the end of pursuit and of persecution. It reveals evil as well as the impracticability of many dreams. It changes feelings. Once one dies, he/she is not a threat any more, and the living are free to feel sorry and pay "respect" to him/her.

Unlike death, living forever, instead of solving old problems, creates new ones. Young people who have not lived long enough evidently want to live. But once they have lived long enough they feel, like Qoheleth, that there is no taste for anything anymore. There is nothing new in life anymore and boredom is the constant companion (cf. Eccl 1, 7-11; etc.). Immortality may be a dream of young people. But death is a welcome guest to those who cannot see any future for themselves.

As a test case, suppose, for example, that after a long life there is a choice for someone to repeat the whole odyssey of his/her life without making it the least bit different from the one already lived, or to die. How would the majority of people choose? It seems that most people would rather die than go through the same life again. Would they not?

But the real problem arises if we imagine eternal life as something rational in the light of our present knowledge. Suppose that eternal life is like the present one. Analyzing the present life we can discover that it is simply not structured for eternal life, as Qoheleth noticed long ago. But if it is different, can a different life satisfy us? If there are no activities familiar to us, like buying, building, repairing, courting, making money, etc., there will be nothing to do. There everything is expected to be done already. There will be no one to help, since no one will need our help; nothing to learn, since we are expected to know everything which can be known. No one needs to love, or to be loved, since love supposes communication, but there will be nothing to communicate, because everyone has everything. People would be like the Aristotelian God, knowing no love.

But this is not all. Eternal life raises another kind of problem which challenges our present notion of a person. How can we conceive someone as a human person who has nothing to plan, nothing to decide and, therefore, no future? A being without a future is not a person at least the way we know a person now. Such a being would be just a retrieval system with perfect memory of the past, which would create new problems. If we keep our past, in eternal life there would be, for example, too many Chinese, since now about one-third of the population of the earth are Chinese. What is the value of being English, or Chinese in heaven or in hell? But if we do not keep our past, how can we talk about personal identity and be sure, for example, that I am the same person in heaven as the one I was on earth?

As if this were not enough, there is a further difficulty with faith in eternal life. We believe that both eternal life and eternal damnation are determined by human actions performed in time. But how can a human being make a decision which has an eternal dimension and thus becomes irrevocable? How can we understand that a creature living in time has such a great power for establishing his/her destiny forever, when the characteristic of human freedom is that it is changing, is revocable and reversible? This is all the more so if we believe that there is original sin, which debilitates human freedom. Even the soul, considered as being separated from the body, still remains a creature. How then can a created soul make an irrevocable and irreversible act to establish his/her destiny forever? Is this not against the temporal nature of everything that exists besides God?

And how about the age-old question of the unborn children who lost the chance of becoming persons, with memories and individual pasts? How can their death determine their lot forever without them ever being given another chance? Moreover, is it not unfair that the number of those "who will have eternal existence" is decided so often by the "impulse of the flesh," or by a calculating human being using birth-control?

In brief, we can say that whereas death is a problem-solving event, eternal life is a problem-raising event. The eschatology of eternal life has indeed the structure of a question rather than of an answer. But as Gadamer noticed, the question is the primary hermeneutical condition of understanding (Gadamer, 1975, p. 266). Once the problem of eternal life has asserted its validity in its problem-raising power, in the event of death the forceful questions might just point to eternal life. What is death, indeed, which solves problems of this life and prompts questions of another kind?

Death is a common human experience yet it cannot be observed. It escapes observation because it cannot be communicated with others. How do we know what death is, if death is essentially non-communicable? What we can observe are only symptoms of death, like dying, and the states of clinical, biological, legal or psychological death, all closely connected with death. They are only signs of death, but they are the only means we have for guessing what death can be in its authenticity.

4.1.2.1.2. Dying

Dying is to be distinguished from death. It does not make communication impossible as death does. Dying can be observed as suffering, pain, dependence, helplessness, loss of dignity, disintegration of personality, change of oneself and of world-image with a radical crisis of faith, charity and hope. The various stages were described by Elizabeth Kübler-Ross as denial of dying, anger, bargaining, depression and finally acceptance (Kübler-Ross, 1969). Dying brings the self-defence mechanism into operation and the various forms of its actuation are the topics of psychological research (Holmes, 1984; Toman, 1979).

4.1.2.1.3. Clinical, Biological and Psychological Death

A very advanced stage of dying is clinical death, the description of which is based on the close interdependence of the function of the brain, lungs and heart. Thus, for example, the heart stops, breathing ceases, there is no blood in the brain. In such a case, doctors say that the brain is dead, though respiration can be sustained by a respirator for a long time after that. "Brain death" as a legal definition of death has been implemented in the legislation of various states and countries.

The cessation of brain function should not be seen necessarily as a sign of biological death. Clinical death is less than biological death. Biological death is described by R.M. Veatch as an irreversible loss of integrated organic functioning (Veatch, 1976, p. 77). The references to Elijah (1 Kgs 17, 17-24), to Elisha (2 Kgs 13, 20-21) and to Jairus's daughter (Mk 5, 21-43) can be considered as cases of clinical death, whereas the case of Lazarus fits more into the description of biological death (cf. by now there will be a stench, Jn 11, 39). Legal death is when the body shows no response to adequate resuscitation efforts (Grisez and Boyle, 1979, p. 371). Biological death occurs when all the tissues begin to degenerate. The signs are rigor mortis, frigidity, lividity, decomposition, etc.

Freud's hypothetical death instinct, *thanatos* (Wittkowski, 1978), is based on the assumption that all biological matters are destined to return to an inanimate state under the control of the repetition-compulsion principle, which would be like a blind impulse to repeat earlier operations and return to the stability of the inorganic state. Critics of the theory of death instinct claim that, unlike other instincts, the destructive instincts have no foundation in the physiology of the organism. The hostile and destructive impulses come from the life instinct and are the source of life rather than of death.

Psychological death can occur long before clinical or biological death is observed. It consists in the severing of all relations with others. It is the end of personal communication with others. However, psychological death can precipitate clinical and biological death. Some experiments indicate that rats as well as human beings die from a reaction of hopelessness. If the situation of hopelessness is removed, rats confined to glass jars become aggressive again, showing no signs of giving up the attempt to free themselves (Richter, 1959, p. 312). Observations made on certain pre-literate people show also that under the influence of a "voodoo" or "hex" previously healthy individuals may die within less than 24 hours, despite any effort to save them. Walter Cannon suggested that these people might have died from an excessive stimulation of the sympathico-adrenal system (Cannon, 1942). Based on his experience in a Nazi death camp, Victor Frankl supports the view that psychological death prompted by helplessness and despair can be reversed by "will to meaning" or Logotherapy (Kovacs, 1982).

4.1.2.1.4. Biblical Interpretation of Death

Besides the analysis of the symptoms closely connected with death, we can interpret death according to different contexts. Scripture recognizes several contexts, and consequently the scriptural interpretation of death changes as revelation progresses from the Old Testament to the New (Wachter, 1967; Bailey, 1979; Kaiser and Lohse, 1981; Léon-Dufour, 1986).

Death as a human condition, when "dust returns to dust," is interpreted in Yahwistic tradition as punishment for sin (Gn 2, 17-3, 19; cf. 1 Kgs 17, 18). This description of death reminds us of the repetition-compulsion principle of *thanatos* which assumes that all biological bodies return to an inanimate state of dust (cf. Gn 3, 19; Eccl 12, 7). According to other biblical sources death is the climax of lifelong efforts and suffering to subdue the world (Gn 1, 28; 3, 17-19).

Qoheleth (12,7) describes death in terms of Gn 3, 19 and Gn 2, 7 (cf. Sir 3, 20-21; 1 Kgs 17, 21-22). The breath of life returns to God who gave it. This is, however, not an idea of immortality of any kind, since Qoheleth knows nothing of personal immortality (cf. Sir 3, 19-21; 9, 10). Beasts and human beings all have the same breath and one has no advantage over the other. Sheol is the end of all. The author nevertheless believes that both death and life are God's gift. In death God takes back life, which he gave. Yet Qoheleth is a critic of the theory of death instinct. He does not accept that all biological matters have the destiny of returning to an inanimate state. Rather they have the destiny to return to the "animate" state, sc., to God, who created all.

The Wisdom of Solomon (1, 16; 2, 24) reflects the teaching of Genesis 3, 14. Death entered the world by the Devil's envy. But it is not physical death he is talking about but the spiritual separation from God, expressed in the death of the wicked (Wis 2, 24-3, 12). Physical death for him is part of being human. It is a common departure for all humanity (7, 1-6) (Taylor, 1966; Larcher, 1983-85; Kolarcik, 1991, pp. 143-58).

In reviewing the various Old Testament interpretations of death we will find nowhere anything similar to the farewell discourses of

Jesus with their tone of happiness that "I will see you again" (cf. Jn 13, 36; 14, 24; 17, 21-26; cf. also Mk 14, 25; Lk 23, 42-43).

In the New Testament, the Letter to the Romans takes over the interpretation of death that we found in Genesis and makes it universal. Death is the result of personal sin as well as of original sin (Rom 1, 32; 6, 16-21). It is the wages of sin, whereas eternal life is the free gift of God (Rom 6, 23; 7, 5,9-10). From Rom 7, 9-10, it is clear that death for Paul does not mean the same as biological death does. Paul says, for example, that he was dead before he became the apostle of Christ. Death is, therefore, not just a return to dust but a separation from the kingdom of God, the kingdom of life. Death is the death of the sinner. It is pain, suffering and "sin" (Rom 5, 12, 19; cf. also James 1, 15; Heb 2, 14), and as such it is more than what we call physical death. Death in Paul is a cosmic force (Rom 8, 38; 5, 14), the last enemy to be conquered. And Jesus Christ, the risen Lord, overcame this enemy (1 Cor 15, 1-58). As a result death has lost its power and now one can please God before death, in death and after death as well (2 Cor 5, 9). Life and death both are relativized in favour of a higher value, which is to be with Christ. Death after Christ is not the end of being with God, as the Psalmist taught (Ps 88, 10-12). Being with the Lord is independent of being alive on earth or being dead. After Christ's resurrection death cannot separate Paul from the love of God that came to him in Christ Jesus (Rom 8, 28-39).

Here we have a new interpretation of death. Death means to be at home with the Lord, whereas being at home in the body is being away from the Lord (2 Cor 5, 68; Phil 1, 22-23). Death is having the earthly tent destroyed for one built by God in heaven (2 Cor 5,1; 2 Pet 1, 14-15). Mortality is swallowed up by life in order to be clothed by immortality (2 Cor 5, 4).

The scriptural interpretation of death would not be complete without considering Jesus' farewell speech in John's Gospel (Jn 13, 31-17, 26). The biblical farewells, like the ones of Jacob, Moses, Joshua, Samuel, Matthias, have much in common. They recall God's gift to his people, talk about the promised land (Gn 49, 8-12; Dt 32, 36-43) and urge the living to remain faithful (Dt 31, 24- 29, 32, 44-47; Jos 24, 1-27; 1 Sm 12, 1-25) by following the examples of their ancestors (1 Mc 2, 51-56). Finally the departing hand over the tradition entrusted to their followers with an exhortation to carry on their work.

Jesus' farewell has something which the others do not have. Jesus transforms the traditional farewell into "a happy to see you again"

(Jn 13, 36; 14, 17-22,28; 16, 22; 17, 24; Mk 14, 25). This is more remarkable since the farewells of the apostles do not suggest any meeting again with their disciples. They think of meeting with the Lord, but not with their fellow apostles or their faithful friends. The difference is noteworthy. Only Jesus appears as the master of time and eternity, who has received the keys of death and Hades (Rev 1, 18). He opened eternity and will take his disciples there, whither he has gone now.

Thus the interpretation of death in the New Testament is closely related to resurrection. Yet such a unified interpretation of death and resurrection does not diminish the reality of death as an end. Death is still a real "finish" as we read in Jn 19, 28-30.

The verb used in Jn 19, 28-30 is not πληρόω, as in the fulfillment of the scripture, for example (cf. Jn 19, 24,36), but τελέω, "ending up," "being over" in the sense that it will never happen again. The work of Jesus had been accomplished on earth (Jn 17, 4), and he will never do it again. The timely, the earthly is sublated by Christ's death. And this sublation is a terrifying one, not lessened at all by the future resurrection, as the agony of Christ and his cry on the cross illustrate (Mt 26, 36-46; Mk 14, 32-42). His soul was sorrowful to the point of death (Mk 26, 37) asking his Father to let the cup pass him by (Mt 26, 39). And something more. The death agony with the sweating of blood disturbs his relationship with his Father and makes him cry out "My God (notice, the word is not Father but God as in Ps 22, 1) why have you deserted me?" (Mt 27, 46; Mk 15, 34; Lk 22, 44). Since the meaning of these texts seems to contradict the tendencies and interest of the early Church they can be referred to Jesus himself. Moreover, John suggests that the agony and fear of death was not limited to the final days of his life. It disturbed him earlier as well. For example, the image of a dying wheat grain reminded him of his own death and he said: "Now is my soul troubled. And what shall I say? Father, save me from this hour" (Jn 12, 27-28).

Jesus' death, as presented in the gospels, is not a fulfillment of an accomplished life. It is a painful end. A painful end on the cross. In presenting the biblical interpretation of death we should not forget that Jesus did not die a natural death: he was crucified and died on the cross. If we accept that his life and resurrection are the revelations of the mystery of our life in Christ we must accept that Jesus' death on the cross is the revelation of the mystery of our death. According to the scripture Jesus was not carried up to heaven by a chariot of fire, as we read of Elijah (2 Kgs 2, 11), but died on the cross, and into his death we are to die, since his death became the saving entry into eternity (2 Tim 2, 11; 2 Cor 7; 3 Rom 6, 4). Diminution of the reality of death as a real destruction would be the diminution of the meaning and efficacy of Christ's death which, together with his suffering (dying, or *mors in fieri*), is effecting our entry into eternity (see, for example, *S. theol.* 3, 50, 6; 48, 1-6).

The death on the cross is more than a simple end of life (Mt 16, 24). It was a loss of dignity (Heb 12, 2; 13, 13), a scandal (Mt 26, 31; Gal 5, 11), rejection by one's own community (Mt 10, 34-39) and being cursed by the living God (Gal 3, 13). Jesus' death on the cross, therefore, reveals unambiguously that the human reality of death is a shameful, destructive end of life, end of the support of one's familiar community and that of relationship with God. To ignore the human reality of dying on the cross would be as misleading and beguiling as to ignore the visible reality of the sacramental sign or, for that matter, the human reality of Christ.

The human reality of death affected by the human reality of sin signifies Christ's death on the cross, and Christ's death on the cross reveals the human reality of death affected by sin. If Christ is the revelation of eternity, it is not Elijah's being carried into heaven but Christ's death on the cross that illustrates the mystery of giving up our time to enter into Christ's eternity. The reality of the crucified Jesus is the final word of the biblical interpretation of death.

4.1.2.1.5. Interpretation of Death in the Church's Documents

The first Church documents dealing with death were prompted by the Pelagian denial that all that Christ acquired for us was gift and not something we own of ourselves. The provincial Council of Carthage in 418 repeated the interpretation of death of Rom 5, 12 and 2 Cor 5, 1. Death as punishment is the result of Adam's sin (DS 227). Adam was mortal yet he had a gift offered to him which he lost for all of us. We find the same doctrine again in the Council of Orange in 529. Death is punishment for sin, and sin is "the death of the soul" (DS 372). This truth was solemnly defined by the Council of Trent in its Decree on Original Sin in 1546 and made it explicit that this is the case for everyone (DS 1512; 1547; 1521; cf. also 2617 Tanner, 1990, pp. 666, 678, 671). And so we have the first basic tenet of the Church's doctrine about death.

The second basic tenet is that death is the end of earthly life, the end of the time of trial when one can freely turn to God or turn oneself from him for all eternity. We can read this in some editions of the documents of the first Council of Lyons in 1254 (DS 838-39), Lyons II in 1274 (DS 856-59; see the teaching of John XII in 1321, DS 925-26), in the Constitution of Benedict XII in 1336 (DS 1000-1002), Council of Florence in 1439 (DS 1304-06; Tanner, 1990, pp. 527-28), and in Leo X's Bulla in 1520 (DS 1488).

These two tenets are the summary of the Church's teaching about death. Death as the separation of the soul and body is implied but only in the sense of Pauline teaching of leaving the earthly tent. The soul and body terminology used in 374 in the Tome of Damascus (DS 146) suggests that the whole person, body and soul together, is saved by Christ who is, like us, a whole human being having body and soul. Such a unity of soul and body is expressed in the doctrine that one's destiny is decided for eternity during the time when soul and body are united here on earth. The terminology is therefore not to be seen as an exclusively scholastic terminology but rather an adaptation of the Pauline interpretation of death given in 2 Cor 5, 6-8. In Phil 1, 22-24 we find *sarx* "flesh" instead of *sōma* for describing mortal life as home in the body and away from the Lord. The terminology reflects the Old Testament idea of body as flesh (cf. Gn 3, 19; 1 Kgs 17, 21-27; Eccl 3, 19-21, etc.). It should also be recalled that in the Pauline literature body has more than one meaning. Body as *sarx* is a perishable, transitory element which is incapable of inheriting the kingdom of God (1 Cor 6, 14). Body as *sōma* is the member of Christ (1 Cor 6, 15) and the temple of the Holy Spirit (1 Cor 6, 19). Through a painful transformation the mortal body *sōma* can become *psychikon* "the spiritual body" not subject to decay (1 Cor 15, 42-44).

4.1.2.1.6. Theologians' Interpretation of Death

The most influential theologian for the theology of death in the second half of the twentieth century was probably Karl Rahner. Rahner distinguished between the natural and personal aspects of death. The natural aspect is expressed by the idea of the separation of soul and body, and the personal, by the definitive end of our state of pilgrimage (Rahner, 1961, p. 13). The separation of soul and body is not a definition according to Rahner but a classical description of death. The Neoplatonic mentality assumed that after death there is a complete separation from the world, so that the soul becomes acosmic. Rahner wanted to correct this understanding by introducing the term "pancosmic." After death the soul becomes not "acosmic," but "pancosmic," by entering into some deeper, more comprehensive openness "in which this pancosmic relation to the universe is more fully realized" (Rahner, 1961, p. 19).

Rahner admits that death can be considered as something "without purpose, as destructive fate striking one from without, or as the accomplishment of the end towards which one positively strives" (Rahner, 1961, p. 25). He adopts the second meaning, since death serves, according to him, to open a person more widely to the whole world and to have a closer relationship with the real ground of the world's unity with which all things are in common even before they begin to influence each other. Because of death, continues Rahner, a person establishes a pancosmic relationship and becomes a contributory cause to the whole world as the basis of the personal life of other psychosomatic beings. Death is therefore an active consummation from within, a total entry into the possession of oneself. It is the state of having produced the fulfillment of one's being.

In such a description of death the demarcation between death and the Christian idea of resurrection, is blurred. What is said of death is true of the resurrection, which is closely united with death by virtue of Christ's death and resurrection. Yet the two should not be identified. The reality of death should be safeguarded, because it is a human reality that theological consideration should not overlook. Rahner's alternative, death as a destructive fate without purpose and death as accomplishment of the end, is not fully adequate. Death can be considered as a problem-solving device in this world without any further consideration of after-life. Furthermore, considering death as accomplishment without thinking of Christian faith in resurrection obscures Christ's importance and reminds one of the pancosmic oneness suggested by Buddhist liberation from the body by entering into a cosmic oneness at the price of one's personal identity. The pancosmic relation should be interpreted not as a result of death, but as the result of entering into Christ's time through the resurrection of our body (see 4.3, Society, World and Eternity).

These critical remarks concerning Rahner's interpretation of death are valid also for P. Troisfontaines's interpretation. Prior to Rahner, Troisfontaines stated that death is a growth, a passage to being. Death is where becoming becomes being. Approaching the moment of death the weakening body signals that it cannot support the growth of the human person just as the womb cannot provide further growth for the child when it is about to be born. As the child of the womb, a dying person is ready to leave the temporal environment which is no longer capable of supporting one's growth (Troisfontaines, 1960). Yet the death of Jesus Christ is not described in these images by the evangelists. There is no sign of growth, but rather that of an end. And we have to die into such a death of Jesus Christ. For Troisfontaines, as well as for Rahner, death is a change of place in space, rather than a threshold of time and eternity. So too is it for Boros.

The mystery of death as a real end is not central either in Boros's *Moment of Truth* (1965). Following Troisfontaines and Rahner and relying on Blondel, Boros interprets death as a free, final decision, since the body, responsible for darkening the mind, is left behind in death. Thus death is entering into a place where the whole creature awaits God and makes this final decision, which becomes state, since it was not made in the midst of the dualism of our present existence. We can sense here the inspiration of Blondel, who saw death as an unconscious ecstasy towards God reaching the total identity of one's original volition (Blondel, 1950).

These interpretations, being interpretations of the resurrection following death, rather than the human reality of death as such, fail to penetrate the mystery of death and face the crucial theological issue of how can a "non-angelic, non-pure spiritual being," a real human being existing in time and space, make a decision which has an eternal dimension. In other words, why is death the final seal of one's destiny, rendering one's decision definitive and irrevocable.

Two answers can be proposed. The first is appealing to God's will and the second is looking for some intrinsic reason. Those who opt for the first say that there is no intrinsic reason that could explain how it is possible that a temporal human action has eternal consequences. Therefore, the only explanation is the will of God. It is so because God has decided so. Others, like Rahner (1961), Troisfontaines (1963), Blondel (1950), Boros (1965), try to find some internal explanation by analyzing the spiritual nature of the human activity at the moment of the separation from the body. Reversibility and reformability of one's decision comes from matter. Once one is freed from the body, reformability becomes irreformability and reversibility, irreversibility. Death is not a temporal succession, but a demarcation line between two moments, without having any temporal extension of its own. This means that the last moment before death and the first moment after death merge into one another. The moment of the soul "separating" and being "separated" thus coincide (Boros, 1965, p. 5). This theory is called the theory of free option, because it underlines the importance of free will in establishing the final lot that one will have for all eternity. But more precisely it should be called the theory of free option of a spiritual immaterial being since the free option is an act of the soul "being separated."

The main difficulty with the theory of free option is that it ignores the real nature of the meritorious act, which is to be temporal and be performed "in the condition we are now," i.e., before death. According to the tradition of the Church, death, as a temporal act performed in the body and in history, is therefore meritorious, and as such, is decisive for one's eternal destiny.

If we agree that only God is eternal and that every created being material and spiritual, or the composition of both, without exception, is temporal, the solution to the problem of how temporal action can have an eternal dimension must be sought, not in a platonic spiritual activity of the human soul separated from the body, but in the mystery of the Incarnation, which is not a compound of time and time, but a union of time and eternity.

Theologians often fail to consider death as a human reality independently of the resurrection of Christ. Death as human reality is an end of life. It is not a happy walk-over to the next life, leaving one's body behind like an old, worn-out gown. Death affects my whole being, my Self, my Ego, my body, my soul, my theological "I." Death is my act and not something outside, like a sickness, which affects just my body. "I" as a person die, and with me everything that I am, including my faith, charity and hope. Paul knows this. That is why he says that we have to die with Christ in his death by reproducing the pattern of his death (Rom 6, 3; Phil 3, 10). And we saw that Jesus' death was an end, an agony with an experience of being abandoned by God.

The first creeds of the Church went even further by stating that Jesus descended into hell, ascending to heaven only after his resurrection. We should also recall here that the old Christian tradition described death as a great combat with the devil, the symbol of death, who makes a last effort to snatch the soul away from God and carry it to hell. And this tradition resulted from the common experience that sometimes the faith of the dying is suddenly shaken by a terrifying glimpse of an abyss and void assailing the life of the faithful. Death is an end affecting anything that is temporal. This radical change can be observed in the dying of the life of faith, charity and hope as one's time comes to an end. The divine life which is in us shares our death.

The tangible world of what one can see, taste and hold to becomes more self-affirming, and faith, charity and hope seem to fade more and more. This is an experience the older faithful do not want to talk about too much. Yet the crisis is there. Death as human reality affects the deepest centre of our "I" at the very point where we are most what we are.

4.1.2.1.7. Death is the Realization of the Inevitability of Unselfish Love

An interpretation of the human reality of death as an end of "me" should not be labelled atheistic, pessimistic, irrational and inhuman without any positive value in it. Instead, we should realistically admit that death as an end is the lot of everything which is not God. But as any created reality, death too has its own beauty, meaning even its own moral value which is known as altruism, or being for others. Believers and non-believers all share in the human reality of death, and consequently in its virtue. The positive value of death is recommended by the fact that the incarnate God did not refuse to share it. It is true that Christ died for our sins, yet by dying he affirmed that death itself is not sinful. Otherwise God could not have participated in it. On the contrary, by dying Christ revealed that death in its human reality was something which could be a sign, a *word* of his message, and what is more, it is a revelation of the divine life. Because death can be interpreted as the realization of the inevitability of unselfish love, the most characteristic feature of the Triune God of revelation. Death is the end of the selfish struggle for life in the combat of the multiplicity of times. It is the end of selfishness, the end of interfering with the sphere and time of others, leaving room and freedom to others by affirming the other as other, taking up the freedom and the beatitude of others as one's own freedom and beatitude (Horvath, 1980a, p. 2329).

Unselfishness, which was free choice before death, in death becomes an "inevitable" law for everyone. Already in dying one is facing more and more the inevitability of unselfishness by experiencing the progressive annihilation of the self-defence mechanism. As death approaches, the different forms of Ego-defence mechanism are activated: the denial of reality (refusal to admit that death is imminent), day-dreaming (escape to the satisfying world of fantasy), rationalization (fabricating false but socially acceptable reasons), projection (blaming others for personal shortcomings), repression (excluding the thought of painful reality), regression (retreating into infantile behaviour), reaction-formation (denying faulty impulses by going to the opposite extremes), emotional isolation, identification with other people instead of with oneself who is coming to an end (Holmes, 1984, pp. 347-50; W. Toman, 1979, p. 252), etc., all are more and more obviously failing and the Self comes to its final end in death.

Death makes altruism both unavoidable and universal: "Unless a grain of wheat falls into the earth and dies, it remains alone, but if it dies, it bears much fruit" (Jn 12, 24), and "one who loves his/her life, loses it, and one who hates his/her life in the world, will keep it for eternal life" (Jn 12, 25). Again, "No one has greater love than to lay down his/her life for others" (Jn 15, 13). These are all scriptural interpretations of the universality and inescapability of death as the execution of the unselfishness and the law of altruism. If there is an option in death, the option is the acceptance of the inevitability of the complete failure of one's self-defence mechanism before death and the transfer of one's self-defence into the hands of someone else (cf. "God, you are my saviour and not me"), or a desperate renewed effort of self-affirmation in a lost battle. All this is taking place constantly in our lifetime. But at the moment of death, when the end is inevitably there, the usually gamelike rhythmical alterations between "I" and others is progressively and more and more forcefully turned in favour of the others.

In an interpretation of death like ours, theology can fully admit the biological reality of death. Death in itself is not a transition, or a dream in deep sleep, but a "catabolism" resulting from the breakdown of complex materials, the dissolution of protoplasm, the material of the basis of life. Yet theology sees in this "catabolism" more than a biological ending. The biological ending is radicalized by entering into the death of Christ, which was a loving, unrestricted surrender to the Father, the creator of the world, and a free surrender of his time to the time of his Father. Jesus' time came to an end in order that the eternity of the Father might be manifest. The Father lives in him and he lives in the Father. This is the death of which Paul says that all people die in his death. Indeed all human beings are "baptized" into this death, because Christ's death made death a more radical end of selfishness.

Since through Christ eternity is given as a gift, the entering into it means a more radical "catabolism" of the "I" and of all its times. The radicalization of death in Christ is prompted by the event that death is not a leaving of space to others to have a "pancosmic" openness to all other times (since all these are to be annihilated as well), but a leaving of one's space and time in order to take up Christ's time, the way to eternity. It is true that death in Christ is not identical with biological death, yet it does affect the biological death and intensifies it. The time of the world is not eternity. Only God is, and God's personality is guaranteed precisely by his eternity, which radicalizes the personality of the dying person for all eternity.

The radicalization of one's personality in eternity takes place in the mystery of resurrection to be studied later in this work. At this moment we focus on death as the end of time, which is further intensified by Christ's death when he conquered death by sublating the times of everyone. That the Church never failed to consider immortality as a gift of God granted together with original justice is a clear indication that in the mind of the Church God never intended us to live a purely natural life and die a natural death without Christ. Christ's death makes a radical break with time because he sublated it by God's eternity. Since death is a real end when one's time is sublated by Christ's time, there can be no after-life, no immortality of any kind independent of Christ.

4.1.2.1.8. After-life Experiences Are Not After-death Experiences

Belief in survival after death can be traced back to pre-history. Tombs, dwelling places where the dead were believed to pursue a life similar to the living, have been known since the earliest times. Excavations proved that corpses were painted with red ochre, suggesting a belief that the corpse lived on. According to H. Cornelis (1968) belief in afterlife of pre-literate cultures is connected with the conviction of the fundamental unity of all the members of the same group. Each one, but specially certain figures, "culture heroes," had a special relation to the collective life of the community. They survived as individuals in memory and were mentioned in various funeral rites.

About 2500 B.C. the *Egyptian Book of the Dead* (Budge, 1967) described sanctions after death, using the image of weighting of the heart and of a trial with the dead's denial of guilt, etc. The transmigration of the soul, a form of North Asian shamanism that became widespread in India posited that the purification of the soul was to be achieved after death through a journey similar to the ascetic itinerary of the believer. Purifications after death were seen as cosmic movements destined to restore all things by their return to their unity with their beginning.

The Tibetan Book of the Dead, from the eighth century A.D., gives a description of life after death remarkably similar to those collected recently by authors reporting after-clinical-death experiences. Here are the different instances of after-life experiences as presented by *The Tibetan Book of the Dead* (Evans-Ventz, 1960). (1) The dead person is leaving his/her body and (2) receives a shining body capable of floating around and going through objects and walls and (3) observes the mourning relatives without being able to communicate with them. (4) In this new way of existence perception is sharpened and the dead can move almost instantaneously (5) through a long, dark passage (6) to a brilliant and pleasant place where he/she encounters relatives and other spiritual beings together with a clear light, as a sort of angelic being, causing a feeling of peace and happiness. The soul, however, is prevented by a barrier from going further to a permanent state. One (7) is judged according to his/her deeds on earth and sentenced to return to life on earth. The description is always influenced and coloured by the cultural background of the narrator. Thus, for example, in the more recent after-clinical-death experiences a Christian would meet Christ, Buddhists would meet Buddha, and so on.

It is interesting that Carl Jung has a similar description of an experience he had after a heart attack, followed by a sort of vision emerging out of his unconscious:

> I myself was floating in space.... I had the feeling that everything was being sloughed away... stripped away... extremely painful process.... Nevertheless, something remained: it was as if I now carried along with me everything I had ever experienced or done, everything that had happened around me.... I consisted of all that... and I felt with great certainty: this is what I am. I am this bundle of what has been and what has been accomplished.... I had everything that I was, and that was everything (Jung, 1961, pp. 289-91).

The after-death experiences in most cases are pleasant (Rawlings, 1978, pp. 79-101) but there are some unpleasant as well (Rawlings, 1978, pp. 6-7, 102-20). Spiritualism, communication with the dead, necromancy, parapsychology and the like have similar features and might make some further contribution to after-clinical-death experiences.

The great similarities of the accounts we find in the clinical reports of today and the description of *The Tibetan Book of the Dead* suggest that the biological changes in perceptive organs affect similarly the awareness of the Self, the Ego and consequently that of the "I." But this does not mean that we have to assume the reality of after-clinical-death experiences as real after-death experiences. They are what they are, sc., experiences after clinical death, which is reversible by resuscitation. Death in the theological sense means sublation of all times. Therefore there is no after-life as something which could take place after death having communication with those who are in time. Once time is sublated by Christ's time, one enters eternity, which is not a linear continuation of time. Times of Self, times of Ego, etc., without exception, are sublated by eternity.

4.1.2.1.9. The Idea of Immortality is Inconsistent

Since the cosmos, as we know it, is conditioned time, time is a fundamental reality of anything which can be experienced. Natural sciences, therefore, cannot use meaningfully the concept of immortality. Scholastic theology distinguished between metaphysical immortality and physical immortality (Sagües, 1958, p. 685). The first is an essential attribute of God only. The most explicit scriptural reference, 1 Tim 1, 16, supports this distinction. From there it follows that anything else which or who is not God is just creature and consequently has its own time. This can be called *aevum* or the time of a spirit or of an angel or angels. But *aevum* is part of our world. That is why according to the doctrine of the Church, the angels are united with humanity in one supernatural saving history which has its goal in Christ. Consequently angelology is an intrinsic element of Christology (Rahner and Vorgrimler, 1965, p. 21).

If we conceive time as a balance in a multiplicity of sub-times, the times of the angels, or *aeons*, are part of our times so that "before" and "after" can be linked to them (*S. theol.* 1, q. 10, a. 5). Therefore the so called immortality of angels cannot mean anything else but that angels cannot die as human beings do. They do not have biological times, yet they have personal times. Whether this is called by some "substantial immortality" or by others "physical immortality," would not make any difference, since both angels and humans have immortality, not by virtue of their essence, but by virtue of Christ. There is no natural immortality for angels and there is no natural immortality for humans either. As was mentioned above, after-life beliefs and immortality are two different concepts that should not be confused. That the idea of immortality became a theologumenon, a widely accepted paradigm in patristic tradition, is very understandable, and it has a very obvious explanation.

Reflecting on the period between death and the resurrection after the final judgment, the writers of the early Church found that if the soul is separated from the body (Platonic heritage), the soul must be incorporeal. Now if it is incorporeal, it must be spiritual. This reasoning was commonly accepted already by the sixth century, yet the immortality of the soul was argued much later. St. Anselm (1033-1109) did argue, indeed, for the immortality of the soul in his *Monologium* (nos. 69-72). But for St. Anselm immortality was still a grace based on God's will.

Somewhat later, in 1150, Dominic Gundisalvi, in his *De immortalitate animae*, argued from the spiritual operations of the soul to its immortality. Peter Lombard went further and said that the spirituality of the soul can be known without revelation (4, *Sent.* 3, 1; 3, *Sent.* 24, 3). As a result of this trend of thought, immortality was progressively considered as something natural to the soul. Now it is remarkable that even though resurrection was always central to the Christian faith, there was not a great discussion about it. Thomas Aquinas seems to have been the first to raise questions concerning resurrection (Flew, 1967, pp. 139-50) and gave resurrection as the title for his eschatology (*S. theol. suppl.* 69).

Later on, philosophy was frequently called upon to give philosophical foundation to the theological claim that there is life after death. But unfortunately the idea of resurrection was left out of these considerations, and more and more arguments were fabricated to support the immortality of the soul. Since Kant, the arguments have been dismissed as the remnants of an exaggerated Platonic dualism (Hounder, 1970). Ratzinger too argued that immortality cannot be demonstrated from the indivisibility of the soul (Ratzinger, 1972, pp. 127ff.).

The doctrine of the immortality of the soul, as far as it considers the natural condition of the soul, must be questioned. Time is an essential element of any created being, and if a person is mortal one's body and soul is not less so. Moreover the problem, of what happens during the period between death and the universal judgment of the last day will be better solved not by arguing for the immortality of the soul, which as such is effected only by the saving grace of Christ, but by considering the resurrection of the dead from the side of God (eternity) and from the side of the world (time) (see below 4.2.1.3) as a logical result of the eschatological union of time and eternity Christology.

4.1.2.1.10. Authenticity of Death, Authenticity of Resurrection: The Question of the Identity of the Person Who Died and the One Who is Risen

"I die" grammatically means that I, my whole human being, in one word, all that I am, dies. Otherwise, there would remain something in me which would not need to be saved and affected by the death and resurrection of Christ.

Early scholastic theologians accepted the Boethian definition of what a person should be (Michel, 1922, p. 140). Boethius defined a person as "an individual substance of a rational nature" (*De persona et duabus naturis*, n. 3; PL 64, 1343D; Thomas Aquinas, *S. theol.* 1, 29 1.; 30, 1). A person had to be a substance, i.e., a being in itself that is rational and not communicated to another, as, for example, the human nature is communicated to the second divine person of the Trinity.

For Rahner, to be a person is to "possess oneself as a subject in conscious, free relation to reality as a whole and its infinite ground and source, God" (Rahner and Vorgrimler, 1965, p. 351). In Rahner's definition consciousness plays a prominent role. For today's psychology the question of personality can be raised only in connection with body. Whereas Descartes defined person as a mind that has a body, B. Williams, for example, considered person as a body that thinks (Williams, 1973). But if bodies are persons, once the body dies, the person dies as well. Thus the so-called *Ganztodtheorie*, or mortalism, states that with death the human person totally ceases to be. It was this view that prompted the Sacred Congregation for the Doctrine of the Faith to say in its letter that a spiritual element survives and subsists after death, which element is endowed with consciousness and will, so that the human self subsists (*Letter on Certain Questions Concerning Eschatology*, AAS 1979, p. 941). This recalls the scholastic solution which considered the separated soul a person to safeguard the continuity before death and after resurrection. Unlike the Eastern creeds, which profess the resurrection of the dead, the Western confessions talk about the resurrection of the body. But if my separate soul does not die, the resurrection of Christ is irrelevant to my soul. Not my soul, but just my body would need resurrection. But again, if my soul dies together with my body, how can we safeguard the identity of the risen person with the one who has died?

M. Gardner (1983) proposed that if the personality of one is considered as an assemblage of the patterns of his/her brain, then this assemblage, which constitutes his/herself, is kept in God's memory, and God at the day of resurrection just materializes these patterns again. Therefore, the continuity between the earthly person and the risen one lies only in God. But if God has to create the subject again, one could say that the subject is not the original itself but only a duplicate of the original which has disappeared (Greshake and Lohfink, 1982, p. 119).

Let us examine now how we recognize in general that this person is the same person, i.e., the original him/herself. In general, we assume an identity of a person by the identity of his/her body. But what kind of identity marks do we use to recognize a body as the same body? Do we look at the appearance, e.g. red hair, 70 kg, etc., or rather the identity of spatio-temporal relations so that if one appears with a different spatio-temporal relationship we would talk about a duplicate, but not of identity? Does the identity of a person consist in the identity of memory and character, so that if one remembers being the same person today as he/she was 50 years ago, keeping some characteristics, can we say that he/she is the same person today as the one we met 50 years ago? Some would suggest that the identity of a person is dependent on brain information, which includes recalling (no new input), reminding (partial new input) and learning something new (total new input) so that not the physical brain, but brain input determines the identity of a person. In this case, the identity of oneself is not the identity of the body but the identity of information. For example, if all my memory inputs, judgments, feelings, actions, relations, etc., could be placed in a retrieval system and later transferred into another human brain which had no other input whatsoever, I could recognize myself as the same person, though in a completely different body. The difference between this pattern and the pattern of the separate soul is that the first uses the concept of recent information sciences, the second, the idea of substance as something which remains throughout changes to assure the identity of a person.

All those who like to consider bodies as persons, and expect resurrection, have to claim a sort of immortality or resurrection, not just for a human person but for any other bodily being, animals included. And, indeed, some, like Gardner, would like to see animals as part of the risen life. This question will come up in in section 4.3. But here for the moment we want to pursue a Christological consideration which might shed more light on the subject matter.

We said earlier that death as real end is implied in the credal belief that Jesus before his resurrection descended into hell. The descent into hell makes it clear that Jesus' death was not a dream. It was not a clinical or just a biological death but a death in a theological sense. His earthly life was over once and for all, since after death there is no return. Jesus gave himself up for others and so his death became a real death, the realization of total unselfishness. The scriptural doctrine that the sinless died for our sins underlines this even more. He who loved us died for us who did not love him. And this is the climax of unselfishness. Thus Christ could never return to his earthly life, because he died really. He has risen really, because he died really.

Reading the scripture we find that the continuity between the earthly Jesus and the risen Christ is ascertained and witnessed by the faith of the apostles together with other witnesses chosen by God (Acts 10, 40) who recognized that the risen one is the same as the one who died. It was in the faith of the early Church that Jesus "survived," since it was the Holy Spirit who revealed the continuity between the dead Jesus and the risen Christ. The recognition narratives make this clear. The chosen ones, the first members of the Church, recognized Jesus in their faith, the gift of the Holy Spirit.

Later theological development expressed the same by saying that the divinity of the second person of the Trinity, who was hypostatically united with Jesus' human nature in his life, in his death and in his resurrection, has never left his dead body. This is a Christological formulation for the identity of the Jesus who died and the Jesus Christ who has risen. Yet this Christological explanation has an ecclesiological prerequisite, sc., that the Church, as a community of believers under the guidance of the Holy Spirit, existed before his resurrection. It was only in the context of the faith of the Church initiated by Jesus with the grace of the Holy Spirit that the recognition of Christ was made possible. The existence of a new reality, sc., that of the Church, made possible that the resurrection was not just a return to a life before death, but the "risen" life of the "risen" Lord who had died.

In light of this consideration, it is very understandable that not everyone and not even the chosen ones could always see and recognize him. Both resurrection and faith are an elevation of both the risen one and the "believer" into the new dimension of eternal life. The recognition of the risen Jesus is indeed an anticipation of the eternal life. Not only the risen Christ but the "seer," i.e., the "believer" by faith, reaches in some sense the completion of history ahead of "time" (Horvath, 1975, p. 201).

This insight should be taken into consideration in any theological discussion on mortalism, or *"Ganztodtheorie."* It is not just "the mind" of God but the community of believers, the Church, taught by the Holy Spirit, that is the reality which guarantees the identity of the dead person and that of the risen one. Christians and non-Christians who died before, during or after the lifetime of Christ will recognize themselves and will be recognized as such in and through the impact or contributions they made to the mystical body, the Church, which is an earthly reality yet against which the powers of death cannot prevail any more. As the body of Christ's eschatological union of time and eternity, the Church is already sharing in the eschatological union of time and eternity of Christ. The continuity between the earthly life and the eternal life does not depend on the "immortality" of our soul, but on the *immortality* of the Church, where our real identity is hidden and will be revealed to us when we enter Jesus' time at the moment of our death (cf. Eph 3, 9-12). It is not in our immortal soul, but in the "immortal body" of Christ, the Church, with its communitarian reality, that we recognize ourselves both as ourselves and not as ourselves.

For this dichotomy of recognizing ourselves as ourselves and not recognizing ourselves as ourselves we find a hint in Matthew's description of the last judgment, when both the righteous as well as non-righteous ask: "But Lord, when did we see you?" (Mt 25, 37,44). It is further confirmed by the traditional doctrine of the state of mortal sin and of the the revival of merits. What counts for eternal life is not what we do, but what we do in and for the Church of Christ, the historical reality and the sacrament of intimate union with God, and of the unity of all mankind, in which "neither moth nor rust consume" treasures (cf. Mt 6, 19-20).

The solution we propose to the question of the identity of the risen one brings the real "motherhood" of the Church more into relief. Since death is a real end, resurrection is indeed a new beginning, a new life in the Church, where our identity is determined in virtue of the body of Christ living both in time and space as well as in eternity. In other words, our personal identity, our personal history, etc., will be "saved" by the Church, in the Church. Our Ego, our "I" survives not in itself, but in the Church which gives ourselves to ourselves. This is probably what is meant when we read of Jesus saying that unless one is born from above, one cannot see the kingdom of God. One has to be born again, since what is born of flesh is just time. Only what is born of the spirit is eternity (Jn 3, 1-15). The generative power of the community of Christ is not less real than that of the human community: one is for time, and the other is for eternity.

We can elucidate this even more. Earlier we considered psychology in connection with other disciplines and the notion of time operating in each. Based on those analyses we distinguished in each person not only body and soul, but Self, Ego, and "I," each as its own time, and the balance of all those times makes up what a human person is. Moreover, in discussing Christ as the eschatological union of eternity and time, we described the Self distinguished from the Ego as the source and objective of motivation. The Self is the organizational centre of experiences and of the behaviour pattern as well as the totality of the experiential content and that of the behaviour pattern. We found that the Ego goes deeper than the Self. Ego is known as the centre of the primitive and unorganized desires. Assuming the validity of these considerations we proposed the time of Self as the unifying balance of irreversibility in the midst of reversible changes in motivation and behaviour pattern. Now when the time of the Ego enters into the time of Self, it brings disequilibrium and consequently new energies of which the Self was not conscious, and thus Ego influences, modifies the time of the Self.

We said that both the Self and Ego are bodily centred. There is no Self and Ego without human bodies, and in this sense, we could say that bodies are Self and Ego, or Self and Ego are bodies. Yet there is a difference from the point of view of other disciplines, each studying methodically different, well-determined aspects of reality. The Self and Ego are the proper fields of psychological research, whereas body enters into the domain of biology and physics as well. Accordingly, the body can be described as a unified field of energies which, in balancing a multiplicity of biological times, creates its own biological time. What makes body "body" is the unifying balance of biological times, which we earlier described as a synchronization of a number of cellular clocks regulated probably by some rhythmic centre or master clock which is not independent of cosmic time.

Yet the biological master clock cannot simply be reduced to the universal cosmic time, because it brings into the universal cosmic time a small, yet from the point of view of biological time, significant disequilibrium, which is a new source of energy. It is called the interiorization energy, that is the growing of the more out of the less. This new energy not only balances the multiplicity of the biological times and forms the special psychological times of the Self and Ego, but brings to the surface new times which are commonly called cultural, philosophical and theological times. The energy bringing about these disequilibriums is expressed linguistically as the soul of the body and can be described as the unified field of energy (we can use the term "field" since the soul operates in the body and through the body) which by balancing the multiplicity of biological, cultural, philosophical and theological times, creates its own time as the last stronghold of the self-defence mechanism that makes up a person.

Cultural, philosophical and theological times are different times. Cultural time is a system of controlling or coping with the contingencies of time. It is an active and passive participation in the history of a community with the intention and effort of defending the survival of the community against time. Philosophical time is the outgrowth of cultural time in order to express cultural time in terms of universal values. In other words, philosophical time is a system of sub-systems to form a concept of time and a language of time and eternity. As philosophical language differs from theological language, theological time goes further than philosophical time. It is a presentation of a solution to the problem of time and that of eternity. All this comes from the new interiorization energy of the "intelligent" being (Szilard, 1929).

In the light of these considerations, a human person should be described as a force which by balancing biological, cultural, philosophical and theological times creates its own time demarcating it from other times, building up not just a Self, and Ego defence-mechanism but an "I" personality against the alienating force of time. "I" therefore differs from the Self, Ego, body and soul by penetrating the deeper structure of time through linguistic hermeneutic experience when eternity as a challenge transpires. Here the force becomes "I" as the most transcendental balance of sub-times in differentiation to other personal times of you and me, he/she and they. As distinct from the Self, Ego, body and soul, the "I" emerges only in the confrontation of time and eternity. It is a philosophical or, more exactly, a theological time when personal time is achieved and expressed in a language like "I am my own time." Whenever this language ability is there, the philosophical and theological "I" is forming personal time and thus achieves personhood.

Now in death all these times, i.e., the time of Self, Ego, body and soul, etc., come to an end. With death the space as a co-ordinate providing reversibility as measurement of irreversibility is removed. The

Self, the Ego and the body lose their power of acting as the self-defence mechanism to keep balance against upcoming sub-times and is taken over by other time(s).

Neither the soul nor the philosophical or theological "I" appears as the ultimate foundation of the reality of all times that could stand before other times. Eternity, which transpires in the heuristic experience of language as an alternative to the end of time, is out of reach and cannot enter into time to save time as time. This is why the meaning of the Incarnation of the Word is not to save time as time but to sublate it into eternity. In virtue of Christ who conquered the death of every human being as well as eternal life for every human being, and made it reality in the life of the Church, each death is not just a death, but a death into the death of Christ, the eschatological union of time and eternity. As a result, death is not just an end of time but an end of time sublated by Christ's time inaugurated in the reality of the Church endowed with consciousnesses and wills making possible that human "I"s subsist.

4.1.2.2. As a Result, the Irreversibility of Time of Any Kind, Individual Cultural—Cultures of Peoples and Nations—Psychological, Existential, Biological, Geological and Cosmic Time, Will Be Measured not by Uniformly Reversible Changes but by Christ's Time, and My Theological "I" is Revealed as the Expression of God's Eternity Within the Church (IV)

Our fourth eschatological assertion implies the following traditional topics of eschatology: "It is not I, but Christ who lives in me"; faith, charity and hope "remain" in the Church; time and eternal life; and sanctifying grace.

Since Christ conquered every time, there is no time which does not end up in eternity. There will be no other measurement for time except the time of Christ. Because of Christ's Incarnation, death and resurrection are both a possibility as well as an absolute reality for everyone. The time of Self, of the Ego, the body, the soul, the theological "I" as well as cultural, both individual and communitarian, the psychological, existential, biological, geological and cosmic times, all enter into Christ's time. And this means that Christ becomes the source and objective of the motivation of the Self. The unorganized drives and desires (Ego) are sublated by Christ's organized drives and desires (see below, particular judgment). The body, the unified field of energy conditioned by biological and cosmic times, will come under the gravitational force of Christ's risen body, and as a result, the linear direction of entropy flowing from a maximum level of entropy, i.e., the degradation of matter and energy in the universe to an ultimate state of uniformity, will be changed into the direction to a maximum level of energy, elevating the matter and energy in the universe to an ultimate state of active diversity. I will understand myself not in time (by my reversible changes) but in God, i.e., in eternity. This is the new creation, the new knowledge Paul is speaking of in Gal 2, 20: "Christ lives in me. It is no longer I who live."

Likewise my faith, charity and hope, my theological "I" will not be measured by uniformly reversible changes as before death, but only by Christ's time. Whereas before death I could have the certitude that faith is true, but I could not exclude that the opposite to faith, sc., non-belief, is impossible (cf. possibility of doubt in faith). Once my faith-time is sublated by Christ's time I can also see that it is absolutely impossible that the opposite to faith (non-belief) is possible. At this instance faith is replaced by beatific vision.

And so there is change in my love of God too. Once my charity-time is sublated by Christ's time, I can see myself as God's own, as God's word who loves God as God loves, i.e., with all one's heart, and mind and might.

Finally there is a change in my hope, too. Before death I trusted in God's promise expressed in human words. Now this word is recognized as the word of God, on which one relies forever not as the word of God in human words, but as the words of Jesus Christ, the infallible word of God, the giver of eternal life itself.

Thus the entry in Christ's time means that my personal time, my personal "I" becomes once and for all the inalienable expression of God's eternity in the Church, which always was the mystery of my time and of my life. Eternity will be the fulfillment of my beginning, which is God's free, irreversible, non-repeatable unique will for me, and can be described as the experience of God's unique and personal creative love of me as the expression of his eternity in Christ, the eschatological union of time and eternity which in its fulfillment is establishing the Church. Paul expresses this by *pneuma*, the inner, imperishable one opposed to the other, perishable, decaying "I" (2 Cor 4, 16-18) when the general notion of soul takes on a new communitarian meaning.

For further consideration sanctifying grace can serve as a guiding principle. Sanctifying grace in theology has been considered as a form of anticipation of the beatific vision. By virtue of sanctifying grace I am the son or daughter of God in Jesus Christ. Once my time is sublated by Christ's time, there is a change which can be expressed grammatically by the statement "the son and daughter of God in Jesus Christ I am." Whereas before death "I am" was epistemologically first so that in the light of myself I could see and understand my time in Christ, after death the son or daughter of God in Jesus Christ is epistemologically the first one in the light of whom I can see and understand the time of Christ as my real time and my time as Christ's time.

The following illustration may be helpful. Suppose that I visualize my lifetime in faith as being in a crowd looking at God; then, after death in the beatific vision, "being in Christ's time" I would see myself as one in the crowd looking, as it were, from the point of view of God. I understand myself as God has always understood me. Or, in other words, eternity is understood as the foundation of my time. Unlike before my death, when I understood myself first and then through me and in me God, after death I understand God first and then myself in God. I came to an end when I entered Christ's time, the Church, the realization of the eschatological union of time and eternity, by the sacrament of baptism. My sharing in Christ's time is not independent of the relationship I have established with the world within the Church, because the Church, as the sacrament of the eschatological union of time and eternity, is the only way of entering eternity for a being which is not God. Besides God no one can have eternity unless he/she existed in time "first," because eternity is God and consequently it is one. The possibility of entering eternity for a being which is not God had been opened by the Incarnation of God, which inaugurated the Church as the fulfillment of the Christ's eschatological union of time and eternity.

4.1.3. *Eternity is Inalienable Irreversibility Inalienably Measured by Inalienable Irreversibility*

Boethius's definition of eternity as the simultaneous and complete possession of infinite life (*De consolatione Philosophiae*, L, 5, p. 5; ML 63, 858) is the traditional one. For Rahner eternity is the plenitude of being (Rahner and Vorgrimler, 1965, p. 151), the absolute possession of itself. But Thomas Aquinas's description, pointing to God, is the best: God is eternity (*S. theol.* 1, 10, 2 ad 3). We can appreciate Thomas's description especially if we start not from the idea of being, but from the reality of time. By summarizing all that we have said so far we can say the following.

The relation between time and eternity can be considered in four different ways: eternity is infinite time; eternity is timeless; eternity includes time (Stinson, 1977); eternity is the sublating fulfillment of time. If our description of time is legitimate and our Christology is sound we have to opt for the last one. Since our time comes to an end by entering Christ's time, eternity should be conceived as the sublating fulfillment of time. Christ, the eschatological union of time and eternity, revealed death as the threshold of time and eternity where eternity appears as the meaning of time and time as the expression of eternity. Because the uniformly returning changes, the measurement of time, are not just something external to the nature of time, but really intrinsic, making time what time is, the axis of the opposite, i.e., that of reversibility and irreversibility, time cannot express eternity except by its own sublation. Time can overcome its paradoxical nature by negating itself as irreversibility measured by reversible changes and thus reach eternity as its own fulfillment. Consequently eternity can be expressed in our language as the sublation of the reversible changes, the measurement of my time, by Christ's irreversibility so that irreversibility of my time becomes ultimate inalienability, i.e., the ultimate denial of death as radical alienation.

By entering Christ's time my inalienability emerges as the meaning of my irreversibility, active in every form of my sub-times. As time and eternity, so too irreversibility and inalienability become correlate terms. Thus in brief we can say that eternity is irreversible inalienability (the Father) inalienably measured (the Son) by inalienable irreversibility (the Holy Spirit), which is one model for a theological scrutiny of the mystery of the Trinity: God as inalienability inalienably inalienable (Horvath, 1977, pp. 293-94). In other words, God is measured by God as God and, therefore, inconceivable as non-existent. God is the only one who is and can say: "I am who I am." Eternity is God and God is eternity.

4.2. Individual and Eternity

4.2.1. *Since Death Is the End of Time as well as the Entering Into Christ's Time, It Follows that at the Threshold of Time and Eternity Christ is the Only Judge and the Only Judge for Everyone (V)*

The fifth eschatological assertion includes the elucidation of the following traditional topics of eschatology: individual and universal judgment and the tension between the two.

According to the Old Testament God is the judge who vindicates his right and the right of all those who had been deprived of it. The judgment day, the day of Yahweh meant both a doom and a deliverance. It is described either as historical reality or as a great cosmic catastrophe (Is 13, 1-14, 32; Jon 2, 1-3. 10). Already in the pre-exilic period judgment meant that the old world would be replaced by a new one.

We still read in the New Testament about God as the judge who punishes bad and evil deeds (Rom 2, 3-11; 3, 6; 14; 10; 1 Thes 1, 5) and rewards good deeds, like prayers, fasting and almsgiving (Mt 6, 4, 15-16). But there is a new judge as well, sc., Jesus Christ, who is progressively replacing God as judge (Mt 25, 31-46; 7, 23; Mk 13, 43. Lk 13, 25-27; 1 Thes 4, 6; 1 Cor 4, 4; 11, 32; 2 Cor 5, 10). And the way Jesus judges is also new. John says that Christ did not come to judge but to save (Jn 3, 17). The judgment is carried out by the actions themselves which either follow or do not follow what Jesus said (Jn 12, 47). In other words, the judgment is *ipso facto* by the very work one performs. Therefore, Jesus does not have to utter a sentence. The acceptance or rejection of Jesus brings the judgment upon one (Jn 3, 17-19).

We notice also that the goodness and evil of an action or behaviour come from its relation to Jesus Christ (cf. Mt 25, 31-46). Social or sexual codes of Christian life do not have their final validity and obliging force from a natural order, but from a natural order transformed by the resurrection of Jesus Christ. Words, actions, behaviours, etc., are defined as good or bad, permitted or prohibited as much as they are an ambiguous or unambiguous expression of the risen life of faith, charity and hope based on the trinitarian life of God, the Father, the Son and the Holy Spirit (Horvath, 1977). No one can enter eternity unless he/she takes on the characteristics of the trinitarian life, sc., the generosity of the Father, the integrity of the Son and the authenticity of the Holy Spirit which cannot be achieved except through faith in Jesus Christ with charity of the Father and by hope in the Holy Spirit. Thus judgment is the work of faith, charity and hope, which express themselves in the universal language of integrity, generosity and authenticity which, in their turn, find their fulfillment in faith, charity and hope. The lack of these three is known in ordinary language as pride (the lack of integrity) greediness (the lack of generosity) and incontinence (the lack of authenticity). These latter ones are those which bring about negative judgment, sc., condemnation.

Thus the result of judgment is that all those who have the work of charity (generosity), faith (integrity) and hope (authenticity) will rise to life and all those who have the work of greediness (lack of charity), pride (lack of faith) and incontinence (lack of hope) will rise to condemnation (cf. Jn 5, 28-29). Thus there are two kinds of resurrection: resurrection of life and resurrection of judgment.

It should be noted that in the New Testament judgment is consistently linked with eternal life and with resurrection. Jesus is the judge, because he is risen and has made eternity accessible to any time. Judgment and resurrection are connected and so is death with both, because in death time is sublated by Christ's time. It is precisely because time is sublated by his time that Jesus is the only judge and his judgment takes place on the day of resurrection. He shall come to judge the living and the dead, as we read in the *Apostolic Tradition* of Hippolytus (215-17) (DS 10). As the Apostles' Creed, so the later councils like Lateran IV (DS 801; Tanner, 1990, p. 230) Lyons II (DS 859) reiterate that we appear in our bodies before the Lord so that each may receive good or evil, life or judgment, according to the work one did in his/her body (cf. 2 Cor 5, 10). This judgment is described in Matthew as a judgment on the last day. Here we find the foundation for the tradition of professing judgment, sc., individual and universal judgment.

4.2.1.1. Individual Judgment

It is the faith of the Church, expressed in its documents, that the outcome of appearing before the Lord can be twofold: eternal salvation which might include the intermediate state of purgatory, or eternal damnation (cf. *Benedictus Deus*, Constitution of Benedict XII, DS 1000-1002). Being a judgment *ipso facto* based on the work one did in one's earthly life, the judgment is pronounced by the one on trial. It is a self-knowledge activated by entering into Christ's time. Since death is the experience of one's end in the form of the end of one's self-defence mechanism and since Christ is the only judge for everyone, there can be only two outcomes of being measured by Christ's time. The first is the recognition of the complete failure of one's self-defence mechanism in establishing the ground of one's inalienability and taking up Christ's time as one's real time; thus recognizing one's life as an expression of God's eternity in Christ's body. The second is the refusal to accept one's incapability of establishing the ground of one's own inalienability by holding up one's time against Christ's time as a time for eternity. The first is salvation and is called heaven. The second is damnation and is called hell. One is unselfish altruism, exercised in integrity, generosity and authenticity. The other is selfish egoism, manifested in incontinence, greediness and pride.

Thus salvation will be a once-and-for-all redemption from all the consequences of original sin which, as the basis of any other sin, is nothing but a turning of a creaturely existence destined to be open to others by an unselfish altruism, into a self-centred egoism. Each sin is a reaffirmation of the self-centred egoism as the only ground of survival, as the only ultimate reality and meaning of human existence.

4.2.1.2. Individual and Universal Judgment

Once the Church became aware that death and eternity cannot be separated and that entering into eternity is not in time and that therefore the entering into heaven cannot be postponed until the last day of the universe (cf. *Benedictus Deus* DS 1000-1003), the problem of the relation and distinction between individual and universal judgments emerged. If the soul can immediately after death enter heaven, there must be a particular judgment. Yet the other judgment, i.e., the one on the last day when the soul will appear with its body before the judgment seat of Christ, cannot be disregarded.

But if one enjoys the beatific vision in heaven, how can one stand again before the judgment seat of Christ? How can the last judgment be a real judgment? Is it not just a great parade or show staged of an event which took place long before? The lack of experiencing the resurrection of the body in time, on the one hand, and the firm faith that judgment, resurrection and eternity cannot be separated, on the other, suggested that there must be more than one judgment.

But as time passed the theologians progressively agreed more and more that the individual and the universal judgment cannot be completely separated. The last judgment for the individual should not be something external, but an internal reality based on an internal dialectic between the individual and universal eschatology (Rahner, 1965, p. 150). Anyone who wants to make a contribution to the question of the distinction and unity of the individual and universal judgments should keep in mind that according to the faith of the Church each one will be judged and receive good or evil according to what they have done in the body (cf. 2 Cor 5, 10; Rom 14, 10-12; Mt 25, 31-46, etc.), and that death is the end of time as we know it now and that Christ will judge on the day of resurrection. To uphold this firm belief and to reconcile it with both the doctrine of the two judgments and the revelation of the resurrection of body related to the last day we propose a distinction between the actuality of the resurrection from death from the point of view of God, i.e., from eternity, and that from the point of view of the world still in time.

4.2.1.3. Death, Judgment and the Resurrection of the Dead Are One Event Accomplished from the Point of View of God, i.e., Eternity, but Unaccomplished from the Point of View of the World Still in Time (VI)

If we admit the meaning of time and eternity, as we described above, we have to say that death, judgment and the resurrection of the dead are one event (2 Cor 5, 5; Phil 1, 22-23; 1 Cor 15, 43-44, 53; Rom 8, 18). Of the three, death is the only one which can be verified in time and space. The world in time cannot yet experience the judgment at the resurrection of the dead. It is only when the cosmic world, too, has fully entered into eternity that judgment and resurrection can be experienced by the world (Rom 2, 5) and the life of the risen ones can be manifest (Col 3,4).

Since Christ conquered death and made eternity the end of all times, good and bad will rise (Jn 5, 28-29; Acts 24, 15) following the judgment made final in death. In death the whole human person, including the body as a unified field of energy balancing biological and psychological times, is risen not in the cosmos but in eternity, which obviously cannot be perceived by anyone who is still in time.

The model of the horizon-event of black holes assumed by some astronomers could serve as an illustration. As there is no way to follow the light (a condition of timely perception) beyond the horizon-event, there is even less of a way to follow the light in a dimension where time and space come to an end. To witness in time the resurrection of the body, which is not in time, is just not possible, unless eternity is conceived as endless time, and survival, but not real resurrection, is admitted, a tenet which in our view is not correct.

Only through death can one experience and witness the resurrection of the dead, which is like a "different universe" within our universe, and the relation between the two can be experienced only by leaving one and entering the other by way of no-return. The last sight which one in time can have of someone's entering eternity is the sight of the dead body, the end of time. This does not mean that one passing through death and lingering, much like an astronaut heading for a black hole, might be seen as entering the horizon-event for millions of years afterwards, even though his passage was effected immediately. The model of black holes is not to be considered as a proof of any kind. It is only a means of helping our mind to get out of traps which our visual imagination sets in the way of speculative thinking.

The judgment of the last day only means that what is already an accomplished reality will be expressed, not just in the life of the dead ones, but in the whole cosmic world expected to come to its end when it fully enters eternity. Yet the end of the world should not be conceived as something which is not taking place already. It does take place progressively, since Jesus Christ as the eschatological union of time and eternity by his death and resurrection has inaugurated resurrection time, which is the progressive entering of the whole cosmic world into eternity. This progressive entering of the cosmic world into eternity is due to the active role which the "already" risen ones play with the risen Christ. Being risen already means that the risen body is no longer functioning as a sort of organism producing the required responses to stimuli. Rather, by virtue of Christ, it is a force which communicates new direction to the world by turning its natural "rundown" in an opposite direction, sc., towards the resurrection of the cosmic world (cf. Rom 8, 9-13). This implies that our present world is already entering into eternity, even though we cannot experience it. To express this in a more concrete term, we can say that heaven, where Jesus Christ and his Mother "are" with their risen bodies, is a heaven "made" of our cosmic world and not of some unknown ethereal otherworld.

The close relation between universal and individual judgments is further postulated by our concept of time as a multiplicity of subtimes. With my death, my resurrection is complete, since my personal "I" has reached inalienability in Christ's time. But there are many other times in the world with which my times are still connected in one way or another and the balance of which I was and which determined my entering Christ's time. Thus my resurrection is not complete. The resurrection-time inaugurated by Christ's time is not over because there are people in time who as a consequence of my times benefit or suffer as they move towards eternity. I have entered Christ's time; I am in eternity yet what remains of my times has not entered fully into eternity.

This model will be further developed in dealing with the mystery of purgatory and of the resurrection of human society and of the cosmic world. But now a few words will be in order to explain how our concept of the resurrection of the dead "already" differs from those views which Paul and Irenaeus rightly rejected.

In 2 Tim 2, 17-18 we read of Hymenaeus and Philetus, who claimed that the resurrection has already taken place. Their view was rejected, as was that of Rheginos, a Valentinian from the second century (cf. Irenaeus *Adv. Her.* 5, Cor 5, 1). Hymenaeus and Philetus, like Rheginos motivated by Col 2, 12-13; 3, 1; Eph 2, 6; 2 Cor 5, 1), believed that we are already in heaven and the resurrection has taken place.

Irenaeus's rejection of the belief that ascension to heaven happens immediately after death is understandable, if we consider the gnostic, spiritualistic interpretation of man. The timeless resurrection of the Valentinians was a liberation from the body, which in their view was inaugurated by the mystical resurrection taking place in baptism (Rom 6, 5; Eph 2, 6). Unlike that of Hymenaeus and Philetus and that of Rheginos, the interpretation we present is in the future tense (cf. Rom 6, 3-11; 8, 18-39; 11, 17; 1 Cor 15, 12-34) for all those who live on earth. But for all those who are dead, present and future tenses are of no concern. In 1979 the Sacred Congregation of the Doctrine of the Faith, in its *Letter on Certain Questions Concerning Eschatology* (*AAS* 1979, p. 941), requested that if one proposes an immediate resurrection of the dead after death a distinction should be made between the bodily glorification of the Virgin Mary by her assumption and the bodily glorification of all other faithful. This we will do in the next section.

4.2.1.4. Difference Between the Resurrection of Jesus Christ, the Assumption of Mary and Our Resurrection Following Immediately Our Death and Judgment

All those who died, are judged, and risen in their bodies do not cease to be related to the cosmos in time. But there is a difference between the relation that Jesus and Mary have to the cosmos in time and the relation the rest of the human race has. The Church believes that both Jesus and Mary were without sin (cf. the dogma of the Immaculate Conception, DS 2803); therefore, their times left no traces of incontinence, greediness and pride in the world. Their integrity, generosity and authenticity fully expressed the integrity of the Son, the generosity of the Father and the authenticity of the Holy Spirit. Using our temporal language, we can say that both Jesus and Mary are already co-extensive and contemporary to each time of the universe. Their resurrection is revealed both in the heaven of eternity and in the world of time, not as reality experienced by the senses, but as reality expressed by the revealed word of God. All other times, being sinful, left their traces of incontinence, greediness and pride in time and, therefore, their resurrection cannot be revealed as fully realized until the entire cosmos dies and enters into eternity. Until that event, the cosmos is not yet the expression of our being loved and willed by God the Father forever, as in the case of Jesus Christ and Mary. In other words, Jesus and Mary were judged by both God and the world. The judgment of the world has been revealed by God in Jesus' resurrection and Mary's corporeal assumption into heaven. Consequently, in Mary's case there is no intermediate state between particular judgment and universal judgment. As a matter of fact, the assumption of Mary confirms that the distance between particular and universal judgments cannot be measured by our time but only by Christ's time, the eternity of God. The dogma of Mary's assumption indicates also that cosmic eternity is not measurable by the dimension of cosmic time.

4.2.2. Eternal Life as Heaven is Entering the Trinitarian God's Eternity: The Time of Christ is My Time (VII)

In listing biblical terms describing eternal life, besides heaven and paradise (cf. Lk 23, 43), we have to consider the concepts of kingdom of God, of angels, beatitude, glorification, beatific vision and so on. We will divide them into three categories of language: space, person, and time.

4.2.2.1. Space-Language: Heaven, Paradise

The word "heaven" in the New Testament refers to the kingdom of God (Mt 5, 2). It means the presence of God and his reign where his will is recognized (Horvath, 1975, pp. 152-55). It is the place where the glory of God is experienced as a sort of "weight" of his existence in the form of being captured by God's beauty, goodness and justice, etc. Seeing the glory of God is being fascinated by God's being as the most valuable person for me. The glory of God is beauty, love, and so on, all that one can desire. Heaven is where our Father is (Mt 6, 9: 9, 5,47; 7, 21; 12, 50). The book of Revelation describes heaven as a heavenly city which reflects the nature of God (Rev 21, 9-27) and this is the place also where Jesus is. It is built of jasper, the precious stone that forms the throne of God (cf. Rev 4, 31). There is no need of sun or moon or any light, since the glory of God is its light and its lamp is the Lamb (Rev 21, 23). The city has rivers, trees, crowns, etc., all symbols of eternal life. The inhabitants, we are told, all reign forever and ever (Rev 22, 5) and will be like pillars standing in a sanctuary which will never be destroyed. They will have the name of God written on their forehead and share Jesus' throne (Rev 22, 4).

Luke uses the term "paradise." Paradise is a place to be with Jesus on the day one dies (Lk 23, 43). The statement "Today you will be with me in paradise" is a new and unique statement unknown elsewhere in scripture.

Paul, too, employed the term paradise to describe his ecstatic rapture of being caught up to the heights of heaven without knowing that it was in the body or out of the body (2 Cor 12, 2). We can find the term paradise once more in Rev 2, 7 where the tree of life is placed, an allusion to Gn 2, 9.

Heaven and paradise both mean a place where one can be with Jesus in the presence of God forever. Thus both imply person-language as well.

4.2.2.2. Person-Language: Being with Jesus, Seeing God, Beatific Vision, Angels, Glorification/Ascension, Kingdom of God, Beatitudes

For Paul heaven is not so much a place, but being with Christ. Wherever Jesus is, there is heaven for Paul. Eternal life is being with the Lord (2 Cor 5, 5). His home is to be with the Lord, and this takes place at the moment of death (2 Cor 5, 8; cf. Phil 1, 22-23).

John extends the Pauline view of eternity as being with Jesus in the Trinitarian God. Eternal life is that the Father and the Son and the Holy Spirit will dwell in the believer (Jn 14, 23-26).

Another form of person-language of heaven is seeing God and Jesus face to face. Seeing face to face implies a knowledge of oneself as one is known by God (1 Cor 13, 12). The mutual knowledge between God and the faithful has a Christological connotation, since we find it in the context where Paul talks about the charismatic gifts given to the mystical body of Christ. The seeing of God as salvation is found also in Mt 5, 8; 1 Jn 3, 2; Rev 22, 3-4. In Rev 22, 3-4 seeing God face to face is replaced by seeing Jesus face to face. The doctrine of the Church about the beatific vision relies on this kind of biblical person-language. The scriptural doctrine can then be further illustrated theologically by the scholastic interpretation of understanding.

In the Constitution of *Benedictus Deus* from the year 1336 we read that we can "see the divine essence intuitively and face to face so that as the object is concerned no creature acts as a medium of vision, but the divine essence shows itself plainly, clearly and openly" (DS 1000).

The occasion of the Constitution was the Bull of 1334 entitled, *Ne super his*, in which John XXII, interpreting Rev 6, 9, wrote that the saints remain under the altar and see only the humanity of Christ until the final judgment. In 1336 Benedict XII made public John XXII's revocation of his own interpretation of Rev 6, 9 (Dykmans, 1973, 1975). The Council of Florence in 1439, in its decree on union with the Greeks, reaffirmed the teaching of Benedict XII adding to it a trinitarian note by saying that those who are purified after death "are promptly taken up into heaven and see clearly the triune God himself just as he is, some more perfectly than others according to their respective merits" (DS 1305; Tanner, 1990, pp. 527-28). We should also remember that the Council of Vienna in 1312 declared against Beghards and Beguines that the *lumen gloriae*, "the light of glory," is needed to elevate the soul to see God and to enjoy God in blessedness (DS 895; Tanner, 1990, p. 383).

Scholastic theology tried to elaborate on the meaning of the biblical expression of face to face by using its own metaphysical speculation. Since God has no face, the meaning of seeing God face to face can be that there is no created, finite entity which could mediate a direct knowledge of God, i.e., a knowledge of the way God knows himself. The direct vision of God requires special direct relationship between God and the creature. This special relationship is explained by saying that the beatific knowledge is unlike any knowledge that is gained by the mediation of an act of mind in which and/or from which (like a substitute [*species*] for the object to be known), the object is known. In the beatific vision God takes the place of the act of mind in which and/or from which, as a "substitute" for the object to be known, he is known. One could say that a reality of the mind as a knower (*species impressa*) is the being of God himself. In other words, God immediately unites himself to the risen one following the pattern of the hypostatic union, with the difference that this takes place not on a substantial, existential level, as in the case of Jesus Christ, but on the level of actually knowing and loving. Thus the ones enjoying the beatific vision exist by their own existence, yet they know and love God not only by means of their own being but through God's own being. They know God not only as their cause and end as in the natural order, but as the object of the divine beatitude, being happy by the same numerically one beatitude by which the Triune God is happy. It is a communion of beatitude which is possible only by Christ's grace. The vision of God, as Thomas Aquinas explains it, means really a unity of beatitude with God (Horvath 1966, pp 229-55). And the beatitude, the perfect achievement of happiness, is the perfect unity of knowing and loving with the plenitude of being in God.

It was unfortunate that the later scholastics failed to see the importance of the concept of beatitude in the system of Thomas Aquinas. Their discussions focused more on how the immediate union of God with the knowing mind of the faithful can be understood. Progressively various kinds of mediations known to them through the epistemology of their times were removed from the beatific vision. So they said that in the beatific vision there is no *medium ex quo*, i.e., no medium, the knowledge of which is first required to know something else (therefore the beatific vision is neither a deductive nor inductive knowledge, nor is it a syllogism). There is no *medium in quo*, the similitude of which would lead to the knowledge of something else. In other words, there is no metaphor, no mirror, no sign. They called these mediums *species* and they said that God is not known in the beatific vision through *species* as an act of something else.

Others, like Gabriel Vazquez (1549-1604), admitting this, required a *medium quo*, i.e., something which functions not as an object of knowledge, but something which helps the intellect to be able to understand God as God does. Some, who were afraid that *medium quo* still might imperil the immediacy of God, used instead the expression *medium sub quo* which would be required not because of the object, sc., God, who is the most intelligible subject one can think of, and who can by his omnipotence unite himself to a creature, but by reason of the human intellect, which needs to be elevated and strengthened to be able to be united immediately with God. And this *medium sub quo* is the *lumen gloriae* which the Council of Vienna declared as necessary for us to be able to accept God's great closeness. This light of glory is a sort of created entity capable of growth and thus explains the difference in the way people enjoy the beatific vision.

Modern scholastic theologians like Maurice de la Taille (1928) and K. Rahner (1965) expressed the immediate relationship between God and the just ones by the notion of quasi-formal causality. The new relationship, they argued, cannot be based only on efficient causality, but rather on a formal causality, like the one existing between body and soul, though not exactly the same, because that would imply pantheism. This is why they named it "quasi" formal causality. The beatific vision is, therefore, not a knowledge reaching out of the subject to another object, but rather the knowledge of one's self, a state of being reflected upon oneself and being present to oneself. And this knowledge of God in/of himself is communicated to the faithful.

Another person-language way of describing heaven is angelology. Angelology is part of eschatology and has considerable importance for a better understanding of it. No eschatology and description of heaven is complete without analyzing the meaning of the angels in revelation.

Angelology has a special meaning for Christian anthropology, Christology, theology of God and for eschatology. In Christian anthropology, angelology prevents us from considering human existence as the only rational and spiritual existence besides God. In Christology it underscores that salvation history in its totality has its goal in Christ. Christ is the head of angels as well, who receive their grace through him. Christ is therefore not just an angel. In the theology of God the function of angelology is to prevent theologians from seeing God as just an angel-like being, though such a concept is assumed in 1 Pt 4, 6.

The origin of angelology may be Persian, though an earlier knowledge of super-human spirits is possible. Certainly the Old and the New Testaments take the existence of the angels for granted. Whether the existence of the angels is a revealed truth is disputed by some theologians. Those who believe so refer to the first chapter of the Fourth Lateran Council which is a profession of faith. The Council says "We firmly believe ... that there is only one true God ... the devil and other wicked spirits were created by God good by nature, but they became of themselves evil" (DS 800). From the point of view of the hermeneutics of conciliar theology this statement makes a stronger case for the existence of the angels than the one in Vatican I teaching that God created out of nothing both the spiritual and the corporeal creature, the angelical and the cosmic and later the human creature (DS 3002). As we stated earlier the correct interpretation of a profession of faith ought to be sought not only in the context of the dispute, as, for example, in the case of the Albigenses the idea of metempsychosis (DS 800-802), but in the nature of a Creed which, first of all, affirms that it is God and not a human creature who revealed.

Angelology's relevance for eschatology transcends the question of the existence of angels. First of all, any eschatology that ignores angelology easily ends up in an angelology confusing eternal life with an incorruptible unfailing existence of purely spiritual being in no need of resurrection of the body. Furthermore, it is important to notice that the multiplicity of times we presented before is further supported by the day or "time of the angels" known in patristic theology as *hem-*

era, which is different from the "time" of God as well as from the times of human beings. The time of the angels is not eternity. We are told that angels were given the choice of making an irreversible decision, but without a chance of repentance. The eschatological "days" of the angels are different from the eschatological days of humanity.

Another important role of the angels for eschatology comes from the tradition that Christ will appear on the day of judgment surrounded by the angels. This means not only that Christ is the Lord and head of the angels, but also that there is no eternity for the angels without Christ. It means also that the last day will be the last day of the whole created world as such and not only that of our universe. Time will cease to be, "everywhere" and "forever."

But the most important role of angelology for our eschatology is that we consider it as one more form of person-language describing heaven as seeing God face to face (Mt 18, 10). The risen life in heaven is a life without marriage (cf. Mt 22, 30-32; Mk 12, 25; Lk 20, 36). It is a glorious life in the presence of God (1 Cor 15, 43; Rom 8, 18; 2 Cor 4, 17; Phil 3, 21; Col, 3, 4), powerful (1 Cor 15, 43; Phil 3, 21), invisible in our time (2 Cor 4, 17), spiritual, *pneumatikos* (1 Cor 15, 43), etc., characteristics of the angels as presented in biblical tradition.

As the good angels are models of what heaven is, so the bad angels reveal what hell is. Demonology is another form of personal language describing hell. In Patristic tradition the sin of the angels reveals the real depth of a sin, which is not sexual. It is the sin of envy and jealousy when one repines over the good of the others. It is the sin of the one who sees the good and success of others as a hindrance to one's own singular excellence, threatened by the excellence of the others. It is the opposite to the generosity of God, shared in the beatific vision of God. The angels are expressions of the glory of God and as such are the paradigms of our glorification.

Glorification is another term used in biblical sources to express the presence of God, or rather, the closeness of God in heaven. Glorification is sharing in the glory, the *doxa* of God, which means being esteemed or loved the way God is loved and esteemed. It is having the full radiance of the lovable God, his power and attractiveness. And this is what Jesus prayed for when he asked that he might be glorified in all those who had been given to him by his Father (Jn 17, 4-5,10,22-26). He prayed that the power and beauty of God might be visible in him and through him in all. Thus glorification means that God will be lovable in all who have entered into his presence and who, in turn, share his "awesome" loveliness, the "tremendum" and, at the same time, the "fascinans" being of God.

The glorification which is described in the Acts of the Apostles as Jesus' ascension and sitting at the right hand of the Father is a new presence of Jesus to the world. Sitting at the right hand of the Father means that he has the power of communicating the divine beatitude to everyone else. He is the only Saviour who can save and let us participate in the eternity of God (Horvath, 1975, pp. 242-49). Consequently, one who is glorified in Jesus shares in his saving beatifying power. God's presence is communicated to humans and through them to the world, to the whole universe. To be glorified by God means to share in Christ's role as the Saviour of the world by communicating God's beatitude to the world. This is the program of the beatitudes of the kingdom of God.

The beatitude of the kingdom of God is the last term using person-language to reveal what heaven is. Kingdom in its obvious sense is a spatial model, yet already in the early sources of gospel tradition the kingdom of God is identified with Christ. The kingdom of God is Jesus himself (Horvath, 1975, pp. 145-47). The parables of the kingdom along with the beatitudes are the description of heaven as being with Jesus.

The atmosphere of the kingdom of God is joy (Mt 5, 2-12; Lk 6, 20-23). All who enter will be saved and comforted, rejoice and be gladdened. They are called *makarioi*, blessed, which means that God is praising them with a special warmth of his "heart" (*barak*). This is the fulfillment of Jesus' prayer in Jn 15, 11 that his joy may be shared by his followers and that their joy may be full and that they may have his joy fulfilled in themselves (Jn 17, 13) because of the fullness of God (Eph 2, 14; 3, 19; 4, 13).

Terms opposite to the ordinary meaning of happiness, like poverty, mourning, hunger, thirst and persecutions are connected with the state of happiness in order to suggest the mysterious nature and depth of this new happiness. The puzzles of the kingdom of God reveal the sublime happiness of heaven. In the parables we are able to sense a unique description of heaven. They are in good part dealing with the present situation of the kingdom of God, yet they are images of heaven as well. They describe the kingdom of God as God's doing, which we find more precious than anything else (Mt 13, 44-46). There will be a great variety of differences (Mt 13, 23-32, 47-50) together with a fundamental split in two groups, one "shining forth like the sun" and the other "burning in a blazing furnace." The latter remains in the somewhat familiar condition of the present life, whereas the former accepts *metanoia*, the change in beatitude, the laying down of one's own happiness and the taking up the happiness of others as one's own. Is not this the meaning of the puzzling doctrine of the beatitudes?

The beatitude of God, as Thomas Aquinas saw it, is the fullness of being with the unity of knowledge and love. One cannot be happy unless one has everything, i.e., the plenitude of being which is known and loved as such. Otherwise no one can be happy. From this description it follows that God alone can be happy, and there is no real happiness for a created being except by entering into the happiness of God. And this takes place, according to Thomas Aquinas, in charity (*S. theol.* 2, 2, 23, 1). Charity is a friendship between God and us based not upon a communication of created goods (like the natural love of God based on acknowledging God as our origin and end) but upon the communication of the beatitude of God when we and God are happy with one beatitude, that of God. This is the meaning of *metanoia* in beatitude: I am happy, because God is happy, I am sharing God's happiness (Horvath, 1966, pp. 229-55).

4.2.2.3. *Time-Language: Eternal Life, Time of Christ and the Time of Others As My Time*

Time-language describing heaven is widespread in the different books of the New Testament. We read about eternal life in the Synoptics (Mk 10, 17,30; Mt 19, 16, 29; Lk 10, 25; 16, 9; 18, 18,30), in Pauline literature (Rom 2, 7; 5, 21; 6, 22,23; Gal 6, 8; 1 Tim 1, 16; 6, 12; Tit 1, 2; 3, 7), in Acts 13, 46,48, in Jude 21, but mostly in Johannine writings (Jn 1, 2; 2, 25; 3, 15,16,36; 4, 14,36; 5, 24,39; 6,27,40,47,54,68; 10, 28; 12, 25,50; 17, 2, 3). Without any further elaboration as to what eternal life might mean, we are told that it is the gift of Jesus Christ and it refers to the life of God. The gift of eternal life means the gift of God's life.

Since the space-language describing heaven is less central in the New Testament than time-language, heaven should not be envisioned as an infinite space, but rather God as eternity. In trinitarian terms God as eternity means that God's generosity never will be alienated by his integrity and both will never be alienated by his authenticity. In other words, not one of the three persons in God can be alienated by the other. Each one holds up the "time" of the others. Heaven expressed in time-language is therefore taking up Christ's time with the times of the other sons and daughters of resurrection (Lk 20, 36) as one's own time by sharing the inalienability of the Son. This short statement is the summary of all that we have said about death as a real end as well as a real entry into eternity (see above 4.1.2.-4.1.3; cf. also 3.5).

4.2.3. Eternal Life as Hell is an Effort to Hold Up One's Own Time as Time for Eternity and Time For Others (VIII)

Like heaven, hell too can be described by space-, person- and time-language.

4.2.3.1. Space-Language: Sheol, Gehenna, Fire, Kingdom of Satan, a Place Without God

In the Old Testament Sheol is the abode of the dead, the world of shadows (Jb 30, 23), where no one can praise God (Ps 6,6). It is an obscurity (Ps 87, 7.13), the deepest region of the earth (Dt 32, 22), into which all beings descend (Is 38, 16; Ez 31, 14). Its terrifying aspect increases as Israel's faith in the one God is put more to the test. Korah, Dathan and Abiram (Nm 16, 27), who rebelled against Moses, were swallowed up by Sheol, because they rejected Yahweh. A fire came down and consumed all who followed the rebels (Nm 16, 1-35). The same Sheol would devour all those Israelites who did not keep the commandments of Yahweh (Is 5, 8-30). The image of fire as a means of punishment is frequent (cf. Sodom and Gomorrah in Gn 19, 23; Am 4, 11; Ps 11, 26).The worm will not die and the fire will never be quenched in the valley of Gehenna (Is. 66, 24), a place set up by the anger of Yahweh (Is 30, 33). A later tradition gave a new name to Sheol, sc., Gehenna, which is no longer a place where the dead go, but a place of punishment prepared by Yahweh for his enemies (Gn 19,24), and brought about by his anger (Is 30, 27-33; cf. Is 66, 24; *Assumption of Moses* 10, 19, and *Esdras* 1, 7, 36).

The Old Testament teaching is taken up by the New Testament. Gehenna is generally translated in English by the word "hell," an Anglo-Saxon word which means "hiding." In the New Testament *Hades* is the Greek word for Sheol (Mt 11, 23; 16, 18; Lk 10, 15; 16, 23; Acts 2, 27,31; Rev 1, 18; 6, 8; 20,13,14), more often Gehenna (Mt 5, 22,29; 10, 28; 18, 9; 23, 15,35; Mk 9, 43,45,47; Lk 12, 5; Jas 3, 6) and once Tartarus (2 Pet 2, 4).

Space-language is implicit in other images, like the blazing furnace (Mt 13, 45,50), flames and fire (Mt 5, 22; 18, 8,9; 25, 41; Mk 9, 43,45,47; Lk 16, 24), or a lake of burning sulphur (Rev 14, 10; 19, 20; 20, 10-15; 21, 8) and place of weeping and grinding of teeth (Mt 8, 11; 13, 42,50; 22, 13; 24, 51; 25, 30; Lk 13, 28).

It is remarkable that Matthew's gospel mentions hell, fire and grinding of the teeth more often than the other books of the New Testament. It is not the only one which describes the last judgment and the separation of the blessed ones from the condemned, but we find also that fire and grinding of teeth are added to passages where the parallel passages of the other Synoptics do not mention them (for example, the healing of the centurion's servant, Mt 8, 11, the parables of the darnel Mt 13, 42,50, of the wedding feast, Mt 22, 13, the wicked steward, Mt 24, 51, and the talents, Mt 25, 30).

Matthew's gospel prefers space-language in describing hell. The pains of hell expressed in space-language are those which the traditional theology called the pains of the senses (*poena sensus*) inflicted by the elements of the created world. There are other pains as well, called *poena damni*, i.e., being apart from Jesus Christ, the loss of the vision of God, expressed in person-language describing hell.

4.2.3.2. Person-Language: Being apart from Jesus Christ, Lack of the Vision of God

Whereas the space-language describing hell is borrowed from Old Testament tradition, the person-language describing hell is proper to the New Testament. One of the earliest books of the New Testament formulated it so: their punishment will be exclusion from the presence of the Lord (2 Thes 1, 9). This is the summary of the Matthean last judgment: Go away from me (Mt 26, 41). Since they failed to recognize Jesus in others they cannot be with him in the kingdom of God (1 Cor 1, 16; 6, 9; 2 Cor 2, 15; 4, 3).

Unlike the Old Testament, where belief in hell as threat or punishment seems to be prompted by angry frustration with the inability of keeping people on the way of God's commandments, the New Testament belief in hell results from the faith that there is no salvation without Christ. In other words, hell means that Jesus Christ is the only Saviour, and whoever is saved, is saved through Jesus Christ. That there is a hell is not because God wants to punish disobedient creatures, but because there can be no salvation without Christ. The belief in Jesus Christ as the only Saviour is the positive, and the belief in hell is the negative formulation of the same doctrine. One who does not believe in him is condemned. This means that there is no exception whatsoever to the belief that Jesus is the only Saviour of every human being. Belief in hell makes faith in Christ absolute, admitting no exception. In this way, hell is a Christological event and should be considered as such in Christology.

That hell is a Christological event does not pre-empt the problem of the real possibility and/or of the actuality of eternal damnation. The fact whether people are already in hell and/or whether anyone will ever be condemned has not been revealed. Mk 14, 21 and Mt 26, 24 refer to anyone who denies Jesus and not just to Judas. The passage is a threat rather than a verdict on Judas's individual judgment. The central issue which should be kept in mind in discussing the possibility of being condemned forever is that without Jesus there is no salvation, no sharing in the eternity of God, since he is the eschatological union of time and eternity. Sins can be and sins are, but they can be and are forgiven. But the lack of belief in Jesus Christ is a different matter. There is no other way to God who is eternity except the way God opened, sc., Jesus, who made eternity accessible to all. Good and bad behaviours are distinguished as they relate to Jesus Christ, who has identified himself with all of us. "What you do to any of the least of these, you do it to me" (Mt 25, 40) is the norm distinguishing salvific deeds from the non-salvific ones. This leads us to the time-language describing hell as eternal.

4.2.3.3. Time-Language: My Time is Time for All

The word "eternal," which is often the adjective of life and salvation, is applied only three times to fire (Mt 18, 8; 25, 41; Jude 7) and once to the punishment of hell (Mt 25, 46). Mk 9, 43,47-48 is an uncertain reading. The text saying that the worm does not die and the fire does not go out might refer to the ravine south of Jerusalem, where rubbish was burned and the constantly burning fire symbolized the place for the wicked (cf. Dan, 12, 2; 2 Esdras 7, 36; Enoch 27, 2; 90, 24-26). The place was seen as a symbol of separation from the community, living outside of human habitation.

In the book of Revelation, we find the image of a burning lake, which suggests annihilation rather than everlasting punishment. It suggests a real end after which, unlike after the first death, there is no resurrection, no life. The dead who came back for the judgment at the end of the world are annihilated.

There are two more texts stating that the unjust will rise, sc., Acts 24, 15 and Jn 5, 28 (for judgment), but they do not use the word "eternal."

Several texts say that there is an incompatibility between the two kingdoms, sc., the kingdom of God and the kingdom without God. But this would only mean that the kingdom of God, the time of Jesus, will never be sublated by any other time, whereas any other times which are not that of Jesus will surely pass away. The main point of these passages is, therefore, not so much that there is hell, but that Christ's time is forever (cf. Heb 6, 2 the judgment is eternal). Here is the reason that the Church could not accept the doctrine of apocatastasis.

The idea of being condemned to tormenting fire forever without any possibility of conversion can be seen as incompatible with the idea of a merciful and compassionate God and, for that matter, even with the magnanimity of any noble human being whose life is not threatened (a circumstance which might make the difference). Thus it is understandable that there were early writers of the Church who, inspired by the idea of apocatastasis of Acts 3, 21, defended a final reconciliation between God and the ones living in hell (see 1.2.5). Again and again there is a rebirth of the idea of apocatastasis (Scheffczyk, 1985). Some, like Rahner, hope that all eventually will be saved. There are many more universalist in hope than the adherents to outright apocatastasis, who "believe" that everybody will be definitively saved. But the right word here should not be "believe" but hope. The more so since Christian love demands that we hope for the salvation of everyone.

The Church consistently rejected the idea of apocatastasis, reiterating scriptural texts that punishment and fire in hell are eternal. Against the so-called Origenists the local Council of Constantinople in 543 professed that "whoever says or believes that punishment of evil spirits or godless men is temporal and will cease after a certain period of time, after which a complete restoration (apocatastasis) of evil spirits and of godless men will take place, let him be anathema" (DS 411).

Fides Damasi (fifth century) confessed that "purified by the death and blood of Jesus Christ, we will be raised upon the last day in the flesh we now live in and we have the hope that we will receive from him either eternal life as the reward for good service, or the punishment of eternal damnation for sins" (DS 72). It is noteworthy that the formula introduced the word "hope" and one can wonder whether it refers to both reward and punishment as if one would be allowed to hope for punishment of eternal damnation for sins. In 1215, Lateran IV states again that Christ will judge and the damned will receive eternal punishment with the devil (DS 801; Tanner, 1990, p. 230).

Benedict XII in his Constitution, *Benedictus Deus*, talks about infernal pains, but not about eternal pains (DS 1002). In the *Letter on Certain*

Questions Concerning Eschatology of the Sacred Congregation for the Defence of the Faith, we read that "eternal punishment awaits sinners, that they will be robbed of the vision of God and that the effects of this punishment lay hold of the entire being of the sinner" (*AAS*, 71, 1979, p. 941).

The theological reason why the Church rejected the idea of the temporality of hell was that the final judgment is based on the deeds and behaviour performed in this world and the decision-making is restricted to the world in time and not extended to the next one. Conversion as change of heart after death is not possible. It is precisely this doctrine which shows that the Church always made a clear distinction between time and eternity in the sense that eternity is not a prolonged time. If eternity were just a prolonged time, apocatastasis could be possible. But if death is the end of everything, good or bad alike, and eternity is the sublation of time, then apocatastasis is not thinkable. In death time is sublated by eternity and reversible changes are made impossible. There is no space, no measurement of time by reversible changes.

If time is more fundamental than space, the impossibility of "reconciliation" is a logical corollary. Apocatastasis visualizes eternity as an infinite space, where the left and right sides are identical and convertible. But time is not space and eternity is not endless time. Thus hell is not a place one can leave. Heaven and hell are in us as condition of our human existence in the paradoxical alternative of generosity/greediness, integrity/incontinence and authenticity/pride. Each of us carries his/her heaven or hell in him/herself, and the balance between the two is precarious. The precariousness is radicalized by the Christ-event, making eternity, the sublation of time, within our reach. Time-existence makes death inevitable, but death, the sublation of time, does not make heaven inevitable for everyone. Time-existence condemns all of us to die, but death does not force us to live in paradise. An alternative is postulated by our existence in time. Yet once the "time" of times is over, there cannot be back and forth, because eternity is neither time nor space.

It is noteworthy that Vatican II has connected the apocatastasis of the Acts 3, 21 with the anacephalaeosis of Eph 1, 10 and Col 1, 20 with 2 Pt 3, 10-12. This suggests that the apocatastasis should be interpreted not as a reintroduction of time into eternity, but rather as the cosmic world's entry into eternity, when Christ's time is accepted as time for others, or when one tries to hold up his time as time for others forever. Thus the gates of eternal paradise and the gates of hell are open and much "closer" than one would imagine, yet in spite of having them open no one is "dreaming" there of an apocatastasis of any kind. The judgment taking place at the moment of death is irreversible. By entering eternity, the alternative, the time of Christ for me or my time for Christ, ceased to be as such. Eternity of hell expressed in time-language is upholding one's time irreversibly against Christ's time, the possiblity of which is due to the eschatological union of time and eternity in Christ, who by virtue of his universal redemption has joined the eternity of God to all times (cf. above 3.5; 4.2.1).

4.2.4. Resurrection-Time in Time: An Intermediate State (IX)

An intermediate state can be understood as a state between heaven and hell (limbo), or as a state between my death and my entering heaven (purgatory) or between my entering into God's eternity, i.e., my resurrection (partial judgment) and the entry of the whole cosmic world into God's eternity with the revelation of my resurrection to the whole cosmos (universal judgment).

4.2.4.1. Limbo

Etymologically limbo means border. It was introduced by St. Augustine in response to a Pelagian doctrine concerning the baptism of children. The problem the doctrine of limbo wanted to solve was that, on one hand, there is no salvation without faith offered by baptism (cf. Jn 3, 5) and, on the other hand, there are so many children who die in original sin without having received baptism. It seemed that since these children had original sin, they had to be excluded from the vision of God, yet they should not be punished in hell because they had committed no personal sin. Thus limbo was seen as a place where they could live happily forever without seeing God face to face.

The Church never pronounced a definitive view on the matter. Suggestions were made that there is no need for limbo, if we assume that children immediately before or after death reach the use of reason and thus are made capable of supernatural love of God and so of entering heaven. But there is no experiential sign for the first, and the second encounters the difficulty of a judgment based on actions not performed before death.

The solution to the problem of limbo should be sought in a more adequate concept of time and death. If eternity is a gift of Christ and without Christ's time there is no immortality, there should be no limbo, because children who would die without Christ simply could not be immortal. If immortality is not a natural state of human existence, as we believe it to be, limbo is impossible. So much for an adequate concept of time.

Concerning death we should recall that death is entering Christ's time. Therefore, children, when they die, die as human beings and thus share in Christ's time precisely through their human death. Since death is conquered by Christ, the children cannot cease to be. They enter Christ's time not so much by an act of love, choosing or not choosing God, but by realizing the complete failure of one's self-defence mechanism in establishing inalienability. They are saved by Christ's death and resurrection, the meaning of the sacrament of baptism, like the innocents of Mt 2, 13-18. The Church celebrates these children who did not reach the use of their reason as the ones "who offered praise to God by their death, they suffered for Christ" (Liturgical Prayer on December 28). These children by their existence and death made an impact on the Church. They were judged and recognized on the basis of this impact. Now there is no reason why this cannot be applied to any child's death if death is entering Christ's time that brought about the Church. We all are judged and recognized by God in our being in the Church of Christ. Thus in the sense of a limbo there is no intermediate state between heaven and hell, but there is an intermediate state in the sense of particular and universal judgment in which the children who died without baptism and before the use of reason share with every human being, Jesus and Mary excepted.

4.2.4.2. The Meaning of Intermediate State Between Particular and Universal Judgment: Purgatory and the Intercessions of the Saints

Since our time is a multiplicity of times which includes times of others as well as cosmic time, the resurrection that immediately follows death is a resurrection-time in time. After death we can be in the presence of God, but until the whole cosmos is taken up into eternity, our resurrection is not complete in terms of the cosmic world, which is part of our time. Because of the complex interweaving of many times in our time even after resurrection, we keep our relation to the world in time. Our time has left its marks on the time of others. These marks cannot be ignored by God if he takes the world, which he created, seriously. But that God takes the world seriously is expressed by the Church's teaching on the intercession of the saints and on purgatory.

Indeed, we can distinguish two instances of the intermediate state between particular and universal judgment.

One is that of the "sorrow" and "pain" for the bad effect one's time left in the world, which calls for justice. And this judgment of the world is not overruled by God. Reparation is the task of the whole Church, individually and collectively. True, by taking up Christ's time, God's judgment is done and sins are forgiven, but the relations the risen ones had to the world are not made null and void. This is so because the same God who created the world is the same God who by Incarnation joined himself to the world as it is, sc., in time. To give a chance to the world to "judge," the resurrection-time in time had been inaugurated in order to assume the times of the world into Christ's time progressively and thus reveal Christ's time as the measure of all times.

Resurrection-time in time is not the full time of resurrection. To make it so is the concern of the Church. This concern prompts prayers, good works, etc., called expiatory acts, and relates them to the times of the deceased. The expiatory acts are performed on behalf of those who are not in time by those who are in time. Those who died cannot merit and the merits are of those who are in time. Yet the expiation is for them because in a form of collective reparation it is done on their behalf for their times affected by greediness, incontinence and pride. Their sins are already forgiven by God in the particular judgment, yet their times made an impact on the created world, and the created world demands justice, since in virtue of the Incarnation what is done to the world has been done to Jesus Christ. The so-called expiatory acts and deeds are gestures of the Church showing that the Church takes seriously the judgment of the world as well as the judgment of God. The Church can do this and even has to do it, because being a union of saints and sinners it is in time and in eternity as well. It is in resurrection-time.

The Roman Catholic church defended the existence of purgatory (cf. Council of Lyons II, DS 856; Council of Trent, DS 1850) but Luther rejected it. The reasoning of Luther is logical if one does not think too much of cosmic time as part of resurrection in time. The Oriental Church did accept purgatory but not as a place. Indeed, purgatory is not a place in eternity, but it is a place in this world where the remains of the sins of greediness, incontinence and pride make their impact, and satisfaction is expected before the times of those "places" enter into Christ's time. The differing concepts and views on purgatory reveal the kind of idea one has of time and eternity.

The other instance of the intermediate state between the universal and particular judgment is the instance of happy enjoyment with God and with all those who benefitted from the "good" effects one's time left in the world. These effects remain in the world even though the person has passed beyond the horizon of time and eternity. By taking up Christ's time the risen ones share in Christ's activity of transforming the time of the world into eternity by converting integrity, generosity and authenticity into their fulfillment in faith, charity and hope. And this is the meaning of the traditional belief that the departed cannot merit for themselves, but they can help the living in the communion of saints. The canonization of one member of the Church means that the marks of sin left by him/her on the times of others are removed. The judgment of the world has been respected and no more expiatory acts are needed. The only action that remains for him/her is to bring the resurrection-time together with Christ to its completion. And the same is expected from all those who are not canonized, yet "have been cleansed" (cf. DS 1305; Tanner, 1990, pp. 527-28).

4.3. Society, World and Eternity

4.3.1. *Christ is the Lord of the Times of History and Redeemer of the Cosmic Universe (X)*

Christ, the eschatological union of time and eternity, is not only the judge of every individual at the threshold of time and eternity, but he is also the Lord of history and Redeemer of the cosmic universe. If Christ, as Redeemer, by the event of his resurrection is expected to give eternal llife to human persons, he has to affect not only the time of each earthling but geological, cosmological, etc., times as well, since human time is a balance of the multiplicity of sub-times characterized by irreversibility progressing through reversibilities. He has to interrelate all the different time-levels, beginning with the time of a single cell up to the various societies of human history, with the different cosmic times and assume all of them into his own time.

This kind of universal lordship and redeeming power is the meaning of the following themes of traditional eschatology: Parousia, final coming of Jesus Christ, universal judgment, anacephalaeosis, and apocatastasis.

4.3.1.1. Parousia and the Final Coming of Jesus Christ

Parousia means "arrival" and, usually, it is understood by many as the second arrival or coming of Jesus Christ into the world in which we live now. But more correctly it means the arrival of the whole world into the time of Jesus Christ. Parousia is when the history of the whole world ends up in the world of the glorified Jesus Christ. It is the end aimed at from the beginning of creation.

There are a few events mentioned in the New Testament which were interpreted as signs of the parousia, for example, the preaching of the gospel to the whole world (Mt 24, 14; Mk 13, 10), the conversion of Israel (Rom 11, 1-10), the appearance and the early triumph of Antichrist (Mk 13, 6; 2 Thes 2, 3; 1 Jn 2, 18-22; 2 Jn 7; Rev 13, 1-18) with persecution (Mk 13, 9-13) and cosmic transformation (Mt 24, 29-44; Mk 13, 7; Lk 21, 25-31). All use mostly spatial language, yet the meaning of the passages is that Christ is the Lord of all times and the people of Israel, the world of history and of the cosmos, all, without distinction, will be assumed into the time of Christ.

Though the parousia sometimes is called the "second" coming of Christ, in the biblical sources Jesus' coming at the end of the world (cf. Mt, 16, 27; 19, 28; 2 Pt 1, 16; Rev 1, 8) is never numbered as the second. The coming back "in the same way" of Acts 1, 11 should not be interpreted in the sense that what happened will happen again. Jesus will never appear in the world as he did 2,000 years ago. Time is irreversible, and we know that after resurrection Jesus will never be the same as he was before. It is noteworthy that Thomas Aquinas, in his *Summa theologiae* and *Summa contra gentiles*, has no article on the second coming of Jesus Christ.

There are many passages in the New Testament which express the longing and waiting for the coming of Jesus Christ. They deal mostly with the particular and universal judgment as well as with our resurrection as seen from this world on its way to eternity, when our resurrection can be revealed (Mk 13, 26-32; Mt 10, 23; 19, 28; 24, 29-36; Lk 21, 29-33; Acts 1, 11; 1 Thes 3, 13; 4, 15-18; Jas 5, 8). The correct interpretation of the awesome apocalyptic event should take into consideration also all those passages which describe the same events as revelation, as anacephalaeosis and apocatastasis. Thus, for example, Paul sees the end as an event when Jesus hands over the kingdom of God to the Father after having done away with sovereignties, authorities and power (1 Cor 15, 24; Col 1, 16; 2, 15), and made all these masters of our age (1 Cor 2, 6) his subjects (1 Pet 3, 15; 1 Cor 2, 6; Phil 1, 10; 2,

15; Eph 1, 4; Col 1, 22; 1 Thes 3, 15; 5, 23). The mastering of the sovereignties, powers and dominions means that the Lord, Jesus Christ, is revealed by God (1 Tim 6, 16; 1 Pet 4, 13) and with him we too (Col 3, 4) are revealed in our glory. The way we "were" risen in regard to God, we "will" be so in regard to the world as well. It is this revelation of Jesus and of us in him which is expressed by anacephalaeosis, "recapitulation" (Eph 1, 10) and apocatastasis, "restoration" (Acts 3, 21) of the whole world.

4.3.1.2. Anacephalaeosis and Apocatastasis: Recapitulation and Restoration

According to Eph 1, 10 Jesus is the recapitulation of the whole creation. "Anacephalaeosis" means to place something at the top of a column. In the Letter to the Ephesians it means that by taking up the time of human history and of the cosmic world, Jesus has reconstituted the whole creation and let it share in the eternity of God (cf. Eph 1, 20-23; 3, 9-13; see also 2 Pt 3, 10-13). The meaning of anacephalaeosis should be further clarified by apocatastasis (Acts 3, 21) as Vatican II did in the *Dogmatic Constitution on the Church*, no. 48 Tanner, 1990, p. 887:

> The Church ... will reach her full perfection only in the glory of heaven. Then will come the time of restoration of all things (Acts 3, 21). Then the human race, as well as the entire world, which is intimately related to man and achieves its purpose through him, will be perfectly re-established in Christ (cf. Eph 1, 10; Col 1, 2:, 2 Pt 3, 10-13).

4.3.2. Self-Discovery of the History of Human Society in the Time of Jesus Christ

4.3.2.1. Eschatological Outpouring of the Holy Spirit: Christ the Language of Languages

Christ by his resurrection became the lord of history. As a result, each moment of history, as well as its totality, is no longer under the power of death but under the power of resurrection. The imminent forces of resurrection are inserted in historical time. History, therefore, will reach eternity and become revelation. Faith and reason encounter each other in perfect union and the validity of faith is vindicated by history itself.

History includes the history of different human societies like family, national, business, cultural, and research, mostly differentiated by languages, whether linguistical, professional or technical. Societies based on linguistic differences are the most enduring and lasting form of human communities. Yet they too are in time and finally sublated by Christ's time. Christ is that language which is the end of all languages. This was prognostically realized during the first Pentecost by the eschatological outpouring of the Holy Spirit. The miracle of languages is the work of the Holy Spirit who testifies to Christ as the language of languages. Christ is the language which will be spoken and understood by the nations of history. And if language is the vehicle as well as the realization of any culture or social community, Christ as the language of languages is to be the fulfillment of cultures, i.e., the fulfillment of the progressive development of the intellectual and moral talents to secure human existence, not just in time, but in eternity. The outpouring of the Holy Spirit became the guarantee that history is revelation, and revelation is history and both are linked with faith and resurrection so that the four events, revelation, history, faith and resurrection, can become one. The outpouring of the Holy Spirit is the guarantee that Christian eschatological expectation will be substantiated not only in heaven in the sight of God, but on earth, in the sight of the world of history.

4.3.2.2. Utopianism, Millenarianism

Since the experience of Pentecost there has been a lasting concern for describing the impact of the Christ-event on the history of the world. Several ideal forms of perfect societies were proposed but all turned out to be so far no more than utopias. All took the shape of an empire of Christian universalism. Here are some of the most influential ones: the City of God of St. Augustine in the fifth century, the Christian Republic of Roger Bacon in the thirteenth century, the Universal Empire of Dante in the fourteenth century, the Peace of Faith of Nicolas of Cusa, the City of the Sun of Tommaso Campanella in the sixteenth century, the Pax Romana of Charles François Castel in the seventeenth century, the City of the Philosophers of Leibniz, the City of the Scientists of Auguste Comte of the eighteenth century (Gilson, 1952), the Universal Global Society of our age and the Expansion of Human Life in the Universe, when "a million of human species will explore diverse ways of living in a million different places across the galaxy" (Dyson, 1988, pp. 287-97).

Some tried to argue from Rev 20, 1-6 and invented various forms of millenarianism, the 1,000-year reign of Christ on earth. Millenarianism, or Chiliasm (from the Greek *chilios*, thousand) was one more effort to unite revelation with history and history with revelation. It was expected that the divine dispensation would make it sure that the veracity and the right of the martyrs would be revealed in world history. Those who gave their life for their faith were to be distinguished from all others. This was done by giving them a reign of 1,000 years with Christ on earth before the end of the world. To assure this Satan had to be bound in order to let the Saints reign free of Satan's interference. After 1,000 years Satan would be let loose for a short while before being thrown into the lake of fire, and then the world would enter into the eternity of Christ (Rev 20, 7-10).

From the early centuries on there were always some who interpreted Rev 20, 1-6 not symbolically but historically. Although Papias, Justin, Irenaeus, Tertullian and Augustine argued against it (cf. *City of God*, 20, 7-8), in more recent times there were still some who strongly believed in it, e.g., anabaptists, adventists, Jehovah's Witnesses and some militant TV evangelists, like Jerry Falwell, applauding a military Messiah fighting the nuclear war of Armageddon (Rev 16, 16; 19, 17-18) against the Antichrist (Halsell, 1986).

The millenarists and the pre-millenarists claim that the millenium follows the glorious coming of Christ. The post-millenarists believe that the millenium precedes the glorious coming of Christ. The pre-millenarists are further divided into two subdivisions, the pre-tribulationists, and the post-tribulationists. The first hold that the Church will be removed from the earth and saved from the catastrophic event, whereas the second assume that the Church will not be removed from the earth away from tribulations, but will suffer (Erickson, 1977).

The very first person ever to talk about the messianic kingdom of 1,000 years seemed to be R. Eliezer ben Hyrcan, who calculated his 1,000 years from Ps 90, 15: "Make us glad as many days as you have afflicted us, and as many years as we have seen evil." Now 400 years in Egypt, 111 years of the dominion of foreigners in the time of the judges and 490 years from the beginning of the Exile up to the destruction of the temple by the Romans according to the chronology of the old synagogue would make up 1,000 years (Rochain, 1981). It is possible that this tradition is the source of Rev 20, 1-6.

Millenarianism is another example of the inadequate understanding of time and eternity. If time and eternity are not distinguished correctly, Christ's reign looks no different from the reign of any monarch of absolute power. But Christ is the language of languages, the fulfillment and not the replacement of human societies.

4.3.2.3. Antichrist, Demons and Satan Upholding the Time of the Nations

The biblical Antichrist should not be confused with Satan, the prince of the evil ones (Mk 3, 22). The Antichrist is not, like Satan, who is a sort of counterpart of God, the highest of the evil ones in regard to God. The Antichrist is the head of evil forces in regard to the created world, yet he is not a challenge to God. He is a challenge to the world by trying to make the revocable world irrevocable, the measurement the measured. The Antichrist is to eternalize what is not eternal. In this sense he is the servant of Satan, the god of this aeon (2 Cor 4, 4), who refuses to accept his time as just one's time and tries to assert it as time for others. Being the servant of Satan, the Antichrist is a sign of the ever-growing antagonism between Christ and the world, between the time of the world and the time of Christ; in simple terms, between eternity and time. Rahner considers this growing antagonism as one of the formal principles of eschatology, since he believes that towards the end the forces of evil grow stronger, and the Antichrist, the "embodiment of all these historical forces hostile to God" (Rahner, 1965, p, 29), will increase his power.

The Antichrist in the New Testament is understood sometimes as an individual, e.g., the man of sin who takes his place in the temple and proclaims himself to be God (2 Thes 2, 3-10) or as a pseudo-Messiah claiming himself to be Jesus Christ (Mk 13, 6). But we find Antichrist in the plural as well, sc., as a group of people who refuse to accept Christ as the revelation of God (2 Jn 7). In Rev 13, 1-18 he is the beast rising from the sea (cf. 2 Esdras 13, 1-58) and is identified with the Roman Empire (cf. Dn 7, 9-14).

Now Christ's victory over the Antichrist and over his master, Satan, means that Christ's time cannot be successfully challenged either by an individual or by any society, be it pluralistic or monistic, like the kingdom of Satan. This is why, for example, unlike Buddhist traditions, early Christian writers did not demythologize Satan as a dimension of individual experience. He was always seen as an external power within a societal context (Boyd, 1975, pp. 157-67).

The meaning of Christ's final victory over Satan as the head of a society is that neither individuals nor societies can uphold successfully the time of the nations against Christ's time. Christ is the one who brings peace among nations and lets them enter into eternity.

4.3.2.4. Societies, Nations Enter Eternity (XI)

As the resurrection-time in time progresses towards its fulfillment, the times of the different nations and cultures as created times approach their end and will be measured by Christ's time. As a result, people as a group will see themselves as God saw them and appreciate themselves the way God wanted them to be appreciated. This new self-understanding of societies in the light of the time of Jesus Christ will make possible that everyone's "I" will be transformed into a "We," in the sense that the Arabs will be able to say "we Jews" and the Jews "we Arabs," etc. The Germans can recognize themselves as "We French" as the whites can authentically confess that they are "black" and so on (Horvath, 1975, pp. 274-75).

Such a universal we-community is described in the first three chapters of the letter to the Ephesians as a great mystery hidden from eternity. Christ in his own flesh (Eph 2, 15) unites all peoples in a new community where the social, cultural and linguistic barriers which previously divided societies will be destroyed (Eph 2, 14), and their times taken up into eternity (Eph 2, 18; Col 3, 11). All nations have access in one Spirit to the Father through Christ the head who as such is all and in all (Col 3, 11).

All that is expressed in space-language in the letters to the Ephesians and Colossians can be expressed in time-language by saying that cultural and historical times of all human societies enter into Jesus' time and find the meaning of their historical times in Jesus' time expressed in the Church as his sacrament.

In analyzing social and historical times one can distinguish four instances, sc., self-discovery, mission, institution and philosophizing. Now on account of his Incarnation Jesus Christ went through these four instances of social and historical times. He experienced the instances of self-discovery, of mission, institution (founding a community of followers) and philosophizing/dogmatizing (e.g. without me you can do nothing, Jn 15, 5). But being in this world he has to face again and again confrontation with new discoveries, communications, institutions and philosophies constantly emerging and providing new culture-types, inventions, productions and marketing. As the risen Christ taking up the different times of the created world, he has to go through those instances again and again in every believer's life-time as well as in every nation's and society's life-time (sc., being discovered, proclaimed, organized and systematized by the times of the different peoples and epochs).

By virtue of these two combats, i.e., confrontation with each individual's culture-types as well as with each nation's and society's time, the encounter between Christ and human society is a constant crisis-event. But by being submitted to these times of the human spirit and that of the social and historical times, Christ manifests his transcendence over the four instances not only by constantly recycling between the first and last instances (after being dogmatized, he is to be discovered again, etc.) but also by challenging the definitive value of the four instances. In the combat of the different social and cultural times Christ is to appear as the unique self-discovery which remains as such, enjoying lasting originality and a never superannuated-newness. Consequently the four instances of the social and historical times will not remain just successive communication, organization and dogmatization of the past. They become the realization of an ongoing, once-and-for-all, unique discovery of one's time in Jesus Christ's time.

That the various societies, whether linguistic, economic, cultural, philosophical, etc., enter into Christ's time at the end of the world means that they will cease to be what they think they are and become what they are in Christ. They discover themselves communicating, organizing, re-evaluating themselves as they are willed and discovered, communicated and organized as eternal values in Jesus Christ. Consequently, when we say that in eternity "we" are in Christ, we say that in eternity nobody will be just German, Japanese, Nigerian, etc., because in heaven everybody will be German, Japanese, Nigerian, etc., since being a German, Japanese, Nigerian, etc., will have a universal value and as such belong to the fulfillment of each human being. The reality of the fulfillment of each human being is what God wanted to achieve by creating German, Japanese, Nigerian, etc. The meaning of the nations becomes the meaning of my life. The fulfillment of each one's self-discovery will be the fulfillment of all the times of the different societies of which one was a sub-time or which one had as sub-times, because all these times are fulfilled in Christ, who as the eschatological union of time and eternity entered into every time. Therefore, his knowledge includes the knowledge of all times and of their cause, eternity, which is both their negation and their fulfillment at the same time. Since the time of Jesus Christ is of eternity, the life of Jesus presented in the gospels is to be understood as the meaning of each society as well as that of each individual.

This revelation of Jesus Christ is the parousia of the "last day." But the time of Jesus Christ as an expression of eternity can be understood only in eternity, because an expression of something can be fully understood only if that of which it is the expression is properly grasped. Therefore, eternity can be understood only in eternity and not in time.

4.3.3. Cosmic Times Enter Eternity: Fulfillment of the Resurrection of Christ (XII)

Some authors like Vogtle (1970) and Greshake (1969) assume that resurrection cannot have too much to do with the cosmos. Matter cannot be brought to a final completion. It is essentially *unvollendbar*, not accomplishable. It is an endless dynamic process of transition from one aeon to the other and no end can be expected.

This may be so if space is considered more basic than time. But anyone who considers time more basic will come to a different conclusion. If we believe that time is more basic than its correlate measurement, space, we can understand that the resurrection of the body includes the transformation of the cosmos as well. Scripture supports this assumption.

Concerning the relationship between the present "corrupt" world and the future world there are two traditions in the New Testament. One says that the present will be completely destroyed (Mk 13, 31; 2 Pet 3, 10-12), and the other suggests that the present will not be destroyed but liberated from the bondage of decay (Rom 8, 21). For the second tradition the Pauline literature is the most explicit.

It was the dispute at Colossae that made the early Church aware that Christ is the creator as well as redeemer of the cosmic world. At Colossae there were some who accepted the view that there are certain cosmic powers (Col 2, 16) which govern the world. The author of the Letter to the Colossians realized that such a view challenged the power and the supremacy of Jesus Christ over the cosmic world. To defend Jesus's supremacy he developed a cosmic Christology. Christ, who is the image of God and the firstborn of all creation, is the one through whom and in whom the Powers, Thrones, Dominations, Sovereignties were created. Therefore, he has the supreme power over the world and over everything which had been created. But in addition to this, by his death and resurrection he reconciled everyone to him and to God. Now since the human race is part of the cosmos, the same effect of Jesus' death and resurrection was to be extended to the cosmos. Thus Christ is the one who triumphed over the whole cosmos by saving it from a purely natural end and transformed it into a new cosmos.

The idea is a further development of a much earlier insight which we find in Rom 8, 18-27. The cosmos, unable to attain the purpose given to it by God, is groaning in travail in order to be saved from death, which was caused by sin (Rom 8, 20-21). In Rom 8, 18-27 Paul sees a close solidarity between human persons and the cosmic world so that one cannot share in the redemption of Christ without the other. Therefore, *ktisis* i.e., all that exists besides or apart from human beings, together with humans is to be saved from the "last enemy" (1 Cor 15, 26) by the Spirit of God, the first fruit of Jesus' resurrection. Since the cosmic world is sharing the Spirit of God, for Paul the cosmic time has been transformed and made part of Christ's time.

Some recent translations omit *huiothesian* "adoptive sonship" in Rom 8, 23 because it would be the only instance where adoptive sonship has eschatological sense. Yet the text with the adoptive sonship is very sound. It is true that Christians are already sons and daughters of God in the sight of God, but in the sight of the cosmic world their sonship and daughtership are still in progress by the communication of their sonship and daughtership to the world. Sonship in Rom 8, 23 can therefore have an eschatological sense and means both realization and revelation. The Christian sonship and daughtership are still to be revealed by bringing them to completion. Though we are saved by Christ's death and resurrection, yet the hope of it, the authenticity of its consummation, cannot take place until cosmic time comes to its end and enters eternity. So we suffer now in the present tense, which will last until the last day. But hope, our special relation to the Triune God as Holy Spirit, helps us penetrate the mystery of eternity (cf. the mind of God in Rom 8, 27) and perceive it as something taking place in the present, as something already going on.

That cosmic time enters into eternity as the fulfillment of the resurrection of Christ is further confirmed by "the "Book of Symbols" of the fourth gospel, where the author presents six signs of Christ. The signs are equally divided so that three demonstrate Christ's power over nature (changing water to wine: 2, 1-11; the multiplication of the loaves: 6, 1-15; walking on the waters: 6, 16-21) and three present his power as a life-giver (the cure of an official's son from Capernaum: 4, 43-54; the healing of a sick man at the Sheep Pool of Bethesda: 5, 1-15; opening the eyes of a man born blind: 9, 1-10, 42).

The symbolism of the first, fourth and fifth signs (2, 1-11; 6, 1-5; 6, 16-21) suggests both that Christ is the Lord of the cosmic world and that the cosmic world will be transformed in the new creation in order to become the revelation of God's redemptive love in Jesus Christ towards every human being.

It was the Johannine symbolism which became the foundation of the sacramental theology recognizing the active role of the material world in the salvation of human persons (anthropological consideration of the sacraments), in the life of the Church (ecclesiological consideration), in recognizing the risen Christ's presence in the cosmic world (Christological consideration), and in revealing the Trinitarian God (theological consideration of the sacraments) (Horvath, 1970). Sacramental theology in reality is the prognostic presentation of the cosmic world entering into eternity. The transformation, the sacramental efficacy of conferring grace, the sublation of time, the power of letting one in time enter into Christ's time in order to see the created world as his/her own world expressing God's unique love towards each of us, etc., all are the symptoms of a cosmic world entering into eternity.

4.3.4. Cosmic Eternity is the Expression of the Uniqueness of Each of Us by Being Loved by God in the Church of Christ as No One Ever Before or After (XIII)

The new or the last day (cf. *de novissimis*, the Latin title for the last things, i.e., eschatology) is when the resurrection-time is extended to the whole human society and to the whole cosmos. It is that instance when the whole human society and the whole cosmos enter into Christ's time, which means sharing Jesus' integrity with the generosity of his Father and the authenticity of his Holy Spirit. As a result, the risen intersubjective world of human beings together with the risen cosmos become the authentic expression of faith, charity and hope of the resurrected ones and the authentic expression of the incontinence, greediness and pride of all those who want to establish their inalienability by their reversible changes (i.e., by themselves and not by Christ's salvation).

Therefore "hell" as well as "heaven" will have a new cosmic reality which will be the expression of the uniqueness of each of us in the Church of Christ.

The cosmos now, the world in time, is in pain because of the alienation caused by sin. It is not an authentic expression of the body of Christ, nor of our body, either. The time after the death and resurrection of Jesus until the end of time is a time of conflict between the "old" time and Jesus' time, entering not only the individual, cultural (cultures of peoples), psychological (existential) time, but also the biological, geological and cosmic times as well, and making them Jesus's times. As a result, the cosmic world will become the expression of God's love of each of us, bringing the revelation of our times as expression of God's eternity to its completion.

In the light of our earlier considerations our conclusion can be expressed more pregnantly following the modern view of the universe rather than the classical one.

The classical view of the universe was static. The natural state of things was rest, and motion was considered as the result of being forcefully removed from a "happy" rest. Any eschatology based on the classical view of nature will envision heaven as a rest and earthly life as being pushed out of heaven into an exile as a valley of tears to be overcome by repaying for the offences of sin, the cause of being pushed out of heaven. But we should note that *exitus-reditus*, falling out of heaven and the "wish" to return to heaven which can be found in non-Christian eschatology, is not found in the New Testament tradition. John's gospel makes an exception of Jesus, who was with God, and returned to God in order to emphasize that the Logos and the Jesus of Nazareth is one and the same person. But for the faithful creation-redemption is not a way back to a natural place but rather a call from a natural place, human existence, to a "non- natural" place, the life of the living God, who is beyond the reach of any created effort. In short, it is a call from time to eternity.

In opposition to the classical view of the universe, the modern view is that "the order of the universe is first and foremost a perpetually increasing disorder" (Asimov, 1966, pp. 239-40). This change was prompted by the theory of thermodynamics, which saw order as an accumulation of contrasting energies, and disorder as an accumulation of one-sided energy. Consequently, order as disequilibrium of energies means life, whereas equilibrium of energies means disorder and death. The amount of disorder is called entropy.

Now according to the second law of thermodynamics, in a closed system heat will always flow to the cold region. In the light of this law all spontaneous processes do bring about an increase of disorder or equilibrium of energies, or, in other words, death, unless a special effort is made to reverse the order of things and increase the available energy. It is essential to keep the difference between the total energy and available energy, because if the two are equal entropy reaches its highest point, which is the end of action and life. Any postponement of decay, i.e., survival, requires drawing energies from the environment.

Earlier we noticed that different times are interrelated and none of them is independent of cosmic time, which follows a linear run-down from a maximum level of energy to a maximum level of entropy. If this is true, our universe, which we know has one beginning and one end, as physical process follows the linear course taken by entropy and reveals itself as a universally valid direction of time's flow. There is run-down, no-return succession which we find valid even if there is a cyclic universe.

We should recall also that the four forces, the weak nuclear force (radioactive), the strong nuclear force (nuclear explosion), the electromagnetic force (speed of light) and the gravitational force all have their co-determinating role in cosmic time. Yet the gravitational force, the weakest, is the strongest, since it can bend the light and change our time, conditioned by the measurement of the absolute speed of light. So we can say that gravitational force, in a certain sense, is the time-grounding force. It can bring about a singularity event or an event-horizon which leads to the sublation of cosmic time as well as to that of its various sub-times.

Now when we believe that by his resurrection Christ became the Lord of the universe (Col 2, 10; Eph 1, 21; 1 Cor 15, 23-26; Rom 8, 38) and has the power over the future aeon (Heb 6, 5), this implies that Christ is able to turn time, which runs irreversibly forward to its run-down, to a run-up eternity. This is the cosmic significance of the Incarnation and resurrection.

Evidently Christ's lordship over time can be conceived as letting time run its course to pass away. In this instance Jesus' lordship would be manifest as being the only one that is not passing away (cf. apocalyptic eschatology). But his lordship over time can be conceived also as his entering into time as a new force which progressively is changing the run-down of the world to an upwards movement. Thus time comes to an end but it does not become irrelevant. Eternity is the end of time as its fulfillment. Using this language as a literary form one could say that the presence of the risen Christ can change the direction of the flow from the maximum level of energy to a maximum level of entropy, to the direction of God's presence to all ages by communicating himself (Father) completely (Son) and authentically (Holy Spirit).

Christ's resurrection can be visualized as a gravitational force bending all times and bringing about a singular event, an irreversibility without recurring repetition, since it is grounded in the eternity of God. The eternity of God is experienced as the foundation of my time as well as the realization of the final inalienability of my time and because of my inalienability that of the cosmos as well.

Therefore the cosmic world together with its biological and animal world enters into cosmic eternity as an expression of God's love for each of us and consequently that of the uniqueness of each of us in the time of Christ, the Church. The experience of eternity joins with the experience of being loved by God as a unique "time" in the whole of history, in a non-repeatable, irreversible way. My time is blended into the time of Jesus and we all "begin to do what God 'was always' doing." This is why love can be understood as the threshold of time and eternity (Horvath, 1979b, p. 159).

5 CONCLUSION

Christ, the eschatological union of time and eternity, is a reality for the theologian. For a non-theologian this concept may serve as an imaginary problem-solving paradigm. It surely accentuates the multiplicity and complexity of real time. At the same time, it emphasizes time's universal and transcendental character and opens the way to recognize the possibility of, not a "recycled" conscious (Penrose, 1990) or unconscious (Stephen Hawking) continuation in existence, but that of the singularity event of the Christed resurrection, which makes one's irreversibility irreversibly irreversible. In the instant of resurrection the irreversibility of one's cosmic biological, cultural, philosophical and theological time will be no longer activated and measured by uniformly reversible changes but by Christ's time bridging time and eternity. One's irreversibility will be radicalized in the irreversibility of God. And the human being will be irreversibly a person in the community of all persons, the Eternity-Person included.

Since eternity is the meaning of time, time in its mystery can never be exhausted. The human mind does not need to stop asking new questions. The boundary of its boundaries will be the parameter of Christ, the union of time and eternity, who in an hermeneutic language event can be addressed as "you," inviting human mind to transcend any experienced boundary.

As there is a desire and search for the possibility of a unified theory in physics, so too in theology. And such a unified "theory" in theology is Christ as the eschatological union of time and eternity which, applied to "real" time, opens a way to solve the problems of the "real" times. Yet a theologian cannot agree more with Stephen Hawking in believing that, as the discovery of the unified theory in physics, so too the "discovery" of the unified theory in theology can be only the first stop: "our goal is a complete understanding of events around us and of our existence" (Hawking, 1990, p. 169). Here ends for the moment the discourse between speculative theology and science.

REFERENCES

Abel, A. 1969. *Eschatologie et Cosmologie*. Bruxelles: Éditions de l'Institut de Sociologie. Université Libre de Bruxelles.

Alfrink, B. 1959. "L'idée de résurrection d'après Daniel 12, 1ff." *Biblica* 40: 355-71.

Arnold, W. 1985. "Rhythm and Regulating Cycle." *Ultimate Reality and Meaning* 8: 149-52.

Asimov, I. 1966. *Understanding Physics*. Vol. 1, *Motion, Sound and Heat*. New York: Walker.

Badham, P. and L., eds. 1987. *Immortality in the Religions of the World*. New York: Paragon House.

Bailey, L.R. 1979. *Biblical Perspectives on Death*. Philadelphia: Fortress Press.

Balthasar, Hans Urs von. 1971. *Klarstellungen zur Prüfung der Geister*. Freiburg: Herder.

Barnhart, M.G. 1992. "Hisamatsu's Oriental Nothingness: Ultimate Reality and Meaning from a Zen Perspective." *Ultimate Reality and Meaning* 14: 20-34.

Barr, J. 1962. *Biblical Words for Time*. London: SCM Press.

Barrow, I. 1735. *Geometrical Lectures*. London: S. Austin.

Barth, K. 1957. *Church Dogmatics*, Vol. 1. Edinburgh: T and T. Clark

———. 1962. *Church Dogmatics*, Vol. 4, 3. Edinburgh: T and T Clark.

———. 1965. *The Epistle to the Romans*. London: Oxford University Press.

Bergson, H.L. 1914. *Creative Evolution*. London: Macmillan.

Blondel, M. 1950. *Exigence philosophique du Christianisme*. Paris: Presses Universitaires de France.

Boros, L. 1965. *The Moment of Truth*. Montreal: Palm Publishers.

Boyd, J.W. 1975. *Satan and Mara: Christian and Buddhist Symbols of Evil*. Leiden: Brill.

Brandon, S.G.F. 1965. *History, Time and Deity: An Historical and Comparative Study of the Conception of Time in Religious Thought and Practice*. New York: Barnes and Noble.

Braudel, F. 1958. "Histoire et Sociologie," *Traité de Sociologie* 1,9: 96-97, 83-113. Edited by G. Gurwitch. Paris: Presses Universitaires de France.

Budge, E.A. 1967. *Egyptian Book of the Dead*. Magnolia, MA: P. Smith.

Bühler, C. 1968. "The Course of Human Life as a Psychological Problem." *Human Development* 11: 184-200.
Bultmann, R. 1957. *History and Eschatology*. Edinburgh: The University Press.
_____. 1960. *The World and the Beyond*. Marburg Sermons. New York: C. Scribner.
Cannon, W.B. 1942. "Voodoo Death." *American Anthropology* 44: 169-81.
Casel, O. 1962. *The Mystery of Christian Worship*. Westminster: The Newman Press.
Charles, R.H. 1970 (1899). *Eschatology: The Doctrine of a Future Life in Israel, Judaism and Christianity*. New York: Schocken Books.
Childs, B.S. 1962. *Memory and Tradition in Israel*. London: SCM Press.
Chomsky, N. 1957. *Syntactic Structures*. The Hague: Moulton.
_____. 1965. *Aspects of the Theory Syntax*. Cambridge: M.I.T. Press.
Collins, J.J. 1974. "Apocalyptic Eschatology as the Transcendence of Death."*The Catholic Biblical Quarterly* 36: 21-43.
Congar, Y.M.J. 1983. *I Believe in the Holy Spirit*. New York: Seabury Press.
Conzelmann, A. 1973. *History of Primitive Christianity*. Nashville: Abingdon Press.
Cornelis, H. 1968. "Afterlife." In *Sacramentum Mundi*, edited by K. Rahner, vol. 1, 13-15. Montreal: Palm Publishers.
Cornish, E. 1966. *Prospectus for an Institute for the Future*. Washington, D.C.: World Future Society.
_____. et al. 1978. *The Study of the Future: Introduction to the Art and Science of Understanding and Shaping Tomorrow's World*. Washington, D.C.: World Future Society.
Cullmann, O. 1960. *Christ and Time: The Primitive Christian Conception of Time and History*. Philadelphia: Westminster Press.
Dange, S.A. 1978. "Aspects of Ultimate Reality from the Ṛgveda." *Ultimate Reality and Meaning* 1: 65-66, 71-99.
_____. 1984. "The Upaniṣads and the Ultimate Real One." *Ultimate Reality and Meaning* 7: 252-69.
Daley, B., et al. 1986. *Eschatologie in der Schrift und Patristik*. Freiburg: Herder.
Davies, P.C.W. 1976. *The Physics of Time Asymmetry*. Berkeley:University of California Press.
de la Taille, M. 1928. "Actuation créée par acte incréé," *Recherches de science religieuse* 18: 253-68.
De Vaucouleurs, G., and D.W. Olson. 1982. "The Central Velocity Dispersion in Elliptical and Lenticular Galaxies as an Extragalactic Distance Indicator." *Astrophysical Journal* 56: 346-69.
Dodd, C.H. 1936. *The Parable of the Kingdom*. London: Nisbet.

DS-Denzinger, H., and A. Schönmetzer. 1963. *Enchiridion symbolorum definitionum et declarationum de rebus fidei et morum.* 32d ed. Barcelona: Herder.
Dupuis, J. 1979. "Comments." *Vidyajyoti* 43: 530-34.
Durkheim, E. 1954. *The Elementary Forms of Religious Life.* New York: Free Press.
Dykmans, M. 1973. *Les sermons de Jean XXII sur la vision béatifique.* Rome: Gregorian University Press.
─────. 1975. *Pour et contre Jean XXII. 1337.* Rome, Citta del Vaticano: Biblioteca Apostolica Vaticana.
Dyson, F. 1988. *Infinite in All Directions.* New York: Harper & Row.
Ebeling, G. 1950. "Die Bedeutung der historisch-kritischen Methoden für protestantische Theologie und Kirche." *Zeitschrift für Theologie und Kirche* 47: 1-46.
Ehret, C.F. 1983. "Coherence and Correspondence on the Classical Composition of the Temporal and Structural Levels of Organization of Living Systems." Lecture. Second Biennial Meeting of the Institute for Ultimate Reality and Meaning. Toronto, August 17-20, 1983.
Ehret, C.F., and E. Trucco, 1967. "Molecular Models for the Circadian Clock." *Journal of Theoretical Biology* 15: 240-62.
Einstein, A. 1961. *Relativity. The Special and General Theory.* New York: Crown Publishers.
Eisenbach, F. 1982. *Die Gegenwart Jesu Christi in Gottesdienst.* München: Grünwald.
Eliade, M. 1954. *The Myth of Eternal Return.* New York: Pantheon Books.
Erickson, M.J. 1977. *Contemporary Options in Eschatology.* Grand Rapids, MI: Baker Book House.
Escribano-Alberca, I. 1987. *Eschatologie. Von der Auklärung bis zur Gegenwart.* Freiburg: Herder.
Evans-Wentz, W.Y. 1960. *The Tibetan Book of the Dead.* New York: Oxford University Press.
Feifel, H. 1959. *The Meaning of Death.* New York: McGraw-Hill.
Ferkiss, V. 1974. "Christianity, Technology and the Human Future," *Dialog* 13: 258-63.
Firth, R.W. 1951. *Elements of Social Organization.* London: Watts.
Fischer, U. 1978. *Eschatologie und Jenseitserwartung im hellenistischen Diasporajudentum.* Berlin: de Gruyter.
Flew, A. 1967. "Immortality." In *Encyclopedia of Philosophy*, edited by P. Edwards, vol. 4, 139-50. New York: Macmillan.
Fraisse, P. 1964. *The Psychology of Time.* New York: Harper & Row.
Fraser, J.T. 1978. *Time as Conflict.* Basel: Birkhauser.

Gadamer, H.-G. 1975. *Truth and Method*. New York: Seabury Press.
Gardner, M. 1983. *Why of a Philosophical Scrivener*. New York: W. Morrow and Co.
Gilbert, L.T. 1985. "Time: The Concept, the Problem of Today and the Visions of Tomorrow." Paper Presented at the Third Biennial Meeting of the Institute for Ultimate Reality and Meaning. Toronto, August 20-23, 1985.
Gilson, E. 1952. *Les métamorphoses de la cité de Dieu*. Louvain: Publications Universitaires.
Gnilka, J. 1955. *Ist 1 Kor 3, 10-15 ein Schriftzeugniss für das Fegefeuer?* Dusseldorf: Triltsch.
Gorman, B.S., and A.E. Wessman. 1977. "The Emergence of Human Awareness and Concepts of Time." In *Personal Experience of Time*, edited by B.S. Gorman and A.E. Wessman, 3-55. New York: Plenum.
Gotesky, R. 1978. "God and Reality in Samuel Alexander's Space, Time and Deity." *Ultimate Reality and Meaning* 1: 130-52.
Gould, S.J. 1987. *Time's Arrow, Time's Cycle: Myth and Metaphor in the Discovery of Geological Time*. Cambridge, MA: Harvard University Press.
Greenberg, J.H. 1971. *Language, Culture and Communications*. Essays selected by A.S. Diel. Stanford: Stanford University Press.
Greshake, G. 1969. *Auferstehung der Toten*. Essen: Ludgerus Verlag.
_____, and G. Lohfink. 1975. *Nahewartung, Auferstehung, Unsterblichkeit*. Freiburg: Herder.
Gressmann, H. 1905. *Der Ursprung der israelitisch-jüdischen Eschatologie*. Göttingen: Vandenhoeck und Ruprecht.
Gribbin, J. 1979. *Timewarps*. New York: Delacorte Press.
_____. 1986. *In Search of the Big Bang, Quantum Physics and Cosmology*. New York: Bantam.
Griffin, D.R. 1986. "Introduction: Time and the Fallacy of Misplaced Concreteness." In *Physics and the Ultimate Significance of Time*, edited by D.R. Griffin, 1-48. Albany: State University of New York Press.
Grisez, G.G., and J.M. Boyle. 1979. *Life and Death with Liberty and Justice: A Contribution to the Euthanasia Debate*. Notre Dame: University of Notre Dame Press.
Gunkel, H. 1895. *Schöpfung und Chaos in Urzeit und Endzeit*. Göttingen: Vandenhoeck.
Gurwitch, G. 1964. *Spectrum of Social Time*. Dordrecht: Reidel.
Halsell, G. 1986. *Prophecy and Politics*. Wesport, CT: Lawrence Hill.
Hanson, P.D. 1975. *The Dawn of Apocalyptic*. Philadelphia: Fortress Press.
Hartocollis, P. 1983. *Time and Timelessness, or the Varieties of Temporal Experiences*. New York: International Universities Press.

Hasel, G.F. 1980. "Resurrection in the Theology of the Old Testament Apocalyptic." *Zeitschrift für alttestamentliche Wissenschaft* 92: 267-84.

Hawking, S.W. 1976. "Breakdown of Predicability in Gravitational Collapse." *Physical Review* 14: 24-60.

———. 1990. *A Brief History of Time*. New York: Bantam.

Hebblethwaite, B. 1979. "Time and Eternity and Life 'After' Death." *The Heythrop Journal* 20: 57-62, 187-88.

Heidegger, M. 1962. *Being and Time*. London: SCM Press.

———. 1971. *On the Way to Language*. New York: Harper & Row.

Hengel, M. 1974. *Judaism and Hellenism*. London: SCM.

Hick, J. 1976. *Death and Eternal Life*. London: Collins.

Hodgson, D.C. 1971. *Jesus—Word and Presence: An Essay in Christology*. Philadelphia: Fortress Press.

Holmes, D.S. 1984. "Defense Mechanism." In *Encyclopedia of Psychology*, edited by R. J. Corsini, vol. 1, 347-50. New York: J. Wiley and Sons.

Horvath, T. 1966. *Caritas est in ratione. Die Lehre des hl. Thomas Aquinas über die Einheit der intellektiven und affektiven Begnadung des Menschen*. Münster: Aschendorffsche Verlagsbuchhandlung.

———. 1970. "The Sacrament of Marriage as Revelation of God." *The Heythrop Journal* 11: 388-407.

———. 1971. "The Sacrament of Ordination as Revelation of God." *The Heythrop Journal* 12: 44-52.

———. 1975. *Faith Under Scrutiny*. Notre Dame, IN: Fides.

———. 1976. "Revelation, Combat of Culture-Types, Thermodynamics: A Fundamental Theological Analysis of Crisis Event." *Traditio-Renovatio aus theologischer Sicht*, edited by J. Bernard and R. Mohr, 445-53. Marburg: N.G. Elwert.

———. 1977. "A Structural Understanding of the Magisterium of the Church." *Science et Esprit* 29: 283-311.

———. 1979a. *The Sacrificial Interpretation of Jesus' Achievement in the New Testament*. New York: Philosophical Library.

———. 1979b. "Marriage: Contract? Covenant? Community? Sacrament of Sacraments? Fallible Symbol of Infallible Love, Revelation of Sin and Love." In *The Sacraments: God's Love and Mercy Actualized*. Proceedings of the Theology Institute of Villanova University, edited by F.E. Eigo, 143-81. Villanova: Villanova University.

———. 1980a. "Tod" (Death). In *Lexikon der Psychologie*, edited by W. Arnold, H.J. Eysenck and R. Meili, vol. 3, 2329. Freiburg: Herder.

———. 1980b. "The Structure of Scientific Discovery and Man's Ultimate Reality and Meaning." *Ultimate Reality and Meaning* 3: 144-63.

Hounder, Q. 1970. *Das Unsterblichkeitsproblem in abendländischer Philosophie.* Stuttgart: Kohlhamer.

Huffmon, H.B. 1966. "The Treaty Background of Hebrew yada." *Bulletin of the American School of Oriental Research* 181: 31-77.

Jaeger, J. 1947. *The Theology of the Early Greek Philosophers.* Oxford: Clarendon Press.

James, W. 1980. *Principles of Psychology.* New York: Holt.

Jastrow, R. 1977. *Until the Sun Dies.* New York: W.W. Norton.

Jung, C. 1961. *Memories, Dreams, Reflections.* New York: Random House.

Jüngel, E. 1964. *Zur Ursprung der Analogie bei Parmenides und Heraklit.* Berlin: de Gruyter.

———. 1967. *Paulus und Jesus. Eine Untersuchung zur Präzisierung der Frage nach dem Ursprung der Christologie.* Tübingen: Mohr.

———. 1974. *Death: The Riddle and the Mystery.* Philadelphia: Westminster.

Kahn, H., and B. Bruce-Briggs. 1972. *Things to Come: Thinking About the Seventies and Eighties.* New York: Macmillan.

Kaiser, O., and E. Lohse. 1981. *Death and Life.* Nashville: Thomas Nelson.

Kolarcik, M. F. 1991. *The Ambiguity of Death in the Book of Wisdom 1-6.* Rome: Editrice Pontificio Instituto Biblico.

Kovacs, G. 1982. "Ultimate Reality and Meaning in Victor E. Frankl." *Ultimate Reality and Meaning* 5: 118-39.

Kübler-Ross, E. 1969. *On Death and Dying.* New York: Macmillan.

Kuhn, K.G. 1969. "Maranatha." In *Theological Dictionary of the New Testament,* edited by G. Kittel, vol. 4, 466-72. Grand Rapids, MI: Eerdmans.

Kunz, E. 1980. *Protestantische Eschatologie. Von der Reformation bis zur Aufklärung.* Freiburg: Herder.

Larcher, C. 1983-85. *Le Livre de la Sagesse ou la Sagesse de Salomon.* Vols. 1-3. Paris: J. Gabalda et Cie Éditeurs.

Lash, N. 1979a. "Eternal Life: Life After Death?" *The Heythrop Journal* 19: 271-84.

———. 1979b. "Time and Eternity and Life 'After' Death. A Comment." *The Heythrop Journal* 20: 57-63.

Layzer, D. 1985. "The Arrow of Time." *Scientific American* 236(6): 59-69.

Lehmann, K. 1970. "Christliche Geschichtserfahrung und ontologische Frage bei jungen Heidegger." In *Festschrift für M. Heidegger. Perspektiven zur Deutung seines Werkes,* edited by O. Pöggeler, 140-68. Köln: Kiepenheuer.

Léon-Dufour, X. 1986. *Life and Death in the New Testament.* New York: Harper & Row.

Leonard, E. 1988. "Experience as a Source for Theology." *Proceedings of the Catholic Theological Society of America* 43: 44-61.

Lewis, H.D. 1981. *Jesus in the Faith of the Christians*. London: Macmillan.

Lindbeck, G. 1984. *The Nature of Doctrine: Religion and Theology in a Postliberal Age*. Philadelphia: The Westminster Press.

Lindblom, J. 1963. *Prophecy in Ancient Israel*. Oxford: Blackwell.

Linstone, H.A., and W.H.C. Simmonds. 1977. *Future Research: New Directions*. London: Addison-Wesley.

Loye, D.1978. *The Knowable Future. A Psychology of Forecasting and Prophecy*. New York: J. Wiley.

Lunear, R. 1979. "What Can African Tradition Tell Us About Hereafter?" *Concilium* 123(3): 15-21.

MacCulloch, J.A. 1920. "Eschatology." In *Encyclopedia of Religion and Ethics*, edited by J. Hastings, vol. 5, 373-76. Edinburgh: Scribner's.

McDannell, C., and B. Lang. 1988. *Heaven: A History*. New Haven: Yale University Press,

Malalasekera, G.P. 1974. "Theravada Buddhism." In *Historical Atlas of the Religions of the World*, edited by I.R. al Fārūqī, 161-83. New York: Macmillan Publishing Co., Inc.

Maloney, G.A. 1982. *The First Day of Resurrection*. New York: Crossroad.

Marsh, J. 1952. *The Fullness of Time*. London: Nisbet.

Martin-Achard, R. 1960. *From Death to Life: A Study of the Development of the Doctrine of the Resurrection in the Old Testament*. London: Oliver and Boyd.

Matthews, W.H., III. 1971. *Invitation to Geology*. New York: Natural History Press.

Mbiti, J. 1969. *African Religions and Philosophy*. New York: Praeger.

———. 1971. *The New Testament Eschatology in an African Background*. London: Oxford University Press.

McKenzie, J.L.M. 1957. "Royal Messianism." *Catholic Biblical Quarterly* 19: 25-52.

———. 1968. "Aspects of Old Testament Thought: Eschatology." In *The Jerome Biblical Commentary*, edited by R.E. Brown, J.A. Fitzmyer, and R.E. Murphy, vol. 2, 764-67. Englewood Cliffs, NJ: Prentice Hall.

McTaggart, J.M.E. 1967. "Time." In *The Philosophy of Time*, edited by R.M. Gale, 86-97. New York: Humanities.

Melott, A. 1981. "The Invisible Universe." *Astronomy* 9: 66-71.

Michel, A. 1922. "Hypostase." In *Dictionnaire de Théologie Catholique*, edited by A. Vacant and E. Mangenot, Vol. 7, 69-437. Paris: Letouzey.

Moltmann, J. 1967. *Theology of Hope*. New York: Macmillan.

———, and R.J. Z. Werblowsky. 1991. "Eschatology." In *The New Encyclopedia Britannica. Macropaedia*. 15th ed. vol. 17, 401-408. Chicago: Encyclopedia Britannica.

Morris, R. 1984. *Time's Arrows: Scientific Attitude Toward Time.* New York: Simon and Schuster.
Mowinckel, S.O. 1956. *He That Cometh.* Oxford: Blackwell.
Mühlen, H. 1964. *Una Mystica Persona.* Die Kirche als das Mysterium der Identität des Heiligen Geistes in Christus und den Christen. Eine Person in vielen Personen. München: F. Schoning.
Müller, M. 1949. *Existenzphilosophie im geistigen Leben der Gegenwart.* Heidelberg: F.H. Kerle.
Münsterberg, H. 1916. *Grundzüge der Psychologie.* Leipzig: J.A. Barth.
Nalimov, V.V. 1982. *Realms of the Unconscious: The Enchanted Frontier.* Philadelphia: ISI Press.
Neale, R.E. 1976. *The Art of Dying.* New York: Harper & Row.
Nickelsburg, G.W.E. 1972. *Resurrection, Immortality and Eternal Life in Intertestamental Judaism.* Cambridge: Harvard University Press.
North, R. 1972. "Prophecy to Apocalytic via Zacharia." *Vetus Testamentum Supplementum* 22: 47-71.
Noth, M. 1952. "Vergegenwärtigung des alten Testaments in der Verkündigung." *Evangelische Theologie* 12, 6-17.
Pannenberg, W. 1968. *Revelation as History.* New York: Macmillan.
_____. 1970. *What is Man?* Philadelphia: Fortress Press.
Park, D. 1981. *The Images of Eternity.* New York: New American Library.
Pawlik, K. 1972. "Ego, Syn, I Self" In *Encyclopedia of Psychology*, edited by H.I. Eysenck and A. Arnold, 313-19. London: Search Press.
Penrose, R. 1990. *The Emperor's New Mind Concerning Computers, Minds, and the Laws of Physics.* London: Vintage.
Peters, T. 1978. *Future—Human and Divine.* Atlanta: J. Knox Press.
Peterson, E. 1959. *Die Frühkirche, Judentum und Gnosis.* Freiburg: Herder.
PG. 1857-1866. *Patrologia Graeca.* Edited by J.P. Migne. Paris: Migne.
Piaget, J. 1971. *The Child's Conception of Time.* New York: Ballantine Books.
PL. 1878-1890. *Patrologia Latina.* Edited by J.P. Migne. Paris: Migne.
Price, H.H. 1972. *Essays in the Philosophy of Religion.* Oxford: Clarendon Press.
Prigogine, I. 1980. *From Being to Becoming.* San Francisco: W.H. Freeman.
Rad, G. von. 1965. *Old Testament Theology.* Edinburgh: Oliver and Boyd.
Radcliffe-Brown, A.R. 1961. *Structure and Function in Primitive Society.* New York: Free Press.
Raghavan, V. 1974. "Hinduism." In *Historical Atlas of the Religions of the World*, edited by I.R. al Fārūqī, 69-96. New York: Macmillan Publishing.
Rahner, K. 1961. *On the Theology of Death.* Montreal: Palm Publishers.
_____. 1966a. *Die vielen Messen und das eine Opfer.* Freiburg: Herder.

———. 1966b. "Hermeneutics of Eschatological Assertions." *Theological Investigations*, vol. 4, 323-46. Baltimore: Helicon.

———. 1966c. "On the Theology of Incarnation." *Theological Investigations*. vol. 4, 105-120. Baltimore: Helicon.

———. 1966d. "Life of the Dead." *Theological Investigations*, vol. 4, 347-354. Baltimore: Helicon.

———. 1971. "Experiencing Easter." *Theological Investigations*, vol. 7, 159-68. New York: Herder.

——— and H. Vorgrimler. 1965. *Theological Dictionary*. Montreal: Palm Publishers.

Ratzinger, J. 1977. *Eschatologie. Tod und ewiges Leben*. Regensburg: Pustet.

Rawlings, M. 1978. *Beyond Death's Door*. Nashville, TN: T. Nelson.

Richter, C.P. 1959. "The Phenomenon of Unexplained Sudden Death in Animal and Man." In *The Meaning of Death*, edited by H. Feifel, 302-13. New York: McGraw.

Rikson, M.J. 1977. *Contemporary Options in Eschatology*. Grand Rapids, Ml.: Cannon Press.

Robinson, H.W. 1936. "The Hebrew Conception of Corporate Personality." *Beihefte zur Zeitschrift für die alttestamentliche Wissenschaft* 66: 49-62.

Robinson, J.A. 1957. *Jesus and His Coming*. London: SCM.

Rochain, G. 1981. "Le regne des milles ans." *Nouvelle Revue Theologique* 103: 831-56.

Sacred Congregation for the Doctrine of the Faith. 1979. *Letter on Certain Questions concerning Eschatalogy*. Rome. Acta Apostolicae Sedis 71: 939-43.

Sagües, I.S. 1958. *De Deo Creante et Elevante Sacrae Theologiae Summa*, Madrid: Biblioteca de Autores Christianos, 1. 2, 443-981.

Schafer, P. 1984. *Eschatologie. Trient und Gegenreformation*. Freiburg in B.: Herder.

Scheffczyk, L. 1985. "Apocatastasis, Fascination and Paradox." *Communio*, 12: 386-97.

Schmid, H.H. 1967. "Das Verstädniss der Geschichte im Deuteronomium." *Zeitschrift für Theologie und Kirche* 64: 1-15.

Schmidt, J.M. 1970. "Vergegenwärtigung und Uberlieferung." *Evangelische Theologie* 30: 169-200.

Schupp, F. 1974. *Glaube, Kultur, Symbol*. Düsseldorf: Patmos.

Schwartz, H. 1971. "Eschatology or Futurology: On the Interdependence Between Christian Eschatology and Secular Progress." *Theologische Zeitschrift* 27: 347-64.

Schweitzer, A. 1910. *The Quest of the Historical Jesus*. London: Adam and Charles Black.

Slaatteg, H.A. 1980. *Time and Its End: A Comparative Interpretation of Time and Eschatology*. Washington: University Press of America.

Sorokin, P.A. 1964. *Sociocultural Causality, Space, Time*. Dordrecht: Reidel.

Stanley, D.M., and R.E. Brown, 1968. "New Testament Eschatology." In *The Jerome Biblical Commentary*, edited by R.E. Brown, J.A. Fitzmyer and R.E. Murphy, vol. 2, 777-82. Englewood Cliffs, NJ: Prentice Hall.

Stever, R. 1983. "The Dynamic Earth." *Scientific American* 249(3): 46-55.

Stinson, S. 1977. "On the Time-Eternity Link: Some Aspects of Recent Christian Eschatology." *Religious Studies* 13: 49-62.

Strasser, S. 1964. *Phenomenology and the Human Science: A Contribution to a New Scientist Ideal*. Pittsburgh: Duquesne University Press.

Strawson, W. 1970. *Jesus and the Future Life*. London: Epworth Press.

Szilard, L. 1929. "Über die Entropieverminderung in einem thermodynamischen System bei Eingegriffen intelligenter Wesen." *Zeitschrift für Physik* 53: 840-56.

Tanner, N.P. ed. 1990. *Decrees of the Ecumenical Councils*. London: Sheed and Ward.

Taylor, J. 1975. *Black Holes*. Toronto: Collins.

Taylor, R.J. 1966. The Eschatological Meaning of Life and Death in the Book of Wisdom." *Ephemerides Theologicae Lovanienses* 42: 72-137.

Thomas Aquinas, 1934. *Summa contra Gentiles*. Roma: Libreria Vaticana.

———. 1948. *Summa Theologiae*. Torino: Marietti.

Tillich, P. 1963. *Systematic Theology*. Vol. 3. Chicago: University of Chicago Press.

Toman, W. 1972. "Ego III." In *Encyclopedia of Psychology*, edited by H.I. Eysenck, W. Arnold, p. 316. London: Search Press.

———. 1979. "Defense, Defense-mechanism." *Encyclopedia of Psychology*. Edited by J.J. Eysenck, W. Arnold and R. Meili, 252. New York: Seabury Press.

Troisfontaines, R. 1963. *I Do not Die*. New York: Desclée.

Veatch, R. M. 1976. *Death, Dying and Biological Revolution*. New Haven: Yale University Press.

Vogtle, A. 1970. *Das Neue Testament und die Zukunft des Kosmos*. Dusseldorf: Patmos.

Volz, P. 1966. *Die Eschatologie der jüdischen Gemeinde im neutestamentlichen Zeitalter*. Hildesheim: Olms.

Wachter, L. 1967. *Der Tod in alten Testament*. Stuttgart: Calwer Verlag.

Watt, M. Montgomery. 1982. "Muḥammad's Contribution in the Field of Ultimate Reality and Meaning." *Ultimate Reality and Meaning* 5: 26-38.

Wegenaer, P. 1958. *Heilsgegenwart: Das Heilswerk Christi und die virtus divina in den Sacramenten unter besonderer Berichtigung von Eucharistie und Taufe.* Münster: Aschendorff.

Wellhausen, J. 1961. *Prolegomena to the History of Ancient Israel.* New York: Meridian Press.

Westermann, C. 1964. "Vergegenwärtigung der Geschichte in den Psalmen." *Forschung am Alten Testament.* Theologische Bücherei 14, 306-35. München: Kaiser.

Wheeler, J.A. 1980. *Beyond the Black Holes.* Austin: The University of Texas at Austin, Center for Theoretical Physics.

Whitehead, A.N. 1969. *Process and Reality.* New York: Free Press.

Whitrow, G.J. 1975. *The Nature of Time.* Baltimore: Penguin Books.

Wilch, R. 1969. *Time and Event.* Leiden: Brill.

Williams, B. 1973. *The Problems of Self.* New York: Cambridge University Press.

Wittgenstein, L. 1961. *Tractatus logico-philosophicus.* London: Routledge and Kegan Paul.

Wittkowski, J. 1978. *Tod und Sterben: Ergebnisse der Thanato-psychologie.* Heidelberg: Quelle und Meyer.

SUBJECT INDEX

Aeon, 106
After-life, 104-106
   spiritualized, 40
   endless life and eternal life, 4
Anacephalaeosis, 5, 142
Angels, 22, 128-29
   angelology and eschatology, 128-29, 148
Antichrist, 74, 145
Apocalypse, 84
   apocalyptic literature, 7
Apocatastasis, 15-16, 135-37, 142
Ascension, Christ's resurrection, Mary's assumption and our resurrection, 123-24

Beatific vision, 19-20, 125-27
Beatitude, 127, 130-31
Body, as unified field of energy, 76, 78, 89, 112-14

Christ, Jesus, *see* Jesus Christ
Cosmic eschatology, 25, 75, 140, 148-53
   "run-down" world and "run-up" eternity, 152

Death, as a real end of time, 89-116
   clinical, biological, psychological death, 93-94
   biblical interpretation, 94-97
   church documents, 97
   theologians' interpretations, 98-102
   final option theory, 100-101
   mortalism, 111
   realization of the inevitability of unselfish love, 102-104
   thanatos, 94
Descent into hell, 89, 101-102

Devils, evil ones, 22, 128, 145
   reveal what hell is, 129
Dialectical tension between universal, cosmic and individual existential eschatology, 21-22, 32-36, 120. *See also* Jesus Christ as the eschatological union of time and eternity

End, 8-12, 78, 85
   "flesh" has an end, 30-31
Eschatology, 85-86
   advent of salvation, 12
   history of, 5-22
   salvation of non-Christians, 16
   structure and method, 23-26
   Synoptic eschatology, 5-12
   theology of eternal life, 13-14
   Vatican II, 20-22
Eternal life, 114-16
   foundational value of Christianity, 1-4
   God's self-giving, 4
   meeting with the risen Jesus Christ, 5
Eternity, 116-17
   is God and God is eternity, 8, 31-32
   language event as way-making for eternity, 60-64
   societies, nations enter eternity, 146-48
   time and eternity, 62-64
Expectation of what is to come, 8-12

Faith, charity and hope, 79-80, 118-19, 140. *See also* Trinity
Future, 13-14
Futurology, 13, 81, 82-84

Glorification, 129-30
Grace, sanctifying, and beatific
  vision, 115-16
  problem of the past event and
    present sanctification, 12-13
  salvation of non-Christians, 2, 16,
    70-73

Heaven, entering in the Trinitarian
  God's eternity, 124ff.
  being with Christ, 6-7, 16, 19
  space-, person- and time-
    language, 124-32
Hell, 16, 19
  as eternal life, 132-35
  Christological meaning, 70-71,
    133-34
  space-, person- and time-
    language, 132-37
Hermeneutics of eschatological
  statements, 14, 87-88
  informative, affirmative, optative,
    14, 20
  its first principle, 65-80
    foundation of 13 basic eschato-
      logical statements, 81-153
Historicity, 3-4
  historically datable events, 86
  importance of the destruction of
    the temple in Jerusalem, 10-11
History
  historical existence 8, 22
  historical time, 53-54
  history-resurrection-revelation
    link, 5-12
  nature of the originating paschal
    experience and an early
    Christology, 11
Holy Spirit, 79-80, 110, 118, 124, 150
  Christ the language of languages,
    142-43
  eschatological outpouring, 142-43

Imminence of the end, 5, 9, 10, 14,
  18, 86
Immortality
  collective, 39-40
  Greek concept of, 38-39
  an inconsistent idea, 106-107
  Old Testament and scholastic
    theology, 39-41
Intermediate state, 20, 137-40
  resurrection-time, 137-39
"It is not I but Christ who lives in
  me," 114-16

Jesus Christ
  conqueror of death and of eternal
    life, 88ff.
  eschatological union of time and
    eternity, and first principle in
    Christian eschatology, 65ff.
    home of time and way-making
      for eternity, 68
    hypostatic union, 73-78
    kerygma, 65, 78
    parable test, 67
    sin and redemption, 68-70
    Trinity, 79-80
  eschaton, 5
  love of, as fundamental reality of
    Christianity, 2-4, 65ff.
  pattern of eternity, 14
  transcending the time between
    the past and the now, 65
Judgment, universal and particular,
  8, 19-22, 117-24
  goodness and evil of an action or
    behavior, 118-19

Kingdom of God, 6-7, 67-68, 130-31

Last things (*eschaton*), 7, 11-13, 74-75
Limbo, 19, 137-38

Mary, the first "flowering" of the
  Church, 21
  assumption and resurrection,
    123-24
Millenarianism, 143-44

Non-Christian eschatology, 15,
  85-86, 99
Now, 9, 10, 36-37
  relation between the past and the
    historical now, 32-36
  Mass and the redemptive act of
    Christ, 35-36

SUBJECT INDEX

Paradise, 6, 125
Parousia, 10, 141-42
Person, 76-77, 108ff., 113
   a force by balancing various times creates its own time demarcating it from other times against the alienating power of time, 113
   body, 76, 78
   Ego, 76, 78, 89, 112
   Self, 76, 78, 89, 112
   soul, 76, 78 89, 112
   theological and philosophical "I," 77-78, 89, 112-16
      emerges in confrontation of time and eternity, 113
   personal identity, psychology of, 52-53
      of the one who died and the one who is risen, 108-14
Purgatory, 17-18, 20, 21, 138-40

Resurrection of the flesh, 7, 15-17, 40
   death, judgment and resurrection from the view of God and from the view of the world, 121-23
   intercession of the saints, 137
   resurrection is history, 6
   resurrection of the body and Mary's assumption, 123-24

Sacraments, 2, 16
   and Christ as eschatological union of time and eternity, 71-73
   sacrament of faith, the faith of the sacrament, 16
Satan, 22, 145
Scientific picture of the world, 25-26
   atomic clock, 45
   biological clock, 51-52,
   biological time, 76
   black holes, singularity events, 25-26, 47, 153
   conflict of times or balance in a multiplicity of sub-times, 60-65
   cyclic or not cyclic universe, 45-47
   Einsteinian universe, 14, 25, 48-50
   geological clock, 42-44
   Hawking's unified theory, 50-51, 155
   internal (psychological) clock, 53
   radioactive run-down, 43
   second law of thermodynamics, 151-52
   spatialized time, 29-32
      and timed space, 28
   time's arrow, 4, 6-47. *See also* time and eternity
"Second" coming of Christ, 5-76
   as final coming, 141-42
Self, 76, 78, 89, 112
Sheol, 94, 132
Soul, 76, 78 89, 112
   the separated, the existence of, 21
   transmigration, of, 15, 17
Spirit, spiritual existence, 7
   spiritual sense of salvation, 12

Temporality, 30-32, 64, 78, 108
Time, 60-64
   de-temporalized, 37-41
   and eternity, 22, 81, 116
   biblical notion, 29
   biological, psychological, cultural, philosophical and theological times, 77
   Christological, 41-42
   concept of:
      humanistic studies, 52-60
      in sciences, 42-52
      in theology, 29-42
   past-, present-, future-oriented time, 32-37
Trinitarian God, 79-80
   and eternity, 8, 31-32
   mystery of salvation, 13

Utopianism, 143-44

World, time of, and eternity, 5
   its judgment, 123-24, 140-56

NAME INDEX

Abel, A., 85
Alexander, S., 84
Anselm of Canterbury, 107
Aristotle, 34, 41
Arnold, W., vii, 51
Asimov, I., 151
Augustine of Hippo, 143, 144

Bacon, R., 143
Badham, P. and L., 39
Bailey, L.R., 94
Baius, 39
Balthasar, H.U. von, 36
Barnhart, M.G., 38
Barr, J., 29, 41
Barrow, I., 46
Barth, K., 9, 15, 36, 41
Benedict XII, 20, 98, 119, 126, 135
Beraza, B., 39
Berdyaev, N., 41
Bergson, H.L., 85
Blondel, M., 100
Boetius, A.M.T.S., 108, 116
Boros, L., 17, 100
Boyd, J.W., 145
Boyer, C., 39
Boyle, J.M., 93
Brandon, S.G.F., 39
Braudel, F., 54
Brown, R.E., 86
Bruce-Briggs, B., 82
Budge, E.A., 104
Bühler, C., 53
Bultmann, R., 8, 9, 36

Campanella, T., 143
Cannon, W.B., 94
Casel, O., 35
Castel, C.F., 143

Cassidorius, 15
Charles, R.H., 39
Childs, B.S., 33
Chomsky, N., 57, 58
Collins, J.J., 40
Congar, Y.M.J., 35
Conzelmann, A., 9
Cornelis, H., 104
Cornish, E., 82, 83
Cullmann, O., 9, 36

Dange, S.A., 17
Dante, A., 143
Darwin, C., 13
Davies, P.C.W., 64
de la Taille, M., 127
Deneffe, A., 39
Descartes, R., 108
De Vaucouleurs, G., 44
Didymus the Blind, 15
Diodore, 15
Dupuis, J., 22
Durkheim, E., 55
Dykmans, M., 126
Dyson, F., 26, 85, 143

Ebeling, G., 33
Ehret, C.F., 51
Einstein, A., 47-49
Eisenbach, F., 36
Eliade, M., 86
Erickson, M.J., 144
Evans-Wentz, W.Y., 105

Falwell, J., 144
Ferkiss, V., 82
Fischer, U., 40
Flew, A., 107
Fraisse, P., 52
Frankl, V.E., 94

NAME INDEX

Fraser, J.T., 60
Freud, S., 93

Gadamer, H.-G., 24, 60, 62, 92
Gardner, M., 108, 109
Gilbert, L.T., 83
Gilson, E., 143
Gnilka, J., 18
Gorman, B.S., 53
Gotesky, R., 85
Gould, S.J., 44
Greenberg, J.H., 57
Gregory of Nazianzus, 15
Gregory of Nyssa, 15
Greshake, G., 109, 148
Gressmann, H., 75
Gribbin, J., 47
Griffin, D.R., 64
Grisez, G.G., 93
Gundisalvi, Dominic, 107
Gunkel, H., 86
Gurwitch, G., 53, 54

Hall, H., viii
Halsell, G., 144
Hanson, P.D., 83
Hartocollis, P., 53
Hasel, G.F., 40
Hawking, S.W., 26, 47, 50, 155
Hebblethwaite, B., 37
Heidegger, M., 28, 58
Hengel, M., 40
Hick, J., 37
Hippolytus, 119
Hodgson, D.C., 28
Holmes, D.S., 92, 103
Horvath, T., 6, 8, 28, 32, 38, 41, 55, 69, 72, 75, 87, 102, 110, 117, 118, 126, 131, 145, 150, 153
Hounder, Q., 107
Huarte, G., 39
Huffmon, H.B., 33

Innocent III, 16
Innocent IV, 17, 18
Irenaeus, 144

Jaeger, J., 38
James, W., 53

Jastrow, R., 85
Joachim of Fiore, 13
John XXII, 125, 126
John of Damascus, 74
Jung, C., 105
Jüngel, E., 41
Justin, 7, 144

Kahn, H., 82
Kaiser, O., 94
Kant, E., 48, 107
Kolarcik, M.F., 94
Kovacs, G., 94
Kübler-Ross, E., 92

Langevin, G., viii
Larcher, C., 94
Lash, N., 37
Layzer, D., 46
Lehmann, K., 28
Leibniz, G.F., 143
Leo X, 98
Léon-Dufour, X., 94
Leonard, E., ix
Lercher, L., 39
Lewis, H.D., 37
Libby, W.F., 43
Lindbeck, G., ix
Lindblom, J., 75
Linstone, H.A., 82
Locke, J., 42
Lohfink, G., 109
Lohse, E., 94
Lombard, Peter, 107
Loye, D., 82
Lunear, R., 86
Luther, M., 34, 139

MacCulloch, J.A., 85
Macdougall, A.J., viii
Malalasekera, G.P., 38
Marsh, J., 29, 31
Marx, K., 13
Martin-Achard, R., 40
Matthews, W.H., 43, 44
Mbiti, J., 38, 86
McKenzie, J.L.M., 74, 86
McTaggart, J.M.E., 29, 32, 62
Melott, A., 47

Michel, A., 108
Moltmann, J., 37, 85, 86
Morris, R., 64
Mowinckel, S.O., 74
Muḥammad, 31
Mühlen, H., 35
Müller, M., 36
Münsterberg, H., 53

Nalimov, V.V., 28, 56
Newton, I., 42, 48
Nickelsburg, G.W.E., 40
Nicolas of Cusa, 143
North, R., 40
Noth, M., 33

Olson, D.W., 44

Palmieri, D., 39
Pannenberg, W., 37
Papias, 144
Pawlik, K., 76
Penrose, R., 46, 47, 155
Peters, T., 82
Peterson, E., 5
Plato, 38, 39, 60
Plotinus, 34
Price, H.H., 37
Prigogine, I., 64

Rad, G. von, 32
Radcliffe-Brown, A.R., 55
Raghavan, V., 17
Rahner, K., 17, 35, 36, 42, 69, 86, 87, 98-100, 106, 108, 127, 116, 120, 145
Ratzinger, J., 9, 10, 107
Rawlings, M., 105
Richter, C.P., 93
Robinson, H.W., 33, 35
Robinson, J.A., 29
Rochain, G., 144

Sagües, I.S., 38, 39, 106
Scheffczyk, L., 135
Schmid, H.H., 33
Schmidt, J.M., 33
Schupp, F., 42
Schwartz, H., 82
Schweitzer, A., 8
Simmonds, W.H.C., 82

Slaatteg, H.A., 41
Socrates, 38
Sorokin, P.A., 53
Stanley, D.M., 86
Stever, R., 44
Stinson, S., 37, 117
Strasser, S., 34
Strawson, W., 82
Szilard, L., 113

Tanner, N.P., 15, 17-22, 34, 39, 42, 97, 98, 119, 126, 135, 140
Taylor, J., 26
Taylor, R.J., 94
Tertullian, 144
Theodore of Mopsuestia, 15
Theopompus, 40
Thomas Aquinas, 27, 32, 41, 71, 107, 108, 116, 126, 127, 131, 141
Thucydides, 38
Tillich, P., 36
Toman, W., 76, 92, 102
Troisfontaines, R., 99, 100

Vazquez, G., 127
Veatch, R.M., 93
Vernet, F., 39
Vigilius, Pope, 15
Vogtle, A., 148
Vorgrimler, K.H., 36, 106, 108, 116

Wachter, L., 94
Watt, M.M., 31
Wegenaer, P., 35
Wellhausen, J., 74
Werblowsky, R.J.Z., 86
Wessman, A.E., 53
Westermann, C., 33
Wheeler, J.A., 48
Whitehead, A.N., 13, 64, 85
Whitrow, G.J., 44-47, 49
Wilch, R., 30
Williams, B., 108
Wittkowski, J., 93

Yubertus, 16

Zeno, 62

www.ingramcontent.com/pod-product-compliance
Lightning Source LLC
Chambersburg PA
CBHW052031070526
44584CB00016B/1996